From Hopalong to Hud

From Hopalong to Hud

Thoughts on Western Fiction

---

by C. L. SONNICHSEN

Texas A&M University Press
COLLEGE STATION AND LONDON

Library of Congress Cataloging in Publication Data

Sonnichsen, Charles Leland, 1901–
    From Hopalong to Hud.

    Bibliography: p.
    Includes index.
    1. American fiction—20th century—History and
criticism. 2. The West in literature. I. Title.
PS374.W4S6   813′.0874   78-6371
ISBN 0-89096-052-6

Manufactured in the United States of America
Second printing

For my friends and fellow inhabitants of the little world of the Arizona Historical Society, with respect and affection.

Contents

Thanks are due to the editors of the following periodicals for permission to reprint revised and updated versions of the essays listed below.

"Western Fiction: Index to America" (originally "Fiction as History"), *Wilson Library Bulletin* 43, no. 3 (November, 1968): 248–255.

"The West That Wasn't," *The American West* 14, no. 6 (November–December, 1977): 8–15; copyright © 1977 by the American West Publishing Company, Cupertino, California. Reprinted by permission of the publisher.

"The Wyatt Earp Syndrome," *The American West* 7, no. 3 (May, 1970): 26–28, 60–62; copyright © 1970 by the American West Publishing Company, Cupertino, California. Reprinted by permission of the publisher.

"Too Tough to Tame" (originally "Tombstone in Fiction"), *The Journal of Arizona History* 9, no. 2 (Summer, 1968): 58–76.

"The Ambivalent Apache," *Western American Literature* 10, no. 2 (August, 1975): 99–114.

"The Two Black Legends," *Southwestern American Literature* 3 (1973): 5–21.

"The Private World of Miss Sue Pinckney," *Southwest Review* 29, no. 1 (Autumn, 1943): 80–92.

"The Sharecropper in Western Fiction" (originally "The Sharecropper Novel in the Southwest"), *Agricultural History* 43, no. 2 (April, 1969): 249–258.

"Sex on the Lone Prairee," *Western American Literature* 13, no. 1 (May, 1978): 15–33.

From Hopalong to Hud

Western Fiction:
Index to America

IN fiction—particularly Western fiction—we see our own faces. To watch how the system works, consider Edward Abbey's irreverent, bawdy, hilarious, and utterly serious 1975 novel *The Monkey Wrench Gang* as it talks about the ecological situation in Arizona. George W. Hayduke, semi-sane survivor of the war in Vietnam, joins three other zealots in a plot to blow up the great Glen Canyon Dam, which to them typifies the rape and ruin of the American land. "All this fantastic effort . . . to keep alive that phosphorescent putrefying glory (all the glory there is left) called Down Town, Night Time, Wonderville, USA."

"Seldom Seen Smith," so called because he has a wife in each of three towns and thus makes only brief appearances in any one of them, looks up at the dam and asks God to help:

> "Dear old God," he prayed, "you know and I know what it was like here, before them bastards from Washington moved in and ruined it all. You remember the river, how fat and golden it was in June, when the big runoff came down from the Rockies. Remember the deer on the sandbars and the blue herons in the willows and the catfish so big and tasty and how they'd bite on spoiled salami. . . . Remember the cataracts in Forty-Mile Canyon? Well, they flooded out about half of them too, and part of the Escalante's gone too. . . . Listen, are you listenin' to me? There's somethin' you can do for me, God. How about a little old *pre*-cision type earthquake right under this dam? Okay? Any time. Right now for instance would suit me fine."

A guard approaches. Smith signs off:

> "Okay, God, I see you don't want to do it now. Well, all right, suit yourself, you're the boss, but we ain't got a hell of a lot of time. Make it pretty soon, goddamit. A-men."

"I'm sorry sir," says the guard, "but you can't pray here. This is a public place."[1]

Abbey's novel has been widely read. The word went out that he was disillusioned about some of his Mormon characters, and booksellers in Salt Lake City, it is said, had a hard time keeping it in stock. The main reason for its appeal, however, was its assault on the road builders, the subdividers, and the Army Corps of Engineers (which is said to hate the sound of running water). He put into vivid language what many people were thinking. This was quite normal and natural. Fiction has always reflected, as well as shaped, popular tastes, prejudices, and admirations. Propaganda novels like Abbey's do it openly and obviously, but stories with no apparent axe to grind do it also. A writer who seems not to be taking a stand on anything, aiming only to amuse, reflects more than he realizes of the basic attitudes of his time. Thus the assembled fictional output of any specific period contributes to social and intellectual history because it offers a guide to what people think and believe, thereby providing a key to what they do, or would like to do. Future generations can learn from *The Monkey Wrench Gang* how one segment of our generation looked at itself and how it felt impelled to act.

It is a Western novel, but it is talking to and about people all over the country. Western novels have a habit of doing that. Southern writers speak for the South; Eastern writers speak for the East; but the West belongs to everybody, including the Swedes and the Italians, and speaks for everybody. It comes closer than the fiction of any other region to providing an index to America.

But why bother with fiction? Novels have been going downhill for years. Readers are much more interested in economics and sociology and foreign affairs and the endangered environment, and the sales prove it.[2] People want answers, and they want their answers documented. It takes a small miracle for a beginning novelist to break into print. True, Louis L'Amour sells in the millions, but there is only one Louis L'Amour. And in spite of him and a few more big names, the Western novel has fallen farther and faster than any other type. Not even libraries try to keep abreast of publication, though they

---

[1] Edward Abbey, *The Monkey Wrench Gang*, pp. 38, 153–154.

[2] *Publisher's Weekly*, February 14, 1977, p. 39. Hard-cover fiction was "making a comeback" in 1976.

try to keep up with everything else. When somebody writes a book about *Man's Best Friend: The Armadillo*, it goes on the nature shelf and children wear it out. Every time an ancient pioneer tells lies about his acquaintance with Wyatt Earp, his memoirs are accessioned, issued, and read. The dull and disjointed history of the least important county in any Western state is welcomed by the library staff. But a novel, good or bad, depicting life in the same area will probably be overlooked and after ten years will be almost impossible to find. The popular titles will be on the shelves because people ask for them, but nobody asks for something he never heard of.

Western novels are indeed here today and gone tomorrow, and there are some special reasons for reader indifference. One is the feeling that we have been conned by the storytellers and scenarists who give us wrong answers about how the West was won. They have ignored the land grabbers and exploiters and played up as frontier Galahads a gang of barroom characters and part-time peace officers whom the Kansas and Arizona historians have revealed in their true insignificance.[3] Even unsophisticated readers have reacted against the romanticizers, and it is worth noting that the magazines which have replaced the vanished pulps bear such names as *True*, *True West*, and *Real West*. Even educated and informed book buyers—the kind who read *The Monkey Wrench Gang* or *Dancers in the Scalp House*, by William Eastlake—are disillusioned about the romantic West and want their fiction to be realistic and tough.

To show how far the flight from fiction, including Western fiction, has gone, take the case of Larry McMurtry, a properly disillusioned writer. His novel *Horseman, Pass By* (*Hud* in the movies) won the Jesse Jones Award of the Texas Institute of Letters in 1962. It picked up for McMurtry a Wallace Stegner Fellowship at Stanford, a Guggenheim Fellowship, and an instructorship in English at Rice University. With all this impact, one would think, it would have sold fifty or a hundred thousand copies. It sold about fifteen hundred (the publishers will admit only that this figure is "not far off").[4] Probably only a few of the fictional titles issued in 1961, or any other recent year, did any better. The big publishing houses seem willing to

[3] Nyle H. Miller and Joseph Snell, *Why the West Was Wild*.

[4] M. S. Wyeth, Jr., executive editor, Harper & Row, to CLS, October 8, 1968: ". . . you are not far off, though perhaps a bit low."

gamble that one novel out of ten will catch on, interest the movies, or be picked up by a paperback house for mass production.

It would seem, indeed, that anyone who writes about Western novels is beating a dead horse. All but a few of each year's crop achieve little note and are not likely to be long remembered. So why bother with them?

Two reasons. First, the social historian finds them more and more significant and they may be resurrected at any moment for what they show about the country which produced them and the people who read, or did not read, any or all of them. Henry Nash Smith's enormously influential *Virgin Land* leaned heavily on the dime novel for its conclusions, and Smith's many successors do the same. Leo Marx's *The Machine in the Garden*, for example, takes up where Smith's pioneer effort leaves off. Marx, like Smith, relies on fiction for source material and announces early in his study that he intends to "consider examples which have little or no intrinsic value." He is looking, he says, for "cultural symbols" and sees them in products of our "collective fantasy life."[5]

From this point of view no novel is ever dead, not even the "genre" or commercial westerns (spelled with a small *w* in many discussions, including this one), sometimes called horse operas, shoot-em-ups, hayburners, or oaters by historians of Western books and movies. They too are part of Western fiction, and from the cultural historian's point of view they can be more revealing than serious works. This volume, now in your hands, also seeks for meaning in books which were never widely read or much respected as well as in literary successes. "Cultural symbols" is a rather pretentious phrase for what Marx and I are looking for, but I do agree with him and would only add that works of "no intrinsic value" may be significant because the unsophisticated novelist is sometimes trying to get something said, while the superior writer is mostly interested in selling his book to Hollywood.

In the second place, fiction is worth attention notwithstanding its present low estate because its decline may be only temporary. In years to come the novels which are overlooked today may be historically important as a link between what was and what is to be.

[5] Leo Marx, *The Machine in the Garden*, p. 4.

Fiction has weathered storms and drouth before and has altered with the times when necessary. Students of regional writing know that an important change took place in 1902 when Owen Wister's *The Virginian* divided the high road from the low road of popular Western novels. From that time on superior writers like Stewart Edward White, Eugene Manlove Rhodes, Emerson Hough, Conrad Richter, and Walter Van Tilburg Clark produced Western fiction with literary merit and more-than-ordinary significance. On the low road the Zane Greys, B. M. Bowers, Ernest Boyds, Luke Shorts, and William Mac-Leod Raines held forth, while somewhere in between were the Alan LeMays, Ernest Haycoxes, and Jack Schaefers. There is still a high road with new faces and new ideas.

The year 1918 was another Great Divide in the history of Western writing. After World War I there was a noticeable improvement in both quantity and quality. Better writers appeared, and better publishers sought their work. Harvey Fergusson and Oliver La Farge turned out superior fiction for a national audience. Paul Horgan and Tom Lea, Frank Waters and A. B. Guthrie, Wallace Stegner and Ben Capps followed them. Good writers like Edward Abbey and J. P. S. Brown are at work now. Fads in theme and approach and subject matter have come and gone, but the Western novel has not disappeared or even been seriously weakened. It will be with us for a long time to come.

It may even achieve equality with the Western movie, though as things stand now, the director gets all the credit, and the authors who write the books on which the movies are based are seldom mentioned.

The most far-reaching changes have occurred on the low road, where dozens of busy authors once traveled. The pulp magazines have disappeared. The writers have been severely weeded out, and only the best have survived. Some very good ones have turned to popular history. A few, like Louis L'Amour and Will Henry, call themselves historical novelists and claim to be telling it the way it was. A small percentage have gone with the tide and tried for success with excessive sex and violence.

On the high road, where stereotypes are avoided and authors try to be literary artists, other interesting transformations have taken place. Much gritty realism, exemplified in the work of Larry Mc-

Murtry and his disciples, shows how far behind we have left the hopes, ideals, and scruples of our forebears. Max Evans and others introduce us to a new generation of cowboys, sometimes funny in a sad sort of way, but stripped of all romance. We have Chicano novels, Gothic novels, Indian novels (some by Indians), murder mysteries, novels about life in the cities, about religion, about the oil fields, about academic communities, about dynastic families. They are all Western novels because they are set in the West and could not, in most cases, have happened anywhere else.

The field is vast and varied—so vast and so varied that one man can hardly take it all in. The would-be fictional historian must take soundings and samplings and make generalizations with caution. I have been taking soundings and samplings for a good many years, and some of the results appear in the following pages. The first and second chapters attempt to look at Western fiction as cultural history and set forth basic assumptions. Those which follow examine special topics and try to answer the question, "What goes on here?" The final chapter suggests some of the areas that need exploration by students who can find the books (which is not by any means easy) and are willing to read the books (which takes more time and concentration than many are willing to invest).

The curious spade wielder who has the patience to dig deep will find the effort worthwhile. There is no better way to learn what we were and what we are and where we are headed than to consider this particular segment of our fictional output over the last century. And when we remember that the legendary West belongs to the world and not just to us, the subject assumes major importance.

The West That Wasn't

W. H. Hutchinson, the sage of Chico, California, likes to talk about the the West That Was, implying that what we usually get is the West That Wasn't. He has a point. We Westerners, and in a sense all Americans, live in two countries—the real one and the more-or-less phony one that we get in the movies, on television, and in the paperback novels. There is a wide gray area between the two extremes, of course—we can admit that. What seems hard for us to admit is that we are quite comfortable in our two Wests, inhabiting them simultaneously without even realizing it, and unaware that we need both for our national health and well-being.

For an introduction to the West That Wasn't, look at the activities of the Cowboy Hall of Fame and Western Heritage Center in Oklahoma City—an organization which exists to keep pioneer days in the West from being forgotten. It has a lot of money behind it and can afford to keep alive anything it wants to. It has first-class facilities, including an art gallery, a library, a museum, a magazine, and an annual awards night which pays tribute to the best artists, writers, actors, movie makers, and musicians who have worked in the Western field during the preceding year. The 1975 awards gave special recognition to several "classic" movies, including *The Westerner*, starring the late Walter Brennan as Roy Bean, the Law West of the Pecos. A scene from the film was shown in which Bean sentences a man to hang and sees that the sentence is carried out.

This is a fine example of the West That Wasn't, for Roy Bean never hanged anybody. He was a really a small-time sharper whose ultimate ambition was to cheat everybody who passed through Langtry, Texas. He threatened a few noisy offenders with the noose, but it was all bluff. He could have sued the Cowboy Hall of Fame for defamation of character if he had been alive in 1975 and aware of of the situation.

Such tampering with the facts is offensive to many people who don't understand that we need the mythical West. Regional historians have registered their disillusion by exposing some of the most admired Western heroes, particularly Wyatt Earp, Bat Masterson, and others of their era, who have turned out to be anything but the perfect gentle knights their biographers have painted for us. In actual fact they were no braver or wiser or more efficient than many other men, but they do seem to have been better liars.

The rebellion extends to the Western novel, where the opposition between the two Wests is most clearly visible. Many novelists are now reacting strongly against the phony or mythical West, making fun of the familiar stereotypes and turning the hallowed conventions upside down.

Take, for example, Gary Jennings' 1975 opus, *The Terrible Teague Bunch*, about an attempted train robbery in Texas in 1905, which the dust jacket introduces to the reader in these words: "Here is the real Old West; this is the way it was." An early scene begins: "It was a crisp October night, cold for Nacogdoches at this season, and a brisk wind was whipping dust, old newspapers, stable chaff and dried horse manure down the unpaved streets."

Zane Grey would never have written that.

L. R. Foyt, the old cowboy who plays the leading role, wears bib overalls and implies that all sensible cowboys do the same. "More pockets to carry things in." And Foyt conceals his six-shooter in the bib. He explains why:

> Nobody but the actors in Wild West shows ever did that face-off-and-reach-pardner performance. If you had reason to shoot a man, it was far more sensible to dog him unawares and shoot him in the back . . . but if it ever come to a face-to-face encounter, it was blamed foolishness to have your gun hanging out where your opponent could see you grab for it.

The bib-holster method of gun toting made some interesting strategy possible:

> Say that you, an ordinary nonprofessional somebody, had to throw down on somebody. . . . First you looked away from the other fellow,

maybe over his head, and looked thoughtful, as if you'd just discovered you had a flea in your chest hair, then you stuck your hand inside the bib to scratch yourself, and then you brought your hand out full of pistol.

One of Foyt's victims thanked him, as he was carried out, for the lesson in the technique of "itch-scratch-shoot."[1]

Mr. Jennings' attitude is only one example of a fairly general reaction against the familiar and traditional concept of the Wild West —a concept which has been passed on from generation to generation since the days of the dime novel. A fair percentage of the "westerns" that are being screened or published now are burlesque westerns, tongue-in-cheek westerns, satirical westerns. The list starts with *Cat Ballou* and goes on to such examples as *Sureshot Shapiro, True Grit, Little Big Man, Support Your Local Sheriff, The Day Fort Larkin Fell, Dingus Magee, Blazing Saddles,* and many, many more.[2] Super-violent westerns are a form of protest. The antihero is a form of protest. Camp westerns are a form of protest.

The revolt has gone so far that we may soon be seeing a whole new set of stereotypes—concepts which will make the Old West completely commonplace, with horse manure blowing down the streets of Trail Town and cowboys bellying up to the bar in bib overalls.

The cure in such a case would be as bad as the disease. For the romantic West, the West of Zane Grey and Owen Wister, of "Gunsmoke" and "Rawhide"—what might be called the Violent West— was not completely phony. It was real enough; it just wasn't real all the time. The violence was there. Conflicts and feuds and shoot-outs existed. They still do. Nesters and big cattlemen did confront each other. Indians did wipe out whole families of settlers, and wronged individuals did pursue their foes all over the country seeking revenge. The moving-picture West is made up of selected bits of reality, but the implication that the Violent West is the true and complete West is all wrong. Most of the troubles of the pioneer Westerners were nonviolent: isolation, loneliness, boredom, back-

[1] Gary Jennings, *The Terrible Teague Bunch*, pp. 38, 136–137.
[2] Another 1975 example is George L. Voss, *The Man Who Believed in the Code of the West.*

breaking toil, mortgages, grasshoppers, blizzards, drouths, sickness, and old age and death. Only a small percentage of them died of lead poisoning.

This does not alter the fact that the Violent West is more real to most of us than the reality. We have seen it and heard it all our lives. It is all that some Americans know about their history and all that many foreigners will ever know. It has crept into our minds, and it conditions our attitudes toward many things—the Indian and the Mexican, the handgun and the horse, the whole process which we used to call "the Winning of the West." The two Wests can and do exist side by side in our minds, influencing each other and overlapping each other, without causing us any discomfort. As evidence, take Murray Sinclair's column in the *Arizona Daily Star* (Tucson) for July 3, 1974: "Dial 800-255-3050 and you get a special desk in Kansas City where instant assistance can be given in five languages—English, French, German, Spanish and Japanese. The service is free. The oddest question to date (in all seriousness): 'Can you drive through the West without being ambushed by Indians?' "

Even in what is left of the range country, the West That Wasn't is cherished and believed in. One night twenty-five years ago when I was working on a book about the mid-century cattleman,[3] I camped under a bridge on the Rosebud River in Montana, and after supper I walked to a ranch house nearby and got acquainted. I noted that there was a bookcase in the living room and that it was devoted almost entirely to the works of Will James. The real West was taking lessons from a purveyor of the legendary West.

The two Wests are there, both real enough, and we hold dual citizenship in them. At the moment, however, we seem to feel that we ought to make a choice—that we are committing some sort of intellectual bigamy if we don't. The cry is for "authenticity" even in commercial or formula fiction. When William Decker's *To Be a Man* delighted the critics and reviewers in 1967, Wallace Stegner called it "as authentic as sagebrush and dirt." Mr. Stegner was right about it, too, but he was putting himself in the position of praising a chorus girl for her virtue—emphasizing the nonessential. Authentic details in a standard western are usually no more than a few lines and

[3] C. L. Sonnichsen, *Cowboys and Cattle Kings.*

creases on the old familiar face of the Violent West. Fashions change. The pulps disappear. Zane Grey's novels become period pieces for graduate students to analyze. But the West That Wasn't is a rock that withstands all assaults. We won't give it up. We can't give it up. And the question is, Why?

Time magazine found a simple answer in 1959 in a famous essay called "The American Morality Play." The western, the author declared, is an allegory of human life and death in which the forces of good (in white hats) and the forces of evil (in black hats and five-o'clock shadow) fight it out on the huge Western stage. Evil always loses. The viewer or reader goes his way fulfilled and satisfied, convinced that the universe is in good hands.

The year 1956, a turning point in the history of the form, brought the eternal struggle into Everyman's living room. *Time* continues:

> Tail over dashboard, wild as a herd with heel flies, the U.S. television audience is in the midst of the biggest stampede for the wide-open spaces since the California gold rush. T.V.'s western boom began four years ago, and every season since then the hay haters have hopefully predicted that the boom would soon bust. Yet every season it has been bigger than the last. Last week eight of the top ten shows on T.V. were horse operas. . . . This season, while other shows, from quizzes to comedies, were dropping right and left like well-rehearsed Indians, not a single western left the air. Indeed 14 new ones were launched, and the networks are planning more for next year. Sighs a well-known writer of western scripts: "I don't get it. Why do people want to spend so much time looking at the wrong end of a horse?" [4]

Could all this excitement proceed from a desire for assurance that God is in his heaven attending to the management of the world, as "Morality Play" suggests? "Not at all," say the more recent analysts. "That is a monumental oversimplification." And then they come up with ever more ingenious explanations for our attachment to the Violent West—so ingenious and so detailed and so learned that one wonders how much more analysis the old simple, carefree western can stand.

In 1974 three more titles were added to those already on hand, bringing additional scholarship and insight to the subject. *Focus on the Western* is edited by Jack Nachbar, a critic and reviewer of note

[4] *Time*, March 20, 1959.

based at Bowling Green University in Ohio, home of the Popular Culture Press and the *Journal of Popular Culture*. Nachbar thinks that western movies are "the single most important story form of the twentieth century." Westerns "account for twenty-five to thirty percent of American-made features," and they "define for all classes of white Americans their traditional ethics, values and sources of national pride."[5] Thirteen assorted contributors agree with him. Kathryn C. Esselman finds that the western is rooted in "the image of the knight and the concept of the quest." Richard W. Etulain looks for its origin nearer the present in the rise of the cowboy hero and in the back-to-nature movement of the early 1900's. Jon Tuska notes its use as a vehicle for social protest.

Philip French, a University of Texas professor, covers some of the same ground in *Westerns*. He is interested, as was Henry Nash Smith, in the movies as a response to the hang-ups and fantasies of the viewing public—their changing attitudes toward reality. His basic theory, which many readers may not buy, is that most western films since 1950 are social and political commentaries in disguise. Any director with a message, he believes, can get it stated by making a western. *High Noon*, for example, was about "existential man standing alone in the McCarthy era," and *The Wild Bunch* is a commentary on the Vietnam war. Disillusionment with the dominant group has grown steadily, and the "Post Western," particularly as conceived by Sam Peckinpaugh, is "not a harbinger of a brave new world" but "a symbol of a deadening mass society and a dehumanized technology."

The pedagogic function of the western, says French, is best illustrated in moving pictures about Indians as the emphasis changes in the fifties and sixties toward an idealization of the native American, picturing him as a superior human being and his life as "a valid counter culture, a more organic, life-enhancing existence than white society."[6] In short, the western is now part of the literature of protest —possibly of the New Left.

Last comes Jeni Calder with *There Must Be a Lone Ranger*. Calder is sensitive to changing emphases, particularly in filmed westerns; she knows that in the sixties the hero became "mean, vicious

[5] Jack Nachbar (ed.), *Focus on the Western*, p. 2.
[6] Philip French, *Westerns*, pp. 23, 32, 35, 89, 136.

and self-seeking" and that the western challenged "the glorification of the gunfighter and the simple proposition that the cavalry was the good guys and the Indians the bad guys" while it exposed "the rotten morality of commercialism." But these negative reactions, she says, can't destroy the hard core of the myth. It survives "in spite of history, in spite of progress, and in spite of movies destroying the Western hero."[7]

Calder has said most of what needs to be said about the way we remodel history to suit our needs and purposes and why we do it, but the psychologists, sociologists, social historians, and culture buffs won't leave it at that. They show amazing ingenuity in finding new and ever more bizarre reasons for the popularity of the western, and the brilliance of their critical insight is exceeded only by the density of their prose. Dr. Kenneth J. Munden, a psychologist, calls the enmity in a standard western "a classic symptom of the Oedipus conflict."[8] Several critics have argued that the western is an expression of the reader's or viewer's sexual drives and have viewed the six-shooter as a phallic symbol. John C. Cawelti discusses "the ticklish subject of the Western as a dream."[9]

Analysis by such specialists has gone so far that a backlash has set in. "The purpose of the popular Western novel is to entertain," Russell Nye trumpets in a recent survey of the popular arts:

> and it is effective only insofar as it succeeds in doing so. It is written neither to shock nor to titillate; it is neither myth nor epic nor multi-level symbolic narrative. It is an adventure story, good or bad only as it succeeds or fails to come alive as adventure and communicates the Western experience accurately and honestly. Fashionable academic criticism, beginning about 1954, saddled the Western novel with hero myths, fertility rites, quests, ritual killings, and phallic symbolism, very nearly smothering it in a fog of footnotes . . . it is not and never was, as Henry Allen has said, "mythic or Gothic or parapsychological or a meaningful social document."[10]

Who would have thought twenty-five years ago that the humble

[7] Jeni Calder, *There Must Be a Lone Ranger*, pp. 213 (quoting Anthony Penn), 190.

[8] John C. Cawelti, *The Six-Gun Mystique*, pp. 14–15.

[9] Ibid., pp. 81–85.

[10] Russell B. Nye, *The Unembarrassed Muse: The Popular Arts in America*, p. 303.

western could rise to such a pinnacle of importance or call forth such conflicting opinions? But it has. And as sometimes happens in a poker game that seems to be getting out of hand, there are calls for a new deck. Leslie Fiedler thinks it is time for a "New Western" and gives thanks to half a dozen authors, including himself, for having broken away from outworn conventions. He defines a western as any book with an Indian, or at least a dark man (a Negro will do), in it. He includes *The Sotweed Factor, Midnight Cowboy,* and *One Flew over the Cuckoo's Nest* in his list of new westerns, and he classifies Ernest Hemingway's reminiscent stories about his boyhood in Michigan as "crypto-westerns" because Indians are in them.[11]

Mr. Fiedler is probably wasting his breath. The western story seems to be monolithic and indestructible—in no danger of being replaced. "At regular intervals," says Jeni Calder, "the demise of the Western is announced, but the myth retains its vitality."[12]

The question is still, Why?

All the critics and historians realize that the answer lies somewhere in our group consciousness—in our awareness of ourselves as a people or a nation—but they don't get much beyond that. Calder tells us that the western in all its forms "enriches a brief past for the benefit of a possibly barren present."[13] Henry Allen (Clay Fisher, Will Henry) believes with Hal Borland that "when legends die, society goes next and quickly."[14] John C. Cawelti notes that "the Western formula does allow serious attempts on the part of creators and audience to relate contemporaneous conflicts to the American past."[15] Everybody is aware that the western is responding to a basic need, but nobody tells us exactly what that need is.

I suggest that this basic need is a natural and normal hunger for a heroic past. We want to have roots in ancient times, like other peoples, but we don't stay in one place long enough to grow them. We move about freely, and some of us live on wheels. Many of us know nothing about our own grandfathers. Pride of family is denied

[11] Leslie Fiedler, *The Return of the Vanishing American*, pp. 13, 24, 26, 144–146.

[12] Calder, *There Must Be a Lone Ranger*, p. 218.

[13] Ibid.

[14] Ann Falke, "Clay Fisher or Will Henry?" in *The Popular Western*, ed. Richard W. Etulain and Michael Marsden, p. 644/52.

[15] Cawelti, *Six-Gun Mystique*, p. 74.

to all but a few of us. Pride of race has to be built. Any group with a thousand-year history has these things provided, but the American is a newcomer and not yet completely at home in his vast country. All he has is the mythical West, and he needs it desperately.

As we look around at the inhabitants of this planet, we note that every group thinks itself specially favored, specially endowed, specially capable. Other groups seem inferior, if not subhuman. The Jews were the Chosen People, and all outsiders were gentiles. To the Greeks all non-Greeks were barbarians. All tribal subdivisions of the Athapaskan stock on our continent use a word for themselves which translates as "the people." Thomas Berger's *Little Big Man*, following Parkman's *Oregon Trail*, notes that the Cheyenne refer to themselves as "the Human Beings," implying that all others exist on a lower plane. The book goes out of its way to demonstrate the soundness of this judgment by exhibiting the subhuman, nonhuman, and inhuman characteristics of the "civilized" white man.

It is significant that the word *alien*, although it means only "someone who isn't me," has overtones of strangeness and not-quite-rightness. An alien is an outsider, and he is probably ignorant and crude. It is true that in our time some of us have developed a tolerance and understanding which would have puzzled our forefathers exceedingly, but the basic confidence is there: *We are the people and what we do and believe is right. Others are suspect and probably need our help and guidance.* Kipling called these others "lesser breeds without the law" and exhorted his fellow Anglo-Saxons to "take up the white man's burden."

We say the same thing in different words. We talk about "underdeveloped nations" and the "Third World" now—no condescending language is permitted—but most middle-class Americans still assume that we should lead the world, police the world, direct the world, and even upgrade the world. It is hard, even impossible, for us to accept the fact that we are Ugly Americans to so many other peoples.

Yet it is right for us to believe in ourselves, to have a sense of mission, to consider ourselves "the people," "the human beings." We are only doing what all ethnic groups have done since time immemorial. A belief in our special gifts and special destiny is natural and therefore right. It can be overdone, like all useful things, but some self-confidence on any level—personal or national—is necessary for survival just as food is necessary. Just because a great many people overeat, one can't ignore the fact that everybody must eat to live.

Some national pride is essential, but Americans have very little of it left. Our general attitude seems to be negative, our thinking guilt ridden. We are ashamed of our past and doubtful of our future. We admit that we are destroying our environment. We see ourselves as greedy and materialistic. We confess that we do not know how to live. We have come to believe that our pioneer fathers before us were no good, either. One contemporary writer calls the first comers to Arizona "the dregs of their respective societies." [16] The Indians, we acknowledge, were better men than the whites who conquered them and took away their lands and their living. Having thus lost our confidence in Columbia's happy land and in the heaven-born band of heroes who created it, we have come close to classifying ourselves among the "lesser breeds without the law." An individual in this condition would be advised to see a psychiatrist. Unfortunately, there is no such thing as a psychiatrist for nations.

We might not be in this situation if we knew who we were; if we had some roots with which to reassure ourselves; if we could look back on—invent, if necessary—a heroic past, the way other peoples do. We need a national myth to help us understand the nature of the universe and our place in it. If our history went back far enough, we, too, could take pride in forebears who slew monsters, put down oppressors, befriended the poor, and in general behaved positively and directly, as we are unable to do.

All we have to fill this basic need is twenty-five years between 1865 and 1890. It was something like a heroic age, and we have done our best to make it into one. Unfortunately, it was too brief and too recent to serve the purpose. Too many survivors remembered it, and the facts were always getting in the way of the legends.

I used to know Mrs. Sophie Poe, wife of John Poe, who was present when Pat Garrett did Billy the Kid in. During the filming of one of the early movies on Billy, Mrs. Poe was called to Hollywood as an expert on the Kid and his times. She watched the director revise the historical facts until she could bear it no longer. As she

[16] John Upton Terrell, *Apache Chronicle*, p. xii.

described the scene to me, she approached this majestic figure and said: "Sir, I knew that little buck-toothed killer, and he wasn't the way you are making him at all."

"Mrs. Poe," came the answer, "I understand your feelings, but this is what the people want."

From his own point of view the director was completely right, and if he had made his motion picture one hundred years later, or even fifty, nobody would have objected. Nobody would have been left who could object.

Even so, the protests in our time might have been sporadic and ineffective if it had not been for television. In the mid-fifties James Arness, Ward Bond, Richard Boone, Hugh O'Brian, Chuck Connors, Dale Robertson, and Clint Walker became part of our everyday lives. "One day," *Time* magazine sums it up, "these he-manly specimens were just so many sport coats on Hollywood's infinite rack. The next they were TV's own beef trust. Their teeth were glittering, their biceps bulging, their pistols blazing, right there in the living room; it was more fun, as they say in Texas, than raisin' hell and puttin' a chunk under it."[17]

Too much exposure, however, was fatal. The growing myth, the upsurge of faith in the West That Wasn't, brought screams of protest, and revulsion spread like a prairie fire. At the heart of the conflagration was Wyatt Earp, as portrayed by Stuart Lake in 1931 in *Wyatt Earp: Frontier Marshal* and by the TV series of the fifties and sixties. Lake invented Wyatt as Geoffrey of Monmouth invented King Arthur, and a frontier character who was not very brave and not very efficient and not very truthful came out as Sir Galahad on a mustang. The book, said the publishers, was "the straight goods, the real facts, far more exciting than any fiction." Wyatt was "the greatest gun-fighting marshal the Old West ever knew."

"Did you ever lose a fight?" Lake asked him.

" 'Never,' he admitted, and one had to know the man to comprehend the innate simplicity of the answer."[18]

At once the Kansas historians began cutting Wyatt down to size. Frank Waters, thundering out of Taos, New Mexico, called Lake's

[17] *Time*, March 20, 1959.
[18] Stuart Lake, *Wyatt Earp: Frontier Marshal*, pp. 150, 358.

book "the most assiduously concocted blood-and-thunder piece of fiction ever written about the West, and a disgraceful indictment of the thousands of true Arizonans whose lives and written protests refute every discolored incident of it."[19] Peter Lyon took Earp for an even rougher ride. "Earp . . . and Bat and the others spent so many nights in Dodge's brothels that they were known as 'the fighting pimps.' "[20] Ed Bartholomew followed Earp's career through two thick volumes and left him with scarcely a shred of credibility.[21] And John Gilchriese of Tucson, who has more material on Earp than any other man or agency, calls Earp "a rather pathetic subject."[22]

Earp was, in one of J. Frank Dobie's phrases, "a man suitable to his time and place," and no doubt he was useful in the various communities where he served. If he had not tried to claim more than he was entitled to, he could have occupied a modest niche in the gallery of notable frontiersmen. But he and his chief biographer were *not* content, and his exposure set off a whole series of skeptics who turned the spotlight of fact on the myth and tried to destroy it.

They did not succeed. Wyatt was shoddy material for the myth, but he was all we had, so we used him and brought him up to specifications. We needed heroes. We needed a glorious past. Our values were more important to us than the truth. Earp had to undergo a change "into something rich and strange" to fit the image of our desire. It was unfortunate that Mrs. Poe and Nyle Miller of the Kansas Historical Society were around to rub our noses in the realities, but we refused to be converted. We dragged Wyatt up out of his frontier gutter and cleaned him up like a mother getting her grubby little boy ready for Sunday school. As a result, most people will probably believe a century from now that "Tombstone was lawless but one man was flawless." Our need for a heroic past is very great.

Jeni Calder agrees. In her opinion, "The days of the Western frontier were brief. For a period of thirty years to produce a figure

[19] Frank Waters, *The Colorado*, p. 226.

[20] Peter Lyon, "The Wild, Wild West," *American Heritage* 11 (August, 1960): 10.

[21] Ed Bartholomew, *Wyatt Earp, 1848 to 1880: The Untold Story*, and *Wyatt Earp, 1879 to 1882: The Man and the Myth*.

[22] John Gilchriese to CLS, Glendale, California, June 24, 1962.

and all his supporting detail that was going to last for more than a hundred years was something like an instinctive necessity."[23]

That is exactly the point. And the reason for this instinctive necessity follows: With the roots we find in the West That Wasn't we have a better chance of being not just people but *a* people. This is the truth that Calder and the others are reaching for: "As long as Westerns are structured with plots and heroes or antiheroes, in other words, as long as it is acknowledged that the Western cannot imitate history and should not, the myth will survive."[24]

Jon Tuska is even farther down the same road in his essay "The American Western Cinema" when he concludes: "I cannot tell you if the Western can survive without heroes. Can you tell me if Western man will survive without them?"[25]

Should anyone have the temerity to announce that the western story is our Old Testament, our *Iliad* and *Odyssey*, our *Nibelungenlied*, he would run into heavy weather. He would, however, have some right on his side. Until we can produce our own epics and sagas, the horse opera will have to do as a substitute.

[23] Calder, *There Must Be a Lone Ranger*, p. 219.
[24] Ibid., p. 215.
[25] Jon Tuska, "The American Western Cinema: 1903–Present," in *Focus on the Western*, ed. Jack Nachbar, p. 43.

The Wyatt Earp Syndrome

IF you like to read westerns (with a small w), the popular, paperback, prefabricated, newsstand variety, you would be well advised to do it on the sly, because the historians and critics of popular fiction think you are sick. Your favorite entertainment, they say, purges the urges of a lunatic fringe of the reading public.

This is a fairly recent development. There was a time, and not long ago, when the horse opera, on the screen or between covers, was accepted as innocent diversion, an opiate for an idle hour. In those days people who knew of your weakness for flaming guns and cross-country pursuits might consider your tastes juvenile, but never depraved. Now all is changed. The western itself has changed. The heart of the old tree may be sound and solid, but some unusual branches bearing strange fruit have been grafted to the trunk. The old ritual violence has been intensified and amplified out of all bounds, thereby drawing the reader deeper into his neurotic jungle.

To make matters worse, all popular fiction, including the western, is being studied as social history, and its variations and vagaries are solemnly observed and recorded by scholars—"pale young men in libraries," as Emerson called them. To critics and historians, including the writer of this essay, the western is not just for fun any more. It is a Significant Document. Functionally, it resembles a fever chart or an electroencephalogram or a Rorschach test. It reveals strange things, uncomfortable things, about the reader of horse operas and all his generation—things our fathers would never have suspected and would not have admitted had they known.

We began hearing about these developments in the mid-sixties when newspaper stories started calling our attention to "The Modern Western—Neuroses on the Range."[1] James K. Folsom sounded the

---

[1] *Houston Chronicle*, October 3, 1964—a discussion of *Rio Conchos* and *Invitation to a Gunfighter*, films shown in that year.

note loud and clear in 1966 in *The American Western Novel*: "The stalwart cowboy . . . who rides off into the sunset leaving a weeping maid behind once seemed pathetic, even tragic; to us he seems ridiculous, and may even be, we whisper, homosexual" (pp. 32–33).

In the golden years of the western such an idea would have provoked raucous laughter. Hopalong Cassidy a member of the gay community? Ridiculous! Impossible! These are new times, however. The writer of fiction produces what is demanded of him, and one of the things he produces is brutality. He does it for money. In the oldest profession this is known as pimping or pandering. Among writers it is called "gauging the public taste." To historians of our culture it means peddling broken bones, torn flesh, and streaming gore to readers with an unnatural appetite for violence.

John C. Cawelti, already quoted, argued convincingly that the western reflects the chaotic crime and brutality that lie just below the more or less peaceful surface of American life.[2] Psychologist Theodore Isaac Rubin approached the problem from another angle in 1968. In an article titled "What the Movies Reveal about You, the Audience," he noted that "many of us are emotional time bombs" and contended that "acceptable identification with heroic violence makes a minute amount of relief possible." All of us, he declared, "contain a little murderous psychology," and this side of our nature responds to the "heroic, unfeeling killing" in western movies and novels.[3] The conclusion we come up with, after sufficient exposure to the Folsoms, the Caweltis, and the Rubins, is that modern man, at least the subdivision that reads westerns, is really in difficulty—is, in fact, a victim of the Wyatt Earp syndrome.

A syndrome, in case a definition is called for, is "a group of concurrent symptoms characterizing a disease." But what has Wyatt Earp to do with it?

Stuart N. Lake has the answer. Thanks to him and his idealized biography *Wyatt Earp: Frontier Marshal* (1931), Wyatt by mid-century had become the perfect example of the gunman-hero. America loved him and believed in him. He was an invincible champion with fists or gun, nerveless, lightning fast on the draw, a killer with a tender heart, a protector of the weak. He was in truth a Christ figure

---

[2] John C. Cawelti, "The Gunfighter and Society," *The American West* 5 (March, 1968): 77.

[3] *Glamour* 60 (October, 1968): 163, 225.

in cowboy boots wielding the thunderbolts of the Almighty. That readers could and did identify in droves with this mythical paragon is proved by the multiple editions through which Lake's book has progressed and by the number of moving pictures and television shows starring Wyatt and his faithful friend Doc Holliday.

The reason for this mystical union between simple citizen and gunman, we are told, is the reader's desire to eat his murders and have them, too. As he reads, he acts out in fantasy his lusts, death wishes, revenge impulses, irrational hates—compensatory imaginings of all kinds. When a few years ago he put down his money for a copy of *Tombstone Showdown* or *Warlock* or *Who Rides with Wyatt?* —when he puts down his money today for a book about Edge the Loner or Steele the Manhunter or Sundance or Cuchillo Oro, he showed and shows himself for what he is—something out of Kraft-Ebbing or the Marquis de Sade. The six-shooter becomes a phallic symbol; the walkdown—a confrontation on the streets of a Western town—is a sacrificial rite. The last frontier, in the words of James K. Folsom, is "finally something more than an aspect of the American West." Its topography comes "to resemble the landscape of the human soul."[4] And a pretty revolting landscape it is.

As the sixties faded and more and more sex and violence were tolerated and even demanded, the landscape became bleaker. The sickness of the western fan seemed more and more acute, and the evidences of his disease more and more apparent. A pathological personality began to emerge. A curious critic could look on the revolving racks in the drugstore, as he can today, and see for himself the curious characteristics which identify this twisted human being.

We can call him Felix Lapgore (in France his name is Coupegorge; in Germany, Schnittfleisch). Outwardly he may seem to be normal, though if you watch him at a bullfight or a bad automobile accident, his eager expression will give him away. He goes to church and belongs to a service club. He is kind to his wife and children. Inside, however, lurks something else—the strange cravings and lusts which make up the Wyatt Earp syndrome. The "concurrent symptoms" would analyze out somewhat as follows:

Loneliness. Felix Lapgore feels in his heart that he is a social

[4] James K. Folsom, *The American Western Novel*, p. 32.

liability and nobody really likes him. He identifies with the Lone Ranger or Hopalong Cassidy or Destry or Shane. In his world of fantasy he becomes a defender of the people, who thereupon accept and love him.

Timidity. He knows he is basically a coward and dreads being tortured or humiliated, so he dreams of being the fastest gun in Texas with complete confidence in his own powers. Here it is possible to bring in the six-shooter as a phallic symbol if one has the urge.

Inferiority. He has never been able to dominate anybody and therefore dreams of being the Pecos Kid, who never gives an order twice.

Moral erosion. He was put down by his mother and is afraid of his wife. He gets even by assuming that the only good woman in his dream world is a bad woman. He is married to a "good" woman and she has turned out to be pretty bad for him. A dance-hall girl with a heart of gold would be better. At least she would not do all the talking.

Bloodlust. His Sunday-school teacher assured him that it was all right for the Jews to smite the Amalekites hip and thigh and spoil the Philistines because they were the enemies of God's people. The Jews were ruthless but righteous killers, like Wyatt Earp. By identifying with them, he could watch all that blood run and at the same time remain a good Christian, a loyal American, and a lover of birds and little furry animals.

This is the average reader of westerns as the critics and historians seem to think of him. Some, at least, of the writers of commercial westerns agree, and plenty of proofs are available that they do so. As Exhibit A, take *The Hour of the Gun* by Robert Kreps. Fawcett Publications issued it in paperback in 1967 as a follow-up to the "towering motion picture" of the same title.

It is about Wyatt Earp and Doc Holliday, the fight at the O.K. Corral, and the aftermath (completely imaginary) of that famous fight. Wyatt is a noble character obsessed by the law, which, in his view, must be upheld at all costs. The concept is not original with Kreps. Oakley Hall took the same view in his much-discussed novel *Warlock* (1958). Making Wyatt a purist in this respect, however, is a sure way of getting inside the reader's defenses, and Kreps has a right to use the technique. Doc Holliday, it should be said, is not taken in. Doc is a sardonic wit who contemplates life with a curled upper lip and distrusts all human pretensions to idealism, including Wyatt's. He feels justified when Wyatt finally takes the law into his own hands after one of his brothers is killed and another crippled for life.

They are not frontier toughs, a fact which sets up an interesting tension between their superior minds and their brutal acts. The Princetonian cast of their conversation appears as Doc hands over his badge after the O.K. Corral fight.

> "Here, son, masked ball's over. No more Hallowe'en till next year."
> "Okay," said Wyatt, heavily, accepting it. "You're incorrigible, Doc."
> "Know why I like you, old lawdog? Cause you know words like *incorrigible*. You were cut out for better things than to stand behind a gun."
> "So were you."
> "*Touché*," said Doc evenly. "*Touché* and check, Wyatt."[5]

The big moment comes when Wyatt and Doc run Ike Clanton, the villain, to earth in Mexico, where he has a big ranch and a palatial *hacienda*. In these times a villain must belong to the establishment, even in a western:

> Wyatt walked south again, along the porch, his eyes flicking each gap between pillars as he passed it. Then Clanton stepped out from his hiding place behind the furthest column, shotgun cocked and held in both hands. And Wyatt came on. . . .
> He smiled. It was perhaps the most dreadful grimace that Wyatt Earp had ever made, compounded of hate and fury and a grim, piti-less, inhuman joy. He walked steadily on toward the man, who waited for him, frozen in his place. Wyatt made not the slightest motion toward the gun in the holster. He simply walked forward coldly until Clanton, his hard lined face pale as milk, jerked the shotgun up to fire.
> Then Wyatt made the draw of a lifetime and the gun bucked and roared in his hand and Clanton was slammed backward, staggering on his bootheels for a yard more, his face astonished, his finger tight-ening on the double trigger so that the blast of the greener tore into the side of his great house; and he whirled and fell on his face, the shotgun caught in the crook of his right arm so that it came with a

[5] Robert Kreps, *The Hour of the Gun*, p. 13.

crunch against the forearm and broke it as Clanton crashed to the floor. Wyatt walked forward and kicked him over viciously onto his back. Clanton was alive, his dark and cynical eye open and glaring at Wyatt, his mouth drooling saliva and a steady low droning noise of agony. Wyatt shot him in the belly twice and stood above him and reloaded his gun, six bullets, and very methodically and without pause shot his head to pieces so that when the hammer clicked on an empty cartridge the thing at his feet looked like a man's body with a shattered pumpkin full of blood and shards of bone stuck atop the neckerchief at his throat.

Then Wyatt reloaded his six-gun and shoved it down hard into the holster and, turning his back on what he had done, went to the door and into the house. . . .[6]

If this sort of action is what the average reader of Westerns yearns for, he is a sick man indeed, and the Wyatt Earp syndrome is no illusion. I submit that he picked up the germ back there in Sunday school when he first heard of the joys of righteous killing. It is more than likely that Samson with his jawbone killed his thousand men much as Earp killed Clanton in Kreps's novel, "very methodically and without pause" knocking their heads to pieces so that they resembled "shattered pumpkins full of blood and shards of bone stuck atop" whatever they wore around their necks.

No intelligent person, of course, would ever believe that Kreps wrote that passage seriously. Of course he didn't! He wrote it cynically with his face straight and his tongue in his cheek, well knowing that the current fashion is to kid the horse opera all over the pasture. For some time, perhaps since *Cat Ballou* (1956), movies, television shows, and soft-cover books have been seasoned with overtones of exaggeration, burlesque, and sly satire, showing how seriously we take our westerns. Satire is never wasted on trivial or insignificant things, and the writers who chip away at the Western myth with their little hammers know what a mighty rock they are attacking and how many people regard it as sacred.

Thomas Berger attacked it in 1964 when he followed Little Big Man through the whole range of frontier history, making him a hero when he lived as an Indian and a sot when he returned to the whites. Typical of his undercutting of Western conventions and stereotypes was Berger's account of Little Big Man's sister Caroline, captured

[6] Ibid., pp. 138–139.

by Old Lodge Skins' Cheyennes. Caroline expected to be ravished, could hardly wait to be ravished, and was intensely disappointed when she learned that Old Lodge Skins had no intention of ravishing her or anybody.

True Grit followed the same trail in 1968, and author Charles Portis was nearly drowned in enthusiastic comment. The motion picture, featuring John Wayne as Rooster Cogburn, provoked even more. Mattie Ross, the heroine, is a "pure" girl with an earnest faith in God and a burning desire to avenge her father's murder. She never suspects that there is any discrepancy between her faith and her desire. Mattie is perfectly realized as she dispenses buckets of blood without a qualm and without compunction. The burlesque of the ritual violence of the western is subtle but unmistakable. *Time* magazine was amused: ". . . the violence is imbued with a bigger-than-camp Bonnie and Clyde quality; the stock two-dimensional figures of the familiar Western landscape become disfigured here with a three-dimensional reality as limbs are chopped off and buckshot imbeds itself painfully beneath facial skin."[7]

What Charles Portis offers is basically what we get from Robert Kreps—violence so hoked up that it can't be taken seriously. The syndrome has become a gag. Felix Lapgore, of course, does not know that he is being satirized. He is too busy watching the blood flow.

In the seventies a tapering-off trend might have been expected, and indeed, the tongue-in-cheek western did give way to new things, but the appetite for human suffering and horrible death never lost ground, and may even have increased. Felix demanded his daily ration, and a number of competent specialists fed his appetite, going far beyond conventional saloon fights and walkdowns to provide extra rations of screams and convulsions.

These specialists tend to follow a pattern. First comes the invention of an extraordinarily ruthless killer, embittered by unspeakable cruelty visited on himself or on those he loves. He has to be expert with all weapons, often including a few unconventional ones, a man of lightning reflexes who possesses an inner monitor which warns him of danger at hand; a man incapable of remorse and unresponsive to love. With a mission of some kind and an adequate sup-

[7] *Time*, June 14, 1968, p. 94.

ply of victims and ammunition, this menacing figure can be turned loose in different parts of the West, emerging each time as practically the only survivor of a carnival of slaughter. He has to endure massive torture himself, but he survives to fight again in the next book. His name—Slade, Hawk, Fargo, Kershaw, Edge—is displayed prominently on each volume of the series, making it easy for Felix to find him on the stands and carry him home to his lair for secret consumption.

A foremost practitioner in this subgenre has been George Gilman, creator of Edge. His first effort, called *Edge: The Loner*, appeared in 1971 with many personal messages for the target reader:

> RAW
> This is the first book in a new western series, but it's more than just another novel of the American West. This is the bloodiest and most violent story that ever erupted from our native territory. Here is mean, bone-chilling raw stuff, a compelling tale you'll never forget.
> EDGE
> His given name was Josiah Hedges, an innocent enough monicker. But one look at the cruel set of his mouth and the icy penetration of his eyes and anyone would recognize pure danger in man's clothing.[8]

"WARNING," says an introductory advertisement: "This story is not for the faint-hearted reader." Lapgore knows this is for him.

The story centers on revenge and pursuit. Captain Josiah Hedges, home from the Civil War, finds his crippled eighteen-year-old brother tortured and murdered. Hedges, or Edge, takes up the trail of the killers and disposes of them in the last chapter, running into many adventures along the way, all ending in agonizing death for someone. We watch buzzards tearing at a dead man and dragging his entrails across the landscape. We see an outlaw queen cut off the genitals of a supposed traitor before he is hanged. We witness an Apache attack in which Edge annihilates the enemy:

> One bullet from the Henry took him in the jaw, smashing upward so that when he screamed his death agony he sprayed jagged pieces of broken teeth before him.[9]

Edge catches up with his quarry in an Arizona village called Peaceville, formerly Warlock. The gang has taken over the town,

[8] George Gilman, *Edge: The Loner*, cover and pretitle page.
[9] Ibid., p. 80.

and one of them has beheaded the sheriff. The shooting and cutting begin at this point and are not over until the last of the murderers has died in screaming agony.

This is heady stuff, made to order for the Lapgores and the Coupegorges and the Schnittfleisches. The book went into a fifth printing in May, 1975. By February, 1977, the twenty-first in the series—called *Rhapsody in Red*—was on the market. By this time, for reasons best known to himself, Gilman had created another extraordinary killer named Steele, a Virginia gentleman who puts on gloves before he moves into danger and has perfect manners to go with his almost complete absence of human feeling. Possibly Steele was conceived because Edge was half Mexican and was referred to very often as "the halfbreed," contrary to current ideas of propriety. Perhaps Gilman felt that after twenty-plus volumes it was time to phase Edge out, though this theory is rendered unlikely by the continuing appearances of Captain Josiah—number twenty-three having been issued in August, 1977. At any rate, Steele was introduced with some new ideas to titillate the secret sadists. He kills with such weapons as a long pin concealed behind his lapel and a scarf with weighted ends which proves most useful when garroting is indicated.

In *The Bounty Hunter*, Steele finds himself in Mexico with the body of a wanted man on his hands. In order to claim the reward, he has to get the disintegrating corpse back across the Rio Grande, and Gilman makes the most of the horrors of this gruesome situation. Number four in the Steele series, *Valley of Blood*, appeared in 1975. The cover art shows the naked bodies of three men draped over a barbed-wire fence. We see them, mercifully, from the rear. They were guilty of rape, and Steele mutilated them suitably before he strung them up.

So it went as the seventies progressed. The sick reader called for more and more blood, torture, and suffering. He became more and more tolerant of filthy language, sexual horrors, and gutter realism, but his real appetite was for bone-wrenching, finger-cracking, eye-gouging violence. His happy hunting ground was the storehouse of paperback novels about the Apache wars, in which the Indian's supposed genius for inventing new and more refined tortures gave the novelist almost unlimited opportunity to present salable sadism. Well over 150 of these novels are in existence, and an analysis of their pecularities appears in another chapter of this book. A victim of the syndrome can always be sure of finding the torn flesh and screams of agony which he needs by watching the fictional Apache in action.

Another favorite locale for skull-shattering violence is northern Mexico. Miners, gunrunners, and fugitives from the law are in danger from *federales* or *rurales*, or the *rurales* are in danger from them. Stories about the Mexican revolution have a built-in storehouse of groans and gore. Behind it all one sees the stereotypes about Mexico and the Mexicans which have existed in the minds of *norteamericanos* since before the Mexican War of 1846 (the subject of another chapter in this book)—preconceptions about Mexican treachery, indolence, and bloodlust; about cruel and contemptuous *ricos*, bandits without soul or mercy, priests with evil intentions and wicked ways. If an American western writer wants to describe painful tortures and agonized deaths, Mexico is the place for him. Felix Lapgore will shudder and believe.

Start with *Apache Raiders*, a 1970 paperback by a writer who calls himself John Benteen. We pick up Fargo, "a man equipped for killing," who is delivering two hundred rifles to Colonel López, one of Villa's men, at a little town "far below the Rio Grande."[10] López, of course, tries to get the guns for nothing by killing Fargo. The gringo outsmarts him, however, and takes refuge in the thicket of desert growth surrounding the town. When his rifle is put out of commission, he waits till his pursuers are only yards away, then blasts them with a sawed-off shotgun, reloading and firing like a machine.

> Thirty-six buckshot slamming point-blank into a dozen men. The air rang with the shrill screams of wounded horses and dying riders. The animals were down, thrashing; others raked by lead reared, pawed, bucked. Cut to ribbons, men fell from saddles or were crushed under dying mounts. What had been a confident band of hunters was now a bloody, squirming mass of butchered flesh; and even as he perceived that, Fargo fired again, both barrels, straight into the turmoil.

López is on the outskirts of the melee, "his face a mask of fury"

---

[10] John Benteen, *Apache Raiders*, pp. 5, 7 (fourth in the Fargo series. Ten had been published in 1971).

as he trains his rifle on the gun runner. Fargo drops his shotgun and draws his Army Colt:

> The shot was a lucky one, but that did not help Lopez any. When the notched bullet caught him in the face, he ceased to have a head. It simply exploded, like an overripe pumpkin, dissolving in a red spray. . . . Fargo saw the headless body fall back over the horse's rump and the Winchester drop from its lifeless hand.[11]

This is in the mainstream of the superviolence demanded by the sick reader—the victim of the syndrome—and even more rewarding examples are provided as Fargo moves back across the line into the Big Bend region of Texas, where he encounters a band of Apaches. An evening with this book will ease the tensions of a susceptible reader and guarantee him a restful and innocent night's sleep.

Not all the Mexican adventure novels are as gory as this one. Several examples come to mind: Frank Castle's *Guns to Sonora* (1962), Glendon Swarthout's *The Cadillac Cowboys* (1964), Walt Slade's *Border War* (1968), Edwin Shrake's *Blessed McGill* (1968), Will Bryant's *Escape from Sonora* (1973), Lou Cameron's *Guns of Durango* (1976), and John Reese's *Hangman's Springs* (1976). There is plenty of fighting and sudden death in these books, just as there is in such popular successes as B. Traven's *The Treasure of the Sierra Madre* (1935) and Glendon Swarthout's *They Came to Cordura* (1958). The violence in such novels is what one expects of the Western adventure novel, soft-cover or hard-cover, and such middle-of-the road production may be expected to continue. The demand for advanced bloodletting, however, seems to have remained constant, and a number of competent practitioners have made a specialty of turning out such bloody books. These artisans follow the pattern by inventing a *macho* killing machine, giving him an appropriate name (two- or three-syllable Anglo-Saxon—nobody named Hitler or Mussolini or Perlmutter need apply), and following his adventures in and out of Mexico in a series bearing his name. A suitable example is Jack Slade's man Lassiter, who appears in a novel called *Guerrilla* (1972), riding "right into the middle of a Mexican revolution to kill a double-crosser." There is some tough fighting on a steamer bound

[11] Ibid., pp. 20, 21.

for Quintana Roo, but the real thrills come during an ill-fated attempt to land on the Mexican coast:

> Two men broke up with the boat. One of the dancing Irishmen got a shattered spike of wood through his belly and lay there screaming in the wreckage of the launch with the surf washing over him. Lassiter didn't know what the other man was. He was dead with a gaping head wound through which blood and brains oozed like boiled-over milk pudding. Lassiter turned the Winchester, jacked a shell and put the dying Irishman out of his misery.[12]

More heads disintegrate before the action is finished, and blood pours "like pumped water" from "huge wounds." Lassiter enjoys himself tremendously. Spencer, a Harvard man who is second in command of the expedition, tells him the truth about himself: "Just the killing. That's what you like. You'd be killing even if the other man didn't have a gun."[13] Spencer never heard of Felix Lapgore, but his words explain why Felix finds it so easy to identify with Lassiter.

An even better example of the gory paperback set in Mexico is Gordon D. Shireffs' 1977 novel *The Marauders*, starring Lee Kershaw, a typical hard-case series hero who kills without compunction and likes his victims to come in droves, platoons, and shiploads. He becomes involved with Beau Valery, a dreamer who leads a filibustering expedition into Mexico hoping to set up an independent commonwealth in Sonora. The commanding officer sends for Kershaw, who at the moment is living on an island in the Gulf of California with a half-Yaqui girl named Ynez, an expert lover, pearl diver, and knifewoman. At the moment only the first two of her talents are being put to use, but her Mexican cousin says of her, "That damned Yaqui hellcat! She could be almost as deadly as Kershaw if she thought Ramon sought to harm Kershaw in any way."[14] It was said of Lee that he was "as cold-gutted as a shark, nerveless as a hunting cougar, and that he bled ice-water when wounded."[15] They make a great combination.

The kind of action provided is well illustrated when Kershaw,

---

[12] Jack Slade, *Guerrilla*, p. 71.
[13] Ibid., pp. 137, 39.
[14] Gordon D. Shireffs, *The Marauders*, p. 18.
[15] Ibid., p. 33.

preparing to sign on with Valery as a spy, encounters Mullion, the second in command, who has just killed a would-be deserter from the expedition. He orders Lee to throw the body into a nearby pigsty, where the occupants are already grunting eagerly. "They'll clean off his face and hands first because they are exposed," he explains. "His own mother won't be able to recognize him by morning."[16]

More gruesome death is piled on when Valery's ship is blown up in the middle of the Gulf of California. The sharks have a rewarding time, and so does the eager reader:

> There wasn't a man alive in the bloody waters now, just terribly ravaged corpses swirling about as the lithe, sinuous black bodies of the sharks tore into them in a macabre feast of death.[17]

The story ends on Kershaw's hideout island. Mullion has now taken over the leadership. Exposed as a United States agent, Lee has to leave the ship and conduct operations from the shore. The pursuers sent to hunt him down suffer dreadful torments as they die one by one. Mullion finds that hell for him is a mangrove swamp:

> The rest of the men hesitantly followed Mullion into the stinking water. Red-hot needles stabbed into their necks as the tiny hard-bodied flies drove in at them for fresh blood. . . .
> The water was now waist deep. Mullion looked desperately ahead. . . . A man screamed somewhere behind Mullion. The screaming died away in a muffled splashing.
> "Something dragged him down," a man screamed.[18]

The end comes when Lee dynamites a cliff and buries Mullion's ship as it tries to leave the harbor. There are no survivors. At their hide-out he finds Ynez dying, and he buries her at sea, as she requests. Our sick man, when he reaches this point, will feel a deep sense of well-being, especially if he is a neat person and hates loose ends. If there are no survivors, there are no loose ends.

It would be possible to turn the spotlight on other distinguished examples of mutilation and meanness in Mexico, and some of the best ones are hard-cover novels, often with a claim to consideration as literature. A particularly revolting example is Forrest Carter's *The*

---

[16] Ibid., p. 62.
[17] Ibid., p. 136.
[18] Ibid., p. 188.

Vengeance Trail of Josey Wales (1976), in which rape and murder reach a sort of *ne plus ultra*. Perhaps the supreme example, however, is Oakley Hall's *The Adelita*, first copyrighted by Playboy Enterprises in 1975 and published in hard-cover format by Doubleday the same year. It tells the story of Robert MacBean, offspring of an American oil tycoon and a Mexican heiress, who moves between his two worlds until the outbreak of the Revolution makes it necessary for him to choose between them. He becomes the lover of La Adelita, a personification of the dedicated revolutionary and supposedly the inspiration for the famous marching song of Villa's men. Hall thinks that revolutions settle nothing and serve only to make corrupt politicians and spoilsmen out of the victors. With this bitter realization in the forefront of his thinking, and the knowledge that war is a brutal and gruesome business, he heaps violence on violence and brutality on brutality:

> They had hung the naked colorado by his genitals from a low branch. His gray flesh stretched by the rope resembled a loose sack in which his body was suspended. One hand made jerking attempts to catch at the rope while the other arm hung down bloody and shattered. His screaming never ceased. MacBean ran to him, drawing his revolver, and shot him dead.[19]

MacBean himself rapes the daughter of a *hacendado* when she defies and whips him. We watch a band of soldiers ravishing a mother beside her child's cradle. We are spectators as the firing squads do their work. We accompany the wounded to the "blood-stinking, blood-slippery, fly-loud butcher shop where stretchers with their freight are loaded five high on either side"—to the operating room of the hospital where Adelita, now pregnant, loses a hand:

> . . . he watched the bright little saw that Alfredo set against the flesh and gagged and closed his eyes. He opened them again to see the doctor cast the sad little remnant into a bucket, tuck the flap of skin over the awful stump, sew it with deft, swift stitches.[20]

One feels that Oakley Hall is genuinely sick at the thought of war and its consequences to human beings. He is not dropping in a pinch of rape here and an amputation there to give a sick reader a thrill. Nevertheless, the sick reader gets what he is looking for.

[19] Oakley Hall, *The Adelita*, p. 39.
[20] Ibid., p. 243.

The book shows the syndrome at work on the upper levels of Western writing in the middle seventies.

The same sort of quivering flesh is a staple item with a group of tough young novelists, many of them Texans, who show the influence of Larry McMurtry. A sort of measuring rod would be McMurtry's *Horseman, Pass By* (the movie was titled *Hud*), in which Lonnie the teen-aged narrator has to watch Hud rape the Negro cook and kill old Wildhorse Homer Bannon, Lonnie's grandfather and Hud's stepfather. Homer, crazed by the loss of his cattle, falls off the porch, breaking his hip, and Hud puts him out of his misery.

Members of the Tribe of Larry do just as well. John Irsfeld in *Coming Through* introduces a sadistic deputy sheriff named Pardee who is brutality personified. A climactic scene involves a fight to the death between him and Tudor Lutts, one of the meanest men ever made. It is all played out against the background of a disastrous flood which Irsfeld uses for maximum effect, counting the bodies and the "four thousand two hundred and seventeen people who were left homeless."

> The dead included Mr. and Mrs. Goodall, both in their seventies, in the bedroom they had shared for more than fifty years. The house was found six blocks from where it had stood on Palo Pinto Street. It had settled in the middle of the street itself, lodged against three jammed automobiles that had been deposited in a heap.[21]

The victim of the syndrome may find much to enjoy in this statistical approach to human suffering. There is also some good killing and raping in Irsfeld's second novel *Little Kingdoms* (1976).

Another member of the tribe is C. W. Smith, but his *Thin Men of Haddam* (1973) has a serious point to make, and the violence is not there for its own sake. It is about the plight of some Texas Chicanos who are getting nowhere in the world and blame their cousin Mendez for it because he works for a rich Anglo ranchman and should be able to find jobs for them. Social consciousness is not what our sick man is looking for, but the novel concludes with a wild and weird chase by night, a manhunt with violent death at the end, which might give him some rewarding moments.

He will be better satisfied with *Brothers*, tribe member Bobby

---

[21] John H. Irsfeld, *Coming Through*, p. 201.

Jack Nelson's 1975 novel about a part-time homicidal maniac in Texas. Curly is just out of the army—that is, out of its detention facilities—and has come home to Langley, an oil town where his brother Jimmy Roy has a job. He is a born troublemaker who goes into homicidal rages and flattens anybody who opposes him. Jimmy Roy loves him, covers for him, pays for him, and believes in him no matter what he does. His adoration is in its way a beautiful thing, but it obviously has no future. Curly is going to kill somebody.

Some of his enemies, who can't hope to whip him themselves, bring in an enormous half-witted fighter to do it for them. The battle is as brutal as they come. Gallagher, the imported gladiator, pulls a knife when Curly proves superior with fists. Curly's only weapon is his belt buckle.

> Gallagher rushed, slashing, and Curly whipped his belt. The knife missed, and the buckle sang in the air and hit with a loud slap, cutting Gallagher's face, and the big guy whirled and lashed out again, but Curly skipped clear.
> Melford was screaming, "Cut him, Gallagher, cut his guts out!"
> I looked for anything I could pick up, a stick, a rock, but there was nothing at hand and I stood helpless to watch.[22]

Curly's buckle turns out to be a murderous weapon, and Gallagher's face begins to disintegrate, becoming a "grisly sight."

> There were wide cuts in his scalp, a flap of skin hanging from his forehead, and a slather of blood sheeting one whole side of his face. One ear was badly ripped and seemed to be hinged only at the lobe. . . . Gallagher was being beaten around the face until you couldn't tell he had any face left. The buckle was striking until the head had to be pulpy and full of dents. When he stumbled and shook his head, the blood sprayed. It became obvious that he couldn't see. He was groping with his arms out as if in the dark, and Curly was moving around on every side fairly butchering the flesh from his skull.
> It was a kind of slaughter.
> And then it was over. With a great roar, Gallagher whirled and threw his arms over his head and sank to his knees. The knife slipped from his fingers and dribbled down his back to the ground, and as he held his head under his arms and rocked, I could hear him whimpering.[23]

[22] Bobby Jack Nelson, *Brothers*, p. 119.
[23] Ibid., pp. 120–121.

To get even, Curly's enemies tie Jimmy Roy to a tree and whip him almost as hard as Curly whipped Gallagher. When Curly sees the result, he goes berserk again, and this time he does kill somebody. The rest of the book is devoted to the manhunt which ends with his death. It is all good, hearty fare for Mr. Lapgore, showing the undiminished vitality of the syndrome well into the late seventies.

It is hardly an adequate defense of Messrs. Coupegorge, Schnitt-fleisch and Lapgore to point out that they may be sick, but others are sicker. That, however, is the case. The cult of violence in the latter half of the seventies showed signs of changing from a spectator sport to a do-it-yourself enterprise. True, the young in spirit identified with the Lone Ranger and Superman, but the rise in interest in violent crime was accompanied by a rise in interest in violent punishment. The reader was able to visualize himself as a one-man vigilance committee fighting crime by wiping out the criminals.

Versatile Western writer Brian Garfield showed the way in *Death Wish* (1972), though only one chapter was set in Tucson, with the rest in New York City. Paul is an unaggressive but very competent accountant whose wife is killed and whose daughter is changed into something nonhuman by a gang of rapists. They get away without leaving a trace, and Paul broods on the injustice of it all until he is ready to prowl Central Park with a gun and kill any creepy creature he encounters, thus becoming no better than the things he kills.

Paul has grievances enough to explain, if not to justify, his actions, but no explanation seems to be necessary. Assassination is becoming a hobby, like bird watching or chess. In May, 1977, according to columnist Bob Greene,[24] the first issue of a magazine called *Assassin* appeared on the newsstands. The cover shows President Carter's face covered by the crosshairs of a telescopic rifle sight. The legend beneath asks, "How Would YOU Do It?" An article within discusses the techniques of "Killing a Head of State," and instructions are included for making a nuclear weapon.

This is the end result of the Wyatt Earp syndrome, or something like it. The western will have to make a supreme effort to catch up.

The writers of traditional westerns, members of Western Writers

---

[24] *Arizona Daily Star*, May 1, 1977.

of America (WWA) leading the van, will have none of this perversion and redefinition of their product. As early as 1963, Nelson Nye, winner of a Golden Saddleman and author of nearly one hundred westerns, stood up to be counted: "The reader of westerns don't want no part of "history" that isn't history—he never was crazy about history in the first place. All he's hunting is a good, absorbing story of he-man adventure. . . . He don't want to be preached to, harangued at, nagged at, taught, or anything that adds up to discomfort. He wants to be entertained, period."[25]

Past President William O. Turner took the same side in the WWA *Roundup* for April, 1968: "The Western story is an adventure story and its truth is the truth of action and open country and the possibility of a man rising above himself and acting heroically. Because of its roots in American history and tradition it has an essential relationship to the American spirit and hence a potential that has not been fully realized. It surely needs writers who see this relationship and articulate it for the modern reader."

Some big guns among Western specialists agree. Wallace Stegner in an article called "History, Myth and the Western Writer," in *American West* for May, 1967, describes these sagas with interchangeable parts and foolproof formulas as "predictable, serene, and timeless fantasies of self-reliance and aggression . . . apparently good for another century and perhaps forever." The victims of the syndrome are outside his purview.

The big guns among the writers of westerns also refuse to pander to the sick reader and vigorously uphold their high calling as guardians of the past. "We chosen few," says novelist Will Henry, "have been charged with keeping alive both the fact and the fiction of the way it was out there along the wild frontier." The pioneers, he says, "were the most extraordinary people who ever built a nation anywhere. . . . Let's quit applying to yesterday's wild and dangerous frontier today's social Bandini. If you put enough manure on anything, you will get fungus and toadstools."[26]

That is what we have been talking about. The fungus and toadstools are flourishing, and the market for them is holding steady.

[25] Nelson Nye, *Roundup* 11 (June, 1963).
[26] Will Henry, "Let's Tell It Like It Was," *Roundup* 24 (December, 1976).

Too Tough to Tame:
Tombstone in Fiction

NO American small town has done better than Tombstone as a subject for fiction—certainly no Western town. The cities may get more attention. Tucson, for example, is the locale of nine fictional works that I know of, and there may be more, but Tombstone is a magic name. It is the scene of major action in at least nine novels, and in stories of the mining frontier, the Apache wars, the cowboy and the gunman it often rates a scene or two. The action of William Hopson's *The Tombstone Stage* comes nowhere near the village limits, but the name in the title probably sold many copies.

And why not? This was the most famous silver camp in the West, the number-one gunman capital, the cradle of a typically American legend: the saga of Wyatt Earp and his brothers and their friend Doc Holliday embattled against the desperadoes of the nearby towns and ranches. The legend makes their warfare an epic struggle between decency and outlawry. Their siege of Troy is the fight at the O.K. Corral. Their *Iliad* and their *Odyssey* are Walter Noble Burns's *Tombstone* and Stuart Lake's *Wyatt Earp: Frontier Marshal*.

Part of the legend was Tombstone itself: too tough to live in the eighties; too tough to die half a century later. It does no good for the historians to point out that half of the village was eminently respectable—that ladies from the East could shop for New York fashions on the south side of Allen Street and that the latest magazines were available in the reading room of the Tombstone Club for gentlemen. We choose to believe that the town was a sink of vice and iniquity and that only a lawman of heroic mould, personified by Wyatt Earp, could save it from itself. The men whose names we know—John Clum, George W. Parsons, Old Man Clanton, Dr. John Henry Holliday, Sheriff John Behan—are not thought of as flesh and blood but as semimythical figures in a familiar saga. Writers reshape them in accordance with their ideas, mindful only of certain stereo-typed patterns. Johnny Ringo, for instance, is always a brooding, mysterious Hamletlike figure; Behan is always a shifty opportunist. Nobody knows what Ringo was really like, and Behan appears to have been a much more complicated person than the stories say. But the Tombstone story is a legend, and that is how legends work.

Actually, the legend, as the fiction writers use it, operates on two levels: Earp and post-Earp. On the first level the Earp brothers and Doc Holliday are somewhere near the center of the picture, and the O.K. Corral fight is likely to be the climactic encounter. On the second level the Earps have fought their battle and departed, and Tombstone has reverted to its original chaos. Somebody has to clean it up, and one sturdy citizen undertakes to do so. He finds, however, that the law's delay and the indifference or timidity of the citizens are crippling him, so he begins using his own methods, ignoring the law as Sheriff John Slaughter is said to have done. The legend of the invincible frontier marshal is reborn in him, and the novelist often invokes the memory of Wyatt Earp to make sure the process is understood.

The cycle was slow in starting. Books and ballads about Jesse James were on the market before Jesse's grave was well grassed over. Buffalo Bill Cody would rush to Eastern cities to star in stage depictions of adventures he had just lived through on the Western plains, and then dash back to the Indian country to have some more salable experiences. Wyatt, however, did not find his Homer until just before the end of his long life, nearly forty years after his departure from Tombstone. His legend was undoubtedly building up behind the scenes, but it took a considerable time to reach the stage.

I find no fictional treatment of Tombstone before the appearance of Alfred Henry Lewis' *Wolfville* in 1897,[1] and in Wolfville I find no trace of the Earp legend—no character or episode which could be related to the Earp-Clanton-McLaury feud.

There is some question, it is true, about whether or not Wolfville is Tombstone at all. The people of Deming, New Mexico, where Cherokee Hall and Faro Nell are said to have lived out the placid autumn of their days, believe that Wolfville and Deming are one

---

[1] The Wolfville series included five other volumes. A recent anthology called *Old Wolfville* has been edited by Louis Filler.

and the same.[2] El Paso newsman Norman Walker, a friend of Lewis',
remarked in 1911 that these stories "started every vale and dale in
Arizona scrapping as to which was Wolfville and which was Red
Dog."[3] It is quite possible, too, that Lewis was attempting to create
a typical rather than a specific community. He even speaks of Tombstone as a place near Wolfville. But the presence of the Bird Cage
Theatre and some other landmarks seems significant, and I have
always believed that the resemblances between Doc Peets of Wolfville and Dr. Goodfellow of Tombstone, between Enright and Allan
English the bibulous barrister, and between the old cattleman (the
narrator) and Uncle Jim Wolf are too close to be accidental. I should
add that Billy King, who married Dick Clark's widow and inherited
the Alhambra Saloon, told me that Mr. Lewis got more stories from
Uncle Billy Plasters than from Uncle Jim, but when it came to naming
his series of books, he found *Wolfville* preferable to *Plastersville*.[4]

Between 1897 and 1913 Lewis published six books in the Wolfville series: *Wolfville* (1897), *Sandburrs* (1898), *Wolfville Days* (1902),
Wolfville Nights (1902), *Wolfville Folks* (1908), and *Faro Nell and
Her Friends* (1913). These stories, which Lewis began to write when
he was working on the *Kansas City Star*, brought him a national reputation and eventually made it possible for him to go back East and
become a political specialist. His popular exposé novel *The Boss* was
the top product of this segment of his career as a writer.

The typical Wolfville story is a picture-frame tale. The narrator
goes to see the old cattleman. A chance remark pushes the old man's
memory button. In a colorful idiom embellished with frontier meta-
phor, phonetic spellings, out-of-place polysyllables, and salty collo-
quialisms, the life of the frontier mining camp unfolds. Time is
measured in terms of first-drink time in the morning, second-drink
time in the afternoon, and so on. The barrooms and gambling halls
are the centers of community life. Killing is casual, but done according to form and ritual. "Jack Moore," says Lewis, "does the rope work

---

[2] For more on these matters see J. Marvin Hunter, *Lottie Deno*; Flournoy
D. Manzo, "Alfred Henry Lewis: Western Storyteller," *Arizona and the West*
10 (Spring, 1968); Bill McGaw, "Deming Woman 'Took' Holliday for $70,000,"
Southwesterner 1 (May, 1962).

[3] *El Paso Herald*, June 1, 1911.

[4] C. L. Sonnichsen, *Billy King's Tombstone*. This story is recorded in my
notes but not in the book.

for the stranglers."[5] The voice of public opinion, influenced and directed by the sages of the camp, seems to be the only law. The few women who appear (Faro Nell, Benson Annie, Tucson Jennie) belong on the north or unredeemed side of Allen Street, but men and women are mostly good, responsible citizens according to their own code. The code, however, is a queer, upside-down, freakish thing calculated to shock and amuse the Eastern reader.

Take the story "The Washwoman's War." Benson Annie opens a laundry in Wolfville, becomes bored by prosperity, and sends over to Tombstone for her friend Sal. A week later the girls fall out, and Sal opens a laundry of her own. The grave and reverend signiors of the camp assemble in the Red Light Saloon and decide that William French must marry Benson Annie and take her out of circulation. French is game:

> "I sees how it is, an' as a forced play I marries Benson Annie in the interests of peace. Which the same bein' settled, if Benson Annie is yere, whirl her up and' I'll come flutterin' down from my perch like a pan of milk from the top shelf, an' put an end to this onhealthful excitement."[6]

This fresh and humorous fantasy on frontier themes, we must admit, was not pleasing to the good people of Arizona. Stewart Edward White in *The Killer* (1920) assigns his story to a time when there was "no railroad into Tombstone yet . . . and there was some indignation against Alfred Henry Lewis's *Wolfville* as a base libel" (p. 4).

It is hard to see anything libelous in *Wolfville* now, but there is certainly nothing heroic about it. The mighty lawmen and magnificent desperadoes of the Earp legend are twenty years in the future. Emerson Hough's *Story of the Outlaw*, published in 1907, never mentions Tombstone.

Something was going on beneath the surface, however, on the level where myths are made. When John P. Clum wrote in 1929 his famous article on the Tombstone troubles for the *Arizona Historical Review*, he was aware of what was going on and commented on the "clever and colorful writers" who had already "added much to the

[5] Alfred Henry Lewis, "The Stinging Lizard," *Wolfville*, p. 19.
[6] Lewis, "The Washwoman's War," *Wolfville*, p. 48.

wild and woolly reputation of Tombstone."[7] Clum's impatience was
no doubt intensified by Walter Noble Burns's *Tombstone*, which had
appeared in 1927. It was that book which erected the pedestal on
which Wyatt Earp's heroic statue was to rise. Burns was a newspaperman who saw his material with a feature writer's eye. He viewed
the Lincoln County War as an epic with Billy the Kid in the role of
dragon slayer. The Tombstone feud reminded him of a story from
the Arthurian cycle. Wyatt was Sir Galahad, without fear and without reproach. His friends were knights of the Round Table (Burns
actually uses the figure), and his enemies were the wicked earls who
had to be laid low before there could be peace in the realm.

Actually Burns's book comes close to being a novel. He works
in scenes like a novelist. He knows what everybody is thinking, and
he reproduces conversations as if he had been there with a tape
recorder. A reasonable estimate would give him about equal parts
fact and fiction. His fictionalizing is well done, however, and only
the most bilious academic critic would stop to ask how Burns knows
all this. A typical chapter begins as follows:

> John Ringo was drunk. For ten days he had been morosely, brood-
> ingly, tragically drunk. As straight as an Indian he stalked about
> Tombstone streets, a tall, silent, sombre figure, looking a little more
> like Hamlet than ever, his hollow black eyes clouded with melan-
> choly.[8]

Ringo, of course, was dead many years before Burns was born.

The Tombstone residents I knew back in the thirties took very
little stock in Burn's slick reconstructions. They were mostly negative
about the Earps and inclined to feel that Sheriff John Behan and the
"cowboys" were better men than the legends allowed. Outsiders
hardly ever sided with these old-timers. The world wants its heroes
to be good and its villains to be evil, and the legend of Wyatt
("Tombstone was lawless but one man was flawless") soon became a
part of our stock of basic assumptions about the frontier West.

Burns touched off a fine run of reminiscent literature. In 1928
came the publication of Billy Breakenridge's *Helldorado*, Eddie Foy's

---

[7] John P. Clum, "It All Happened in Tombstone," *Arizona Historical Review* 1 (April, 1929; reprinted in book form, Flagstaff: Northland Press, 1965).

[8] Walter Noble Burns, *Tombstone*, p. 261.

Clowning through Life and Lorenzo Walters' *Tombstone's Yesterday*. Clum's account of the Earps and their difficulties appeared in October, 1929, and helped to fix the legend in the American mind. The veteran Western historian and novelist William MacLeod Raine included twenty-three pages on "Helldorado" in *Famous Sheriffs and Western Outlaws* in 1929. The publication of George W. Parsons' *Journal* in 1934 and of John Hays Hammond's *Autobiography* in 1935 added to the factual side of the story.

By far the most influential of the makers of legend, however, was Stuart N. Lake, whose book about Wyatt set his man up as a folk hero and made him available to the movies and to television as the embodiment of our dream of the frontier champion of virtue, full-blown and ready to be worshiped. It was this book also, as most of us know, which, by going too far, ignited the indignation of Frank Waters (*The Earp Brothers of Tombstone*), Peter Lyon (*The Wild, Wild West*), Ed Bartholomew (*Wyatt Earp, 1848 to 1880: The Untold Story* and *Wyatt Earp, 1879 to 1882: The Man and the Myth*), and all the others who have reacted with indignation against *Frontier Marshal*. It took twenty-five years, however, for the opposition to get organized, and in the meantime Lake's romanticizing passed for fact and may never be completely dislodged from the position it so long held as a respectable piece of historical writing. There can be no doubt that it has played a major role in creating the assumptions which were the stock-in-trade of fiction writers after 1931.

The first writer to get on the legendary bandwagon did so after the publication of Walter Noble Burns's *Tombstone* but before Stuart Lake's book on Earp. W. R. Burnett's *Saint Johnson* made its appearance in 1930. Already famous as the author of the best-selling *Little Caesar*, Burnett shifted from the gangsters of Chicago to the gangsters of Cochise County, Arizona, without any great clashing of gears. Saint Johnson, as may be readily guessed, is Wyatt Earp, renamed Wayt Johnson. Not even Lake had the temerity to attribute sainthood to his hero, though he did make him almost painfully pure. Burnett does not pursue the odor of sanctity very far, however. Once in the course of the story a bitter enemy calls the lawman "Mr. rectitudinous Johnson . . . he should have been a gospel expounder" (p. 51). Another character calls him "Mister Wayt (Sky Pilot) Johnson" (p. 174). Burnett is thinking more about the man's prowess than about his purity, however, and the novel is misnamed.

As the story begins, the Earps (Johnsons), Doc Holliday (Brant White), and the Clantons and the McLaurys (Northrups and Todds) are heading for a showdown, but the author takes very little historical baggage with him on his fictional journey. Wayt's problem is his brother Jim, who reacts against authority and for a time is part of the outlaw gang. His rejection of his brother brings on the street fight, and the story ends as the Johnson faction takes its time in leaving town. The tale is told in short, often childish sentences intended probably to convey the tight-lipped taciturnity of fighting men. The amount of talk is often too great for the action, and one has a feeling that Burnett is interested mostly in filling pages. As an example of craftsmanship, the book does not get very far.

Even an unimportant novel, however, can start a trend, and this *Saint Johnson* seems to have done. It is the first stage in the fictional apotheosis of Saint Earp. It presents Wyatt as "a big man, blond, aquiline, with broad shoulders and a rawboned, loose-hung frame he had inherited from a long line of pioneer ancestors. He walked with a pronounced slouch and carried his head a little to one side. His dark suit and big black hat were covered with alkali dust. . . ."[9] This is not the lion of some of the later novels, but the lion is on the way.

As Burnett conceives him, Wyatt is slow to wrath, and even his friends forget how dangerous he can be.

> They had never seen him riding slowly up and down the main street of a hostile town, daring anyone to reach for a gun. They had never seen him with his back to the wall, alone, surrounded by a mob of infuriated Mexicans. They had never seen him hit a man with his fist and put two bullets in him before he struck the ground. To them he was merely big, quiet, Wayt Johnson, leader of the Law and Order party; dangerous, of course, but forbearing.[10]

The time comes when Wayt ceases to be forbearing, and the result is the encounter at the O.K. Corral.

Doc Holliday, who always has second billing in the legend, is portrayed as a complete dandy. The best tailor in Houston made his suits:

[9] W. R. Burnett, *Saint Johnson*, p. 84.
[10] Ibid., p. 190.

He was lanky and flat chested, his face was long and pale, and his teeth were three sizes too large but he carried himself as if he thought he was the handsomest man in San Miguel County.[11]

It took eight years for Tombstone to stimulate the imagination of another novelist, but Jack O'Connor's *Boom Town* (1938) was worth waiting for. It may well be the best piece of fiction that has been written about a silver strike. Frank O'Reilley finds his mine much as Ed Schieffelin found his. Larry Richards (Dick Gird) analyzes his few remaining samples just as it happened in real life, and together they persuade Lucky Goldwaser to back them. The boom is on, and the boom town is Tombstone by another name.

No other novel about this famous silver camp treats the mines and miners as anything but stage scenery, but O'Connor, so far as a nonminer can tell, knows what goes on above and below ground:

> In long lines they waited at the timekeeper's window for their work-checks. Others who were just coming off night shift turned theirs in. The hoist engine sputtered and chugged. The double-decked cage shot up and down in the black hole of the shaft discharging night-shift men whose faces were tight and drawn with fatigue. Bill sure did feel funny. He'd never even been near a mine, and the prospect of working in one scared hell out of him. Once while the cage was going down he walked over to the shaft and peered into it. He saw the top of the cage disappearing into the earth, growing swiftly smaller like a stone dropped from a precipice. It was taking the shift to the lower levels and as it fell Bill could see it flash by dim-lit drifts. The cage was falling so fast he wondered if they could ever stop the damned thing and from the depths of the mine rose a cool, damp exhalation of moist rock and rotting wood and stale powder fumes. Then the great drum above his head rattled and screeched as the hoistman put on the brake. Bill saw the tiny miniature of the cage a quarter of a mile below him come to a stop in the vague glow of an open drift. Voices of miners floated up, remote as if from another world.[12]

O'Connor writes well. His style is colloquial, but not self-consciously so. His people are people, every one of them. He writes a novel about the West, but it is not a western. Men get killed, but they don't stalk each other down the middle of the sreet. And when

[11] Ibid., p. 186.
[12] Jack O'Connor, *Boom Town*, p. 175.

Frank O'Reilley passes on, he is not shot to death but is caught in a cave-in caused by improper timbering—the result of too much haste and greed on the part of the Eastern capitalists who now direct the destiny of the mine.

The Earp saga gets no help from O'Connor, though the principals are present. Doc Holliday is there in the shape of Doc Bagby, a consumptive Southerner who gambles for a living but is actually a doctor competent to "snatch" a baby when Mrs. Richards has one to snatch. We watch him as he weakens and gets ready to die, seedier and more courtly with age and subject to hallucinations as the end approaches.

As for Wyatt Earp, he gets twelve lines. He appears on page 268 under the name of Dud Towne:

> Old Dud was a caution. He'd been an officer for twenty years—in Dodge and Silver City and El Paso and Leadville. He'd shot twenty-five men but all of them legal and he was an hombre to stay clear of. Everyone said he liked to shoot just to see folks kick.

Seven years later another fiction writer found the Earps expendable, though they made token appearances. In 1945 Lynton Wright Brent authored an astonishing fictional concoction called *The Bird Cage: A Theatrical Novel of Early Tombstone.* Tombstone's famous theatre is about to open, and Donna Drew is coming with her company from New York to present *The Westerner.* Donna is a ravishing redhead who has every able-bodied male in Tombstone drooling, especially Peter Crawley, professional gambler and impresario; Matthew Prane of the P-Bar-B Ranch; and Matthew's partner, Steve Brammer. Prane himself comes from stage people who were killed and robbed by a gang of desperadoes as they neared Tombstone many years before. Matt was adopted by a kindly old ranchman, but as he grew up, he was obsessed by the idea of killing the murderers. As the story opens, he has disposed of four of them and is looking for the fifth and last.

The show opens and is a failure. Not one of the actors knows anything about the West, and neither did the playwright. Matthew steps in, however, rewrites the play, becomes the leading man, and takes the show to New York, unaware that Brammer has raped Donna in her dressing room and is the fifth man he is looking for. Successful in the East, the troupe comes back for a Tombstone triumph and to a showdown between Matthew and Steve. Donna finds that she is carrying Steve's baby, but nobody seems to be unhappy about that at the end.

The Bird Cage has small merit as a novel. It sounds like East Lynne or one of the old melodramas moved to the Southwest, where the superheated emotions and overblown style are much less tolerable than they would have been elsewhere:

> Matthew felt chilled over Donna's sudden induration. He was well aware that she shared with him an abhorrence for one man killing another man; and here now, she coldly, calculatively, weigh[ed] the theatrical value of his morbid past. Were it not that he understood show folk, he would have been shocked over her enthusiasm. Even so, he was amazed that even gentle, sweet Donna Drew knew no limit to her scheming to put over a theatrical production. He shook his head in firm negation. "It could not be," he said slowly. "I cannot leave Tombstone until I have killed the fifth man."[13]

The Earps and Johnny Behan are in the picture, but they make only token appearances. When two cowpunchers fall out over their claims to the favors of the actress, who has not yet arrived, "Sheriff Johnny Behan and U.S. Marshal Wyatt Earp separated them. But after the two lawmen had departed, the cowpunchers again lambasted each other with profanity over Donna Drew's hypothetical choice of one of them."[14] The legend has taken hold, however. Wyatt is "the tall and stately deputy United States Marshal." He is "reserved in his somber way of speaking; and his sharp eyes roved over the crowd about him." It is only two months since the O.K. Corral episode, and "tension pro and con was at a strained peak."[15] In this novel, however, Wyatt and Doc are only window dressing, as are Fly the photographer, Nellie Cashman, and a few more of the Tombstoners given fame of a sort by Burns and Lake. The Earp legend has been bypassed.

As the fifties got under way, the Earp legend came back into its own. Lake's romantic inventions had convinced even serious historians, and Lake himself was pugnacious and litigious toward people

---

[13] Lynton Wright Brent, *The Bird Cage*, p. 164.
[14] Ibid., p. 12.
[15] Ibid., p. 98.

who presumed to differ with him—and very few chose to differ. At the same time, the television boom, which invaded the American living room in the middle years of the decade, made Wyatt a folk hero and exasperated the local historians in Kansas and Arizona so thoroughly that they began digging into the records and accumulating negative evidence which would have punctured Wyatt's balloon had it not flown so high as to be almost out of reach.

Trouble in Tombstone, by Tom J. Hopkins (1951), shows how far the Earp cult had progressed. Sam Chalmers, a supertough Texan, starts a ranch in the San Pedro Valley near Tombstone with cattle he has "bought" from Bigelow Newman in the Pecos country of New Mexico. At settling-up time he pays Newman with his own notes, purchased at a fraction of their value from small ranchers whom Newman had refused to pay. This transaction creates something less than amity between them, and when Sam finds his enemy living as his neighbor and married to the sister of his own beloved, the clouds begins to gather.

Thunder on the left comes from the outlaw gang led by Curly Bill Brocius and John Ringo, who are stealing everything in sight. Sam believes Newman is behind their operations. He has already done his share of righteous killing and is ready and willing to go after the band, but when Jean marries him, she makes him promise to let the law take its course with no help from him. He keeps his word as long as he can.

The Earps are in the picture from the beginning, larger than life. Sam is in Tombstone when Wyatt makes his first appearance, Doc Holliday by his side. The evaluation of their characters is unusual:

> Wyatt Earp, cold, calculating, nerveless gunman. A man who sometimes avoided fights, but never through lack of courage. A man up to now always on the side of the law and wearing a badge. Yet he had Doc Holliday with him, the cold killer who had been trained as a dentist and had turned outlaw and gambler and gunman extraordinary. . . . That man, with Wyatt Earp, the lawman.[16]

Johnny Behan appears and commands Wyatt and Doc to turn in their guns. Wyatt tells the sheriff to come and get them, and the

[16] Tom J. Hopkins, *Trouble in Tombstone*, p. 54.

feud is on. Sam joins Earp and Holliday in running the rustlers out of town and is nearby when the O.K. Corral encounter takes place, though he has no part in it. He lives through the days when Tombstone is "a roaring hell town,"[17] but stays away from the trouble because of his promise to Jean. When the Earps leave and the thugs and thieves take over, John Clum and George Parsons, foremost citizens, come out to the ranch and ask Sam to pin on a badge:

> "Chalmers, all hell is popping open. We've got the vigilantes organized and the Citizens' Safety Committee, and we need you."[18]

In the end Sam puts duty ahead of domestic bliss and pins on the badge, making his announcement from the stage of Newman's Bird Cage Theatre. The word goes out to the rustlers: *get out or get killed*. Sam starts his campaign at Charleston, the mill town in the San Pedro Valley which has been the outlaw headquarters. The campaign continues until the inevitable showdown comes between Sam and his brother-in-law.

Wyatt is an indomitable but not a mythical figure in this story. "There goes the last chance for real law and order in this town," says a citizen as the Earps ride out for the last time. "At least until we have that election. Maybe then we can throw out Behan and get a real sheriff in here."[19]

One feels some pity for the dapper Johnny, in real life an amorous extrovert who had the misfortune to be in charge at the time of the Earp-Clanton broil. In fiction, the more heroic Wyatt becomes, the worse Behan looks by contrast. And it will be that way as long as the legends live.

A good commercial writer got hold of the Tombstone story next. He was Clarence Budington Kelland, a migrant who exchanged Vermont for Arizona. Like himself, his heroes and heroines were likely to be transplants from New England—probably because he liked to hear them talk. In a 1953 novel which he called *Tombstone* he brought a pretty Vermont girl named Reva Crane to town at the time of the big fire of January, 1881. Who should meet her and escort her to Aunt Abby Newton's place but Doctor Holliday? And what

[17] Ibid., p. 82.
[18] Ibid., p. 105.
[19] Ibid., p. 109.

should Aunt Abby do but ask him in for a cup of tea? And what should Doc do but sit down and drink two cups? The shock was severe, but he survived. Reva goes on to make a lot of money, mostly by selling hats to girls from the tenderloin, but at the end she learns that love is more important than money and she throws herself into the arms of the Wells Fargo undercover man who has taken a hand in the doings at the O.K. Corral.

Being a reasonable New Englander, Kelland is sensible about Tombstone. Speaking for him, Aunt Abby says: "Maybe this town hain't so different from other towns, only it's more so. It's good and it's bad. The good is about normal good, but the bad is extravagant bad."[20] Probably even Tombstoners would accept this estimate. Kelland is reasonable about Wyatt and Doc Holliday, too. Aunt Abby exclaims:

> "Them two! As soon as a town grows peaceful they leave for a new spot that's wild. Mebby they're moved to fetch law and order. I wouldn't know. Mebby there's somethin' in their souls that craves danger and killin'. Could be they're all bad or could be they're all good. . . . They drink and they gamble and they kill. But somehow, seems as though, law follows on their heels. Could be they're a kind of phenomenon of nature, growin' out of such times as these—with a mission to kill off the evil so decent folks can live in peace 'n' abide by the law."[21]

It is some satisfaction to note that Kelland has read carefully a book called *Billy King's Tombstone*, which appeared with my name on it a good many years ago, but the satisfaction is balanced by a feeling of discomfort brought on by his almost total disregard of Western idiom. When Reva Crane appears on the streets of Tombstone, one citizen inquires of another, "Who in tunket is she?" And again, when Billy Clanton, madly in love with the New England girl, wishes to inquire about the state of her health, he asks, "How be ye, Ma'am?"[22] As a matter of fact, all his characters are apt to break out into pure Vermontese.

In 1954, the year after the appearance of Kelland's book, the Earp saga reached a strong climax in a sort of superwestern called

[20] Clarence Budington Kelland, *Tombstone*, p. 13.
[21] Ibid., p. 9.
[22] Ibid., pp. 18, 180.

Who Rides with Wyatt? It was conceived by Will Henry, a prolific
fellow who writes under several names and loves to tinker with history—particularly history with shooting in it. Although he has won
many awards and much acclaim under one or another of his pseudo-
nyms, his work leaves a historically minded reader with mixed feelings. On the one hand he has researched his subjects carefully and
takes himself seriously as a historical novelist. Mostly he seems to
follow Walter Noble Burns, but he has read John Clum's account of
the O.K. Corral battle, and he quotes newspapers and pertinent
documents. On the other hand, he likes to paint in shiny blacks and
stark whites, and he gives a tremendous boost to the perpetuation of
the legend. Here is his picture of Tombstone:

> When they got all through making tough towns they threw away
> the mold and poured what was left of the mix out into the sagebrush
> down yonder on Goose Flats. What cooled out and set up was Tomb-
> stone.[23]

His picture of Wyatt is what you would expect after this beginning. Earp is "the last of the great lawmen . . . the greatest gunfighter of them all. A tall blond man with fish-blue eyes and a sun-
gold mustache."[24] A dance-hall girl named Lily Beloit

> looked at the massive, sure form of him standing there in the box
> shadows, the gaslight cutting bold around his thick-maned head and
> the whole lion's grace and strength of him. . . . A clean, real man. A
> man who would look at a girl like she was his woman for life, not
> his tramp for tonight.[25]

"He did his job," says the italicized little foreword, "in stark
loneliness, spurned by the only woman he ever loved, and in the end
was betrayed by the 'good' citizens whose best interests he had
served."

The "only woman he ever loved," incidentally, is named Evelyn
Cushman. She runs a boarding house and sounds a good deal like
Nellie Cashman, much respected in her own day and part of the
Tombstone legend now. Her surviving relatives will be surprised and
shocked if they ever find out about Henry's idea. In view of what we

[23] Will Henry, *Who Rides with Wyatt?*, p. 30.
[24] Ibid., unpaged foreword.
[25] Ibid., p. 64.

know now about Wyatt's romantic entanglements before, during, and after Tombstone,[26] it seems more than a little absurd to link him with a woman of Nellie's character and ideals.

The author pretends, surely with tongue in cheek, that this is a true account which he got in the summer of 1933 from a nonagenarian living at the Pioneers' Home in Prescott. The old man is supposedly telling the tale as Johnny Ringo told it to him, and Henry declares that he is giving an "unvarnished account . . . without apology in the words of a very old man sitting in the sunshine of his last afternoon and remembering, as best he could, a very old story."[27] A few pages farther on, supposedly still quoting the old man, he describes Lily Beloit of the Bird Cage Theatre looking at Wyatt. She sees "a stark, still-eyed, compellingly lonely figure of a man; fierce and kind and gentle and terrible, all in the same breathless eyeful."[28] Even if the ancient frontiersman were capable of such a conversational style, the odds are against his using such a phrase as "breathless eyeful."

Along with such highly charged writing, Henry gives us a run of metaphors which take the breath away. Here is Johnny Ringo in a poker game with Doc Holliday: "Ringo licked his lips. The oily sweat stood off his forehead and temples like spring water on a wax lily."[29]

The plot fits the style. It starts in San Angelo, Texas, where Earp saves Ringo from the consequences of a killing. Ringo is only a boy, but he is on his way to being a bad one. Wyatt takes him along to Tombstone, hoping to make a man of him, but it is too late. Ringo is too proud of his fast draw to steer clear of trouble. He joins the wild bunch, defies Wyatt, and loses his useless life.

This brings up the matter of the title. It is part of a phrase which Henry invented: "Who rides with Wyatt rides with death."[30]

In the middle fifties Ringo seems to have been on the mind of other Western novelists as a rival for Earp. Leslie Scott in *Tomb-*

[26] For Wyatt's romantic involvements, see Frank Waters, *The Earp Brothers of Tombstone* and Glenn G. Boyer (ed.), *I Married Wyatt Earp*.

[27] Henry, *Who Rides with Wyatt?*, "In the Beginning," unpaged.

[28] Ibid., p. 36.

[29] Ibid., p. 150.

[30] Ibid., p. 20.

stone Showdown, a paperback novel printed in 1957 and reissued in 1964, builds Ringo up as "the only man Wyatt Earp ever feared." He is the brains of the Curly Bill gang and plans all their escapades, at the same time maintaining a private life of his own. He is a loner, making friends only with thoughtful people who read books—not many of whom were available on the frontier. He drinks heavily, plays poker expertly, and broods on the mutability of human existence. He really wants to die and eventually commits suicide. He is Walter Noble Burns's Hamlet, trapped between heaven and earth.

Earp is his implacable rival. "No man ever discounted his desperate courage, not even the grim and puritanical Wyatt Earp, his deadly enemy, who likewise knew fear only as a word with a rather murky dictionary definition." The two were much alike. "Both were cold, calculating, absolutely fearless, complete masters of their emotions in times of stress." Both were close to invincible in combat. But Wyatt was the "exponent of law and order," while Ringo was "strictly the individualist who followed his own code and cared nothing for law or public opinion."[31]

This is the myth at work. The powers of good confront the powers of evil, and wickedness must defeat itself in the end. Satan may be magnificent, but he can't win.

The idea of the western as a dramatic conflict between good and evil—a morality play—has been convincingly stated along with the idea that the television westerns, which began to achieve popularity about 1956, accelerated the myth-making process and made Wyatt our number-one hero.[32] We were too close to our Heroic Age, however, to forget the facts, and before long the Earp legend was in difficulties with one segment of the population. Among the uncritical it still flourishes and probably always will.

Meanwhile, other forces were at work which would influence the legend making. In England the Angry Young Men were having their say, and their counterparts in the United States were carrying the naked and the dead from here to eternity, laying it on the line that the human race was sick—that all men were victims of their frustrations and guilt complexes and there was no health in them. It

[31] Ibid., pp. 8, 67.
[32] "The American Morality Play," *Time*, March 30, 1959.

was bound to hit the West, and eventually it did, surfacing in 1958 in Oakley Hall's monumental *Warlock*. Quite obviously Warlock is Tombstone, and the material is the familiar Earp saga with some important differences.

The action starts with the arrival of Clay Blaisdell (Earp), who has been brought in by a citizens' committee. His job is to stop the wild followers of Abe McQuown (Old Man Clanton) from shooting up the town every time they get the urge. Blaisdell is a Homeric figure—unshakable, unbeatable, always in command—but he has never been up against anything like Tombstone. A merchant named Henry Holmes Goodpasture keeps a diary in which he comments on Blaisdell's progress, his remarks adding flavor to Hall's narrative.

The plot is so complicated that it defies summary. The *Los Angeles Times* calls the story "a vast mural of a novel." It is that. And it would have been a better book if it had been shorter and had not tried to make so many points. The viewpoint shifts from character to character, and the action becomes wilder and more improbable as it progresses. Take, for example, Morgan the gambler (Doc Holliday) who is a very bad man but a loyal friend of Blaisdell's. When the marshal is humiliated and knocked off his pedestal by General Peach (Governor Fremont), Morgan is willing to die to restore his friend's preeminence and prestige. He shoots up the town in order to force Blaisdell to kill him. His ruse is successful, but as a consequence the marshal goes wild. He lays Morgan's body out in the Lucky Dollar Saloon, calls for candles, and makes everybody stand up to sing "Rock of Ages." Then he burns down the saloon. Naturally the book was made into a motion picture, with some very good people taking the leading roles. The producers apparently did not see anything ridiculous in Oakley's hodgepodge.

Reading the book makes one uneasy and uncomfortable. One has a sense of discrepancy or incongruity about what is going on. The heroic Tombstone legend is there, but it has gone sour. Morgan is wicked and bitter and bored by his bootless life. Blaisdell has been God Almighty too long and is haunted by the memory of the times he shot too quickly or killed needlessly. Everybody is either depraved, disillusioned, or scared to death.

Old, drunken, one-legged Judge Holloway, sick and disgusted

with life and the mess men have made of it, talks for Mr. Hall. He says the trouble with men like Blaisdell is that they are not responsible to anybody. "A man like you," he remarks, "has to be always right, and no poor human can ever be that." The lot of humanity, he declares, "is terrible past the standing of it," and if it were not for the "universal solvent" of his whiskey, he couldn't bear it.[33]

And so on one side we have here a story about the mythical West. On the other we have an existentialist philosophy which might be appropriately titled *No Exit*. It is *The Oxbow Incident* with some new neuroses. The two halves do not fit together. It is a breach of decorum, somehow, to mix the heroic, no matter how ill conceived, with bitterness and disillusion. It is hard, perhaps impossible, to reconcile these irreconcilables.

The confusion embodied in *Warlock* may reflect a decline of faith in the Western myth, but the next author acts as if he is trying to get his faith back. It is significant, however, that he does not try to refurbish the Earp legend. Instead, he finds a new hero and tries through him to return to the epic tradition. *John Slaughter's Way*, by James Wyckoff (1963), is the first of the post-Earp novels which picture a Tombstone in the hands of the thieves and desperadoes after Wyatt and his men have departed. *Trouble in Tombstone* (1951) in its later chapters laid the groundwork for the type, but Wyckoff's book is the first clear-cut example, and in it John Slaughter appears with his right name.

It should be noted at once that Wyckoff has done some reading, but he is satisfied with a minimum of fact. Had he read Allen Erwin's biography of Slaughter, he would have blushed at the number of things he did not know and the greater number of things he knew wrong. His greatest mistake, however, involves his inventions. The people he describes actually lived, and they deserve something better than an out-and-out caricature. Here, for instance, is Wyckoff's impression of Old Man Clanton:

> Three Clanton boys and the Old Man were standing around in the round horse corral, and now the father spat, getting some of it on his very white beard, but not noticing, or anyway not caring, and scratched himself fiercely, first in each deep armpit, and then on his

[33] Oakley Hall, *Warlock*, pp. 95, 373.

broad, aged buttocks. With one long spatulated finger he explored his matted beard while his pale blue eyes looked out speculatively across the San Pedro Valley.[34]

The author, we might add, is something of a specialist in scratching and spitting. His unpleasant characters do these things persistently, but even John Slaughter spits. As the hero, he is naturally the best spitter in the area, and when he aims a charge of tobacco juice at a lizard, the poor creature nearly drowns. And when he spits again, he hits exactly the same spot.

Of Wyatt Earp, whose deeds are reported but not described, Wyckoff makes a significant remark: "About Wyatt legend flourished. He was basically a controversial man. Lie and truth were told of him with equal vigor."[35]

Here is evidence that in the post-Earp novels Wyatt is neither sick nor sainted. He is not even very interesting. The legend is not denied; it is merely ignored. But in at least one later book it is resurrected. This is an extraordinary soft-cover thriller by Robert Kreps called *The Hour of the Gun*, a nonserious, not to say cynical, elaboration of the Tombstone story which deserves consideration on account of the height to which the Earp mystique is carried. Some of this height, incidentally, is probably due to the fact that the motion-picture scenario preceded the novel. Both picture and book were released in 1967.

The flyleaf states that all characters are purely fictional, which is really a monumental understatement, for they resemble nobody who ever lived or is likely to live. Nevertheless, Kreps uses all the familiar names and landmarks without disguise. He even allows Fawcett Publications to declare, "This is the story of the bloodiest feud in the West, never before told to its deadly end." Mr. Scott wishes to eat his history and have it, too.

He begins with the O.K. Corral fight. Ike Clanton, a pure and complete villain, watches while his brother and his friends die in their futile attempt to murder the Earps and Holliday. Frustrated, he sends Pete Spence, Frank Stilwell, Curly Bill, and others to do their famous hatchet job on Morgan Earp. Wyatt in retaliation or-

---

[34] James Wyckoff, *John Slaughter's Way*, p. 83.
[35] Ibid., p. 132.

ganizes his posse and wipes out almost everybody. The climax comes in Mexico, where Ike is gathering somebody else's cattle. At his Mexican hacienda Wyatt and Doc eliminate him in a brutal scene full of heavy gunsmoke and gratuitous gore.[36]

For the finale we move the camera to Doc's room in the Colorado sanitarium where he dies. Wyatt has come to say goodbye.

Kreps's book in reality takes the ball away from W. R. Burnett, Oakley Hall, and Leslie Scott and runs with it. Wyatt is a Puritan—a firm believer in Law, capitalized. Without Law, he believes, there is nothing. When his brothers are killed, however, he avenges them, still considering himself a lawman and not a feudist. Doc knows better, but Wyatt is hard to convince. They debate the issue in highly literate language, but their most conspicuous talent is not philosophical discussion. It is their skill in shooting their enemies to very small rags. Wyatt the lion has been replaced by Wyatt the tiger.

After the sixties the production of Tombstone novels slowed to a walk. The books continued to appear at longer intervals, and they were post-Earp in their orientation. In 1971 a write who calls himself Jack Slade published *The Man from Tombstone*, which breaks some new ground. The viewpoint character is a hardy but conscienceless Westerner called Lassiter who is drawn to the town by the scent of easy money. A black pugilist named Magnus Kirton, but known professionally as the Chocolate Kid, arrives in Tombstone for a Fourth-of-July "battle of the century" with Yankee Nolan. Lassiter plans to hold up the box office after the fight, but is hired as the Kid's bodyguard when he shows his mettle by pistol whipping the big black and saving him from trouble with a local six-gun artist. A black tigress named Melissa complicates the action, and Sheriff Johnny Behan complicates it even more. His stock is as low in Jack Slade's estimation as it was in the minds of his predecessors:

> The famous old feud between the Earps and the Clanton-McLowery bunch that ended at the O.K. Corral had made Behan a sort of left-handed legend. Behan had a way of starting trouble and then ducking out when the bullets started to fly.[37]

The sheriff is older now and has "watery, very blue eyes" along

---

[36] Robert Kreps, *The Hour of the Gun*, pp. 138–139.
[37] Jack Slade, *The Man from Tombstone*, p. 48.

with "wrinkles and a droopy mustache."[38] The Earps are ten or fifteen years in the past, but they still crop up in conversation. When Behan warns Lassiter not to make trouble in the area if he wants to stay healthy, he boasts, "I can deputize every man and boy in Cochise County."

> It was out in the open now, so Lassiter said, "That's why the Earps walked around you?"
> "Nothing like being popular," Behan said. "A sheriff doesn't have the support of the community is in trouble." . . .
> Walking back to the hotel, all Lassiter could think of was—"I'll be damned!" He was caught in the middle between the sheriff and the prizefight. . . . That, from old talk, was what had happened with Behan and the Earps. The Clantons and the McLowerys were rustlers and backshooters and stage robbers, but Behan sided with them because they were home folks.[39]

To author Slade, Behan is "the foxy little lawman" with "an elderly child's face" who is smart enough to outwit Lassiter. When promoter Delaney skips out with the proceeds of the fight, Behan and Lassiter pursue and overtake him—then argue about dividing the loot. Lassiter settles for twenty thousand. Behan advises him to head for the border.

> "I'd say that was sound advice," Lassiter agreed. "No wonder the Earps couldn't budge you."
> "Earps weren't businessmen," Sheriff Johnny Behan said.[40]

Todhunter Ballard's *The Sheriff of Tombstone*, which appeared in 1977, is a standard post-Earp opus. John Savage, a hard-nosed cattleman from Louisiana by way of Gulf Coast Texas, starts a ranch in the San Pedro Valley with profits gained from organizing cooperative cattle drives from Texas to the Kansas railheads. On the way west he marries Edna Hannah, one-quarter Cherokee and all woman. They find the standard Tombstone props in place:

> The Clantons, Curly Bill Brocious and his lieutenant John Ringo were the worst of the lot, though the valleys around Tombstone crawled with killers, stage robbers to whom anything they could steal was fair prize, rustlers and bandits raiding from Mexico. Even

[38] Ibid., p. 50.
[39] Ibid., pp. 51–52.
[40] Ibid., pp. 72, 138–139.

Sheriff John Behan was suspect. Rather than curtailing the criminals, he associated with them, even deputizing them on occasion.[41]

Behan refuses to become involved the first time the outlaws raid the Savage herd. What happens the second time the gang moves in brings John Slaughter to mind:

> Savage did not again go to Behan. He took his crew, caught seven of the outlaws in a saloon in Galeyville, hanged them to a clump of cottonwoods and rounded up the stolen animals from the range Clanton claimed as his.[42]

After a third unsuccessful try, which costs them a "significant number" of dead, the outlaws leave Savage alone, but everyone else suffers, and the decline of Tombstone plays into the hands of the badmen. As the mines flood and close, the good people move out, leaving the town to the mercies of the rough element. Something has to be done. Lew Trumble, a Texan friend of Savage, describes the situation:

> Now with the big money gone we've got cheap housebreakers and petty thieves holding up people for a couple of dollars every night. Hell, no one ever locked their doors until now, but it's got so we're broken in on regularly, anything that can be sold stolen night and day. We need your help. The commission wants you for sheriff.[43]

John says no until they tell him that a sixteen-year-old girl has been gang-raped—seized and dragged into a vacant store building in broad daylight. Then he says yes, and his troubles begin.

First of all, his men, mostly Texans, are by nature and inheritance antilaw, and some of them quit when he tells them of his decision. Mario Valdez, his top hand, is one of them. Then the "Tucson Ring," in control of county affairs, tries to bring him to heel. The town toughs are out to get him. His deputy is in league with the enemy. John Ringo attempts to kill him (he fails). And Horace Simpson, the banker, tries to fire him. John refuses to quit, however, until the job is done. He runs the bad men out of town under threat of death, and most of them go. The ones who don't go wind up in Skeleton Canyon with the choice of death from thirst or suicide.

[41] Todhunter Ballard, *The Sheriff of Tombstone*, p. 27.
[42] Ibid., p. 28.
[43] Ibid., p. 32.

The chink in John's armor is his brother-in-law, Verne Hannah, who works for Banker Simpson. Verne is a gambler and is vulnerable. The men in power, led by the banker himself, arrange to have the boy kidnapped and taken out of the country and then accuse him of robbing the bank. The kidnappers try to collect ransom money, however, and John nails them. Then he nails Simpson, and Tombstone is clean again, or at least cleaner than it was.

Characteristically, the Earps are only a memory, but they are recalled clearly and often. Savage thinks of them when he pins on his star. He had watched them as cowtown marshals.

> . . . on the other side of the fence, he had admired the neat and efficient way in which the Wyatt Earps and other lawmen mastered their problems. Earp had been singularly direct. He carried a heavy .45 known as a Buntline Special, given him by the writer Ned Buntline. This gun had a sixteen-inch barrel, an apt weapon for buffaloing, clubbing a man over the head; many an obstreperous trail hand had waked in a cell with a headache he could not blame on rotgut whiskey. It was a popular method among other marshals.[44]

John does not copy Earp's methods, but he carries on in what Walter Noble Burns and Stuart Lake believed was the Earp tradition.

What does all this riding and shooting add up to? It would seem to show an ambivalence in the American mind—at least in the part which takes an interest in Western novels. Only four of these nine novelists—W. R. Burnett, Tom J. Hopkins, Will Henry, and Leslie Scott—follow Walter Noble Burns and Stuart Lake in making Wyatt a champion of virtue defying the powers of darkness. The rest react in various negative ways. Lynton Wright Brent bows respectfully to the Earps and then ignores them. Robert Kreps reduces the whole bloody business to an absurdity. Jack O'Connor takes a straight look at mining-camp life and refuses to be stampeded by the Earp worshipers. Clarence Budington Kelland does a good job of commercial storytelling without taking sides for or against anybody. Oakley Hall brings Berthold Brecht to our creosote-and-cactus stage and says that people in general, including the people of Tombstone, are defeated by circumstances and their own natures—are, in fact, no damn good. The post-Earp stories try to get back to the true roman-

44 Ibid., p. 61.

tic mood by substituting John Slaughter (or Sam Chalmers or John Savage) for Wyatt and letting them give the rustlers hell. Jack Slade introduces Lassiter the *picaro* into the familiar setting and makes a desert *Beggar's Opera* out of the Tombstone legend.

The stock characters remain, either in the background or in the foreground: Wyatt and his brothers, Doc Holliday, the Clantons, Ringo, Curly Bill, and always Johnny Behan, the Loki of the saga. But the novelists do not rush to the altar to sacrifice to Saint Wyatt.[45]

Consumers and producers of fiction dealing with other western folk heroes would probably show similar caution if anyone would take the trouble to find out about them. It would seem legitimate to conclude that these readers and writers are not as stupid as their critics tell us they are.

[45] A sacrifice to the grimy side of the Tombstone legend is *Doc*, the original screenplay by Pete Hamill, in which the great traditions of gutter language and gutter situations are faithfully adhered to.

The Ambivalent Apache

In a 1967 paperback western novel about the Apache wars of the 1880's, Major Albert Morrow delivers himself as follows to one of his officers:

> I give you my solemn promise that Victorio will be destroyed. Perhaps not by me, perhaps not by you, but I swear to God it will be by men who wear blue and ride horses. Where that flag goes, Captain, there goes honor and pride and law and order.[1]

In the same year another practitioner in the same paperback genre took an opposite point of view:

> "It seems a shame," Wichles said, "that the Injuns have got to behave this way when this country's ours. It is, you know. We got more rights than they have, no two ways about it."
> "Who the hell says we got rights?"
> "Why we do," Wichles said, surprised that Travis didn't know. "We make the laws, don't we? Bring civilization, don't we?"
> "What civilization?" Travis asked.[2]

Our ambivalent attitude toward our own history is nowhere more plainly visible than in our assumptions about the nature of the Apache Indian and our relations with him. The old concepts about the white man's role as a bringer of enlightenment to the savage are by no means dead, but a large segment of the population, including many thoughtful and humane people, has come to believe that the white men were the real savages and that the Indians were basically gentle creatures driven to vengeful violence by the brutalities of their conquerors. John Upton Terrell sounds the note fortissimo in his 1972 historical survey, *Apache Chronicle*: "Through the years . . .

[1] Kingsley West, *Apache Lance*, p. 6.
[2] Will Cook, *Apache Fighter*, p. 97.

superior American military power gradually drove the Apache closer to the end of their tether, but it never succeeded in completely defeating them. That was accomplished by the perfidy, the treachery, the inhumanity of bestial white civilians both in Washington and the Southwest, forces which created in them a hopelessness they were unable to combat" (p. xv).

Other tribes—the Comanches, the Cheyennes, and the Sioux, for example—had the same problems with the white man and fought him just as hard, but for various reasons the Apaches get more attention than all the other groups put together. They were the last to battle for their freedom, and their struggles were well reported. Their great leaders were legendary figures. As fighters they were unsurpassed. Their ruthlessness and cruelty make fine grist for the mills of writers and readers with an appetite for violence.

All this gets maximum exposure in fiction—not just the "serious" writing about the West, but also the commercial product that we buy in the drugstore and the supermarket along with the aspirin and the cauliflower. Ever since Henry Nash Smith told us so in *Virgin Land* in 1950, we have known that dime novels and their present-day equivalents are mirrors which faithfully reflect our assumptions and prejudices. They have to do so or we don't read them. The social historian discovers that they are invaluable for the study of American popular culture. He reads them not for what they tell him about the subject matter, but for what they tell him about the reader.

That reader has been suffering from a massive guilt complex about what we have done to the Indian. The Native American owned the country, we tell ourselves; we stole it from him. He was wild and free; we caged him. He was a magnificent pagan in tune with nature; we baptized him and ruined him in the process. To use the word "savage" in connection with any Indian is in the worst possible taste. He is simply "preindustrial."

The consequence of this sort of thinking and writing is contradiction. There is no middle ground. If the Apache is a gentleman of distinguished culture, the white man is a savage, and vice versa. Fiction about the Apache wars is a good laboratory for fact-finding in this area. Close to two hundred novels have been devoted to the Indian uprisings in the Southwest from the close of the Civil War to Geronimo's surrender in 1886—old ones and new ones, paperback and hardback, pro-Apache and anti-Apache. Even a short survey of these books throws light on the changes in our thinking over the last century, our basic prejudices which remain unshaken, our painful progress toward tolerance and understanding.

Since the dominant voices in our time are pro-Apache, it is worth noting that these believers have not discovered anything new. People have taken the side of the Indian and accused the white man since very early times. The Doolittle Commission of 1865 surveyed the situation throughout the West and advised Congress that the red man was abused. Vincent Colyer in 1871 blamed the whites for everything bad that had happened before he took charge of Indian affairs. Government employees, church groups, and even a few military men spoke out about the chicanery and injustice they saw in white management of Indian affairs. Eastern people who had not been in the West but had read the novels of James Fenimore Cooper and Francois René de Chateaubriand sometimes took a romantic view of the aborigine. The press in the West was always complaining about the silly and ignorant people back East who had never seen a live Apache but blamed the pioneers for bringing all the killing and burning and scalping on themselves.

All this sympathy for the desert Indians was reflected in fiction eventually, but it took some time for it to become visible. The first group of novelists to write about the Apache wars had a service background or were in some way close to the service. Captain Charles King had first-hand experience in the Apache wars and made capital of his knowledge in about a dozen of his fifty-odd novels of military life. Gwendolen Overton's *Heritage of Unrest* (1901), the best of the early novels about soldiers in Apachería, is based on the idea that a woman with some Apache blood in her veins will not be able to suppress all her savage instincts. Edward S. Ellis in *Trailing Geronimo* (1908) follows General George Crook in pursuit of "as desperate a band of wretches as ever desolated a community." Forrestine Cooper Hooker, daughter of a colonel and wife of an Arizona cattle baron's son, shudders at the cruelty and blood lust of the tribesmen in *When Geronimo Rode* (1924). It could hardly have been otherwise with any writer close to the Indian-fighting Army.

All this time, however, the pro-Indian sentiment was building up. It appeared in Marah Ellis Ryan's *Indian Love Letters* (1907, 1973), which sentimentalized the Hopis hopelessly, but it did not surface in Apache fiction until 1923, the year of Harold Bell Wright's *The Mine with the Iron Door*. Natachee, the solitary Apache, has been educated in the white man's schools but is bitterly antiwhite. Outcast from his tribe, he asks: "Could you expect one who has been humiliated and shamed and broken to set up the author of his degradation as his ideal and pattern?" (pp. 164–165).

The next torch bearer in the drive to elevate the Apache would be none other than Edgar Rice Burroughs, who spent some time in the Service in Arizona and wrote two pertinent novels: *The War Chief* (1927) and *Apache Devil* (1933). The hero of both is Shoz-dijiji (Black Bear), a white boy reared by Geronimo as an Indian. When he reaches manhood, Shoz is "filled with bitterness against all men who were not Apaches, often brooding over the wrongs and injustices inflicted upon his people." Unaware of his white ancestry, he becomes "a living scourge throughout the countryside."

Burroughs sees the Apaches as fine, sensitive human beings:

> Among themselves they are entirely different people from those we are accustomed to see on the reservation. No one who has watched them with their children, seen them at their games, heard them praying to Dawn and Twilight, to the Moon and Stars as they cast their sacred hoddentin to the winds would ever again question their possession of the finer instincts of sentiment and imagination.[3]

In the thirties the banner was carried by Will Levington Comfort's *Apache* (1931), a classic attempt to get inside the mind and soul of Mangus Colorado; Edwin Corle's *Figtree John* (1934), which tries to understand a less important but no less defiant Apache; and Paul I. Wellman's *Broncho Apache* (1936), a fictional re-creation of the adventures of Massai, who escaped from Geronimo's prison train somewhere in Missouri and made his way, undetected, back to his homeland to wage "single-handed war for two or three years against not only the United States but Mexico and the 'tame' or reservation Indians, whom he despised" (p. 5).

Beginning in the 1940's, the trend went all the way. The white

[3] Edgar Rice Burroughs, *Apache Devil*, p. 37.

man became the Bad Guy; the Apache turned into the Good Guy. Elliott Arnold's *Blood Brother* (1947) and Jane Barry's *A Time in the Sun* (1962) gave the reading public what it wanted to hear.

Arnold's book was a best seller, was made into a moving picture, and called forth several lower-level follow-ups, setting the tone for much later writing. Cochise, chief of the Chiricahuas, is a truly great man, "witty, kind and possessed of an incomparable understanding." He speaks in poetry:

> Are we not natives to this earth about us?
> Are we not of the rocks, the mountains, the air, the forest?
>
> Do not the bodies of our fathers and their fathers lie beneath the earth that belongs to the Apache?
>
> .   .   .   .
>
> Why then do the white men come here?
> Why do they kill our food?[4]

Nobody explains to him that the white man has come to reclaim the wilderness, tame the savage, and bring the blessings of civilization.

Jane Barry's novel, fifteen years later, is even more pro-Apache and antiwhite. It explores the most sensitive area in race relations: intermarriage. The question, "Would you want your daughter to marry one?" is always crucial. Squaw men—whites who married Indian women—were a reality of the frontier and had a place, of sorts, in fiction. Tom Jeffords in *Blood Brother* marries Cochise's sister Sonseeahray with the complete approval of the reader. Before Jane Barry, however, an Indian man who conceived an attachment for a white woman never lived to do anything about it. To aspire was to expire.

Forrestine Cooper Hooker, writing in 1924, allows an Apache warrior to respond to the charms of her heroine, but he dies in battle protecting her soldier lover, thus taking himself safely out of the picture. Natachee, Harold Bell Wright's Apache, is probably emotionally involved with Marta, the white girl, but he never betrays himself by the quiver of a muscle. Edgar Rice Burroughs' Apache Devil is in love with Wichita Billings, but makes no progress until his white origin is revealed.

---

[4] Elliott Arnold, *Blood Brother*, pp. 27–28.

"If Shoz-dijiji was a white-eyed man, you would listen," he said.

"Oh God, I don't know, I don't know," she cried.

"Shoz-dijiji knows. . . ." He wheeled his pony and rode away.[5]

Even in *Blood Brother* (which Miss Barry seems to have had at her elbow as she wrote) Tom Jeffords' Apache bride does not survive. She is shot in the back by a white soldier, and Jeffords loses both her and their unborn child.

By 1962 a mixed marriage has begun to seem tolerable, even intriguing. Anna Stillman in *A Time in the Sun* comes to Arizona to marry her soldier fiancé, is captured by Apaches, and falls in love with Joaquin, half Apache and half Mexican. She marries him, refuses to give him up, and loses him when he is murdered by a couple of rascally white men. A white woman and a red man may come together, but they can't live happily ever after. They still can't. Gail Rogers' *Second Kiss* (1972) ends tragically, like all the others. So does Reuben Bercovitch's *Odette* (1974). So does Robert J. Seidman's *One Smart Indian* (1977). It may take many years more for a successful mixed marriage to violate the taboos which rule our subconscious minds and underlie our fiction.

Jane Barry is unwilling to let her lovers continue their housekeeping, but in other ways she is completely defiant of the old stereotypes. The traditional roles of white man and red are reversed. Anna and Joaquin make the point:

"They burned a man. Burned him!"

He said, "Have you ever seen Apache scalps on Mexican and American saddles? Have you seen them geld and flay our wounded? Or what they do to our dead if we don't recover them?"[6]

The impact of this sort of thinking is felt all the way down the scale from the slickest hard-cover fiction to the lowliest of paperbacks, but its greatest impact is on books which attempt to be historical novels. Even when the Apache is portrayed as a red-handed terror, his "imaginative cruelties" are perpetrated by "the People in their frustration and fight for survival."[7] It has become customary to blame the worst atrocities on "wild young ones whom even the chiefs

---

[5] Burroughs, *Apache Devil*, p. 126.

[6] Jane Barry, *A Time in the Sun*, p. 105.

[7] John Hunter, *Lost Valley*, p. 58.

cannot control,"[8] Apaches who are outlaws among their own people. A good many authors look for a middle ground, trying not to take sides. Will Henry's *Chiricahua* (1972) concentrates on Flatnose, leader of the Chiricahua "wolfpack" who has vowed to "destroy every white life in his path," and on Lieutenant H. C. Kensington, determined to further his career by killing any and all Apaches. In the middle is the well-known Apache scout "Peaches," who functions as a peace bringer. In his dedication the author informs us that his book is intended "to honor in spirit a wild, free way of life, vanished forever." James R. Olson's *Ulzana* reconstructs the character and experiences of a minor but historical Apache leader who is cast in heroic mold. He kills, but he kills in defense of his homeland and to slow down pursuit (white men always stop to bury the dead). The trouble with most such reconstructions is that the authors can't possibly get inside an Indian, and they inevitably make him heroic in white man's terms. Ulzana is Hiawatha with a gun and a horse.

Admiration for the Indian—even for the Apache—is the "in" thing now, and the white men are "the dregs of their respective societies . . . uncouth, ignorant, bigoted, and looking for something for nothing."[9] Little Big Man in the movie version of his novel is somebody to respect and admire when he lives with the Cheyennes. When he returns to white "civilization," he becomes a no-good lush. The white troopers are bloody-handed cutthroats, and General Custer is a narcissistic madman. Thus, the Cheyennes are seen to have good reason for calling themselves "the human beings." They are the only ones who qualify.

This is only one side of the picture, however. There is definitely another. Although the hard-cover novels tend to take the side of the Indian, and have done so for at least twenty-five years, the others— the paperback westerns, the commercial products which ornament the revolving racks in the supermarkets across the land, have resisted today's reversals of the old attitudes. In these novels the Apache is still a savage, an inhuman monster, a cruel and bloodthirsty menace to all civilized people. Vine Deloria's *Custer Died for Your Sins*

[8] Lewis B. Patten, *Apache Hostage*, p. 41.
[9] John Upton Terrell, *Apache Chronicle*, p. xiii.

(1969) and Dee Brown's *Bury My Heart at Wounded Knee* (1971) have had only minor impact on the writers of popular fiction.

There are substantial reasons for this survival. One is the fact that popular fiction has a firm connection with folklore and folk attitudes. The Apache has been put to use in "The American Morality Play," *Time* magazine's phrase (March 30, 1969) for the western novel, which has to be conceived in blacks and whites. Both the good guys and the bad guys are really symbols, not people. When a bad guy dies, deservedly, he is not a dead person. No mother mourns for him. He has no mother. He is a personification of dangerous wickedness. He hurts us and hates us. We fear and hate him. He is GRENDEL, the enemy of God and man.

The pioneers themselves started us down this road. A dispatch from Deming, New Mexico, dated June 13, 1885, to the *Silver City Enterprise* said of the Apaches: "They are the ugliest and filthiest brutes on the globe—lying, thieving, gambling cutthroats, who when a beef is cut up and distributed among them will quarrel over the entrails, and eat the filthy stuff raw."[10]

Today's popular novelists take up where the man from Deming left off—for example, James Warner Bellah in *Apache* (1951):

> It can be a phase of the moon that maddens Apaches, or a word from the memory of a medicine chief, or a strange flower by the trailside, or an omen of blood in a stone; because Apaches hate life and they are the enemies of all mankind. [P. 4]

Often the title indicates what the author has in mind: *Apache War Cry, Apache Ransom, Apache Dawn, Apache Hostage, Apache Massacre.* In many such novels a malignant Apache chief lurks in the background, an irresistible, inhuman presence endowed with almost supernatural malice and cunning. He can be Mangus or Victorio or Geronimo. He can be Tucsos, Chingo, or Meathead.[11] He can even be Diablo, Diablito, or Satanio.[12] His name does not matter. He is

---

[10] Quoted by Charles Fletcher Lummis in *General Crook and the Apache Wars*, p. xiii.

[11] Charles Marquis Warren, *Only the Valiant*; T. V. Olsen, *Savage Sierra*; Richard Telfair, *The Secret of Apache Canyon*.

[12] Wade Everett, *Fort Starke*; Will Cook, *Ambush at Antlers Spring*; Jackson Cole, *Apache Guns*.

the Enemy—the same one John Bunyan's Christian fought all the way to the Celestial City, and just as deeply rooted in folklore.

It is understood that he must be totally bad. No redeeming feature is possible. And if he is not bad enough to suit us, we work on him till he is. How we go about it is clear from even a casual look at the fictional Apache. We give him credit for everything we find intolerable in ourselves.

First of all, he is filthy in his habits and smells bad. He has "a rank, feral breath,"[13] and he gives off "a potent smell of sweat and grease and smoke and bird lime and the Lord knows what all."[14] The Apache warrior is "filthy in his ideas and speech and inconceivably dirty in his person and manners."[15] This sometimes applies to the women as well as to the men: "Apache women's habits leave them offensive and even in the earlier years, few mountain men wanted one for a wife."[16] A sensitive nose could pick up the Apache odor even at a distance:

> "What's the matter boy?" Hardhead said.
> Billy whispered, "Apaches, Pa. I smell 'em."[17]

It should be no surprise to a generation pathologically sensitive to human body odors that the Apache should thus offend. Our consumption of deodorants (roll on, spray on, pat on, rub on), mouthwashes, special soaps, and aids to "feminine daintiness" makes the point. Since we must at best smell good and at worst not smell at all, the Enemy could not smell any way but bad.

Anthropologists tell us that Indians don't really smell bad at all. They just smell different. And if one of them burns mesquite, he smells different from one who burns piñon. Here, however, as in other departments of human affairs, to be different is to be offensive.

Eating habits provide an even better area for making value judgments about the Apache. Since he is evil personified, his table manners must be impossible. One finds such descriptions as these:

> This was not the first time he had observed Apaches eating, yet he was still appalled. They chewed with loud smackings of their lips,

[13] Don Catlin, *Desert Crucible*.
[14] Hal G. Evarts, *The Blazing Land*, p. 132.
[15] James Warner Bellah, *A Thunder of Drums*, p. 6.
[16] Will Cook, *Apache Ambush*, p. 11.
[17] Harry Whittington, *Desert Stakeout*, p. 34.

grease dripped off their chins. A favorite dish was body-hot animal entrails.[18]

Laredo squinted his eyes against the glare. The raiders were gulping that horse meat in huge chunks. He could see a buck stick a large mass in his mouth, hold the rest with one hand, and saw off the bite in front of his lips with a redly glittering knife.[19]

We all know that some of our strongest taboos are related to the consumption of food. We have the lowest possible opinion of people who eat what we reject, like "high" meat or parts of which, as Dickens described them, "the animal has least reason to be proud." Our opinion is even lower of a man whose table manners are at variance with ours. Toothpicks, once tolerated or even encouraged, are taboo. Spitting, even in cases of emergency, is intolerable to us, though an early-day New England etiquette book advised: "When it is necessary to spit, a gentleman will spit only in a corner." Naturally the Apache, as the Enemy personified, cannot be a dainty eater.

Another way in which he can be stigmatized involves his speech. Ever since George Bernard Shaw convinced us in *Pygmalion* that language makes the lady, the importance of genteel inflection has been axiomatic. The Apache tongue must, therefore, be unpleasant to civilized ears. "The Apache lingo was such a barbarous tongue he was never able to get the hang of it," Edward S. Ellis remarked in 1908.[20] Later writers describe it even less kindly as "gobble talk,"[21] or "hissing, guttural Apache."[22] One of them remarks, "The Apache bubbled and slushed," and adds: "What was up was a whole lot of Apache language, like a herd of cows pulling their feet out of the sand."[23]

It would be a safe bet that none of these writers ever heard any spoken Apache, but that, of course, does not matter. The Enemy would not be the Enemy if he spoke good English. The point is established in a backhanded sort of way in S. E. Whitman's *Captain Apache*, in which, through a strange chain of circumstances, a full-

[18] Cook, *Apache Ambush*, p. 49.
[19] Catlin, *Desert Crucible*, p. 83.
[20] *Trailing Geronimo*, p. 319.
[21] George Garland, *Apache Warpath*, p. 116.
[22] Dale Michaels, *The Warring Breed*, p. 18.
[23] Julian Fink, *Major Dundee*, pp. 67, 74.

blooded Apache becomes a captain in the United States Cavalry during the Indian campaigns. Big, tough, and efficient, he is the best man on the post. He has to fight prejudice, but since he is the leading man, he has better manners and talks better English than the West Pointers.

Along with his other deficiencies the Apache naturally has to be lacking in human feelings. The pain and terror of his victims must mean nothing to him. In the folklore which popular writers accept, the Enemy begins by being cruel to animals. He does not love his horse, but rides him to death and then eats him. He "goes in fer mule meat" and enjoys "slicing off thick red slabs of meat" while the mule is "still bawling."[24] When he has to leave in a hurry, and even when he is in no hurry at all, he abandons his old people and leaves them to starve. His finest efforts, however, are devoted to torturing his captives. In this department the modern writer, serving a readership with a highly developed taste for horror and violence, lets it all, as we say now, hang out. This passage is milder than some:

> Lovington was in the barn, still alive, hanging by his wrists from one of the rafters. The Apaches had sliced through his calf muscles and his feet kept twitching. Another had flicked out Lovington's eyeballs with the point of his knife. They hung on his cheeks like boiled eggs dangling from bloody strings.

Lovington asks O'Hagen, the viewpoint character, to put him out of his misery, and O'Hagen, following a well-established pattern, shoots him.[25]

The writers seem to be more ingenious in inventing tortures than the Apaches themselves, but some devices are used so often that they have become standard. Living burial is one, with ants and coyotes as added attractions. Suspension over a slow fire, boiling the brains, is another. The stakeout, however, is by all odds the favorite. A naked man is spread-eagled on the sand, face up, with wrists and ankles pegged to the ground. If the Apaches cut off his eyelids, it is bad enough with the desert sun to blind him. If they stake him out on an anthill, it is worse. If they build a fire on his stomach, the

[24] Lynton Wright Brent, *Apache Massacre*, p. 31; Robert Steelman, *Apache Wells*.

[25] Cook, *Apache Ambush*, p. 7.

reader's stomach starts to turn, and if they mutilate him, the effect is catastrophic. John Benteen's Fargo is unbelievably tough, but this scene is too much for him:

> . . . they had scalped him first. His face was indescribable, the loose skin oozing in a welter of blood down over his eyes.
>
> Of course, that had been only the beginning. Then there was the fire they had built in the middle of his chest. Its embers still smoldered, filling Fargo's nostrils with the stench of burning flesh.
>
> But that was not the worst. His eyes went to the bloody groin; then looked quickly away.
>
> "Jesus Christ," he whispered. "You poor goddam bastard."
>
> He turned away, sure that the man was dead. No human being could have survived all that.
>
> Then he heard the groan.[26]

It is accepted as truth in the paperback novels that the Apache women are the keenest and most resourceful torturers. "Folks," says one of Will Henry's characters in *The Seven Men at Mimbres Springs*, "I'd sooner get caught alive by a hundred Apache bucks than dead by six of their squaws" (p. 119). "This feller's riddled with bullets," observes Tobin the scout in Gil Martin's *Squawman*, "but he's not mutilated. That means they're not toting women. It's the women who work on the bodies. Likely they were in a hurry" (p. 48).

As Martin reports it, the Apache woman may enjoy torturing and mutilating strangers, but she reserves her supreme efforts for a man who has betrayed her. In the book just quoted, Tobin is married to an Apache who suspects him of tender feelings for the white heroine.

> "Two hours ago," she said in careful English, "I would have seen you dead. As a squaw I claimed my right to be the one to torture you, and to watch you die, slowly, inch by inch, along the length of your body. . . ."
>
> "And,"—her voice was almost a whisper—"before you died, I would have cut from you your manhood and you would have seen me hold it up for all the squaws to look upon—for with this you have betrayed me."[27]

The worst fate is reserved for captive white women. James War-

---

[26] John Benteen, *Apache Raiders*, p. 33.
[27] Gil Martin, *Squawman*, p. 127.

ner Bellah is the expert on this aspect of Apache cruelty. "You have to see it to believe what they do to white women. There is a ferocity in it which beggars rationalization," he tells us.[28]

> Nothing is worse than burying women the Apaches have worked over; nothing is worse than an insane girl digging down to her mother's dead face in the starlight.[29]

The ones who die quickly are lucky. The ones who live, if they know what is in store for them, will "pray for death."[30]

> It was the way of the Apaches with a young and desirable female captive that she would belong to the two who had taken her; she would be used by them for a time, then passed on to the others, turn and turn about at their pleasure. If she survived this brutal debasement, she would be a serf in some village, beaten and abused by the Apache women.[31]

Except for sexual abuse, a white woman would not be put to the torture. She might, however, be mutilated after death according to John Hunter's *Lost Valley* (p. 80):

> After [Manah] used a woman to death, he cut a souvenir from her pubic tuft, and he valued these most when the color was golden.

If the white captive survived and had a child by her Apache captor, she was likely to be despised and rejected when she got back to her own people—especially by her husband. Ellen Graf, in Marvin H. Alberts' *Apache Rising*, finds herself in this position:

> "You were even a wife to one of them."
> "Not because I wanted to be."
> "Then why were you? Any decent white woman would kill herself before. . . ." [P. 32]

As any reader can tell you, the way to avoid the worst is to save the last bullet for the woman:

> "If you see we're not going to make it, shoot yourself in the head. Make sure it's a finish shot." [P. 95]

The idea that a woman suffers unspeakable things if she is cap-

28 Bellah, *Thunder of Drums*, p. 6.
29 James Warner Bellah, *Massacre*, p. 166.
30 Garland, *Apache Warpath*, p. 78.
31 Frank Castle, *Guns to Sonora*, p. 102.

tured by Indians is one of our basic beliefs. No popular writer could approach his typewriter with confidence if this cliché were taken away from him. It is so universally accepted by unsophisticated readers that the facts are worth examining. J. Norman Heard, who has assembled and digested all the available accounts of Indian captivity, is convinced that Eastern captives were comparatively safe, but that in the West women were in some danger. He cites Carl Coke Rister's *Border Captives* to support his belief that "white women along the frontier generally regarded death as preferable to captivity." Yet he cites the case of Olive Oatman, who endured much from the Cocopahs during her five-year captivity in the 1850's, but declared when it was over that "it was to the honor of these savages . . . that they never offered the least unchaste abuse to me."[32]

Mr. Heard probably says all that can be said when he remarks that "caprice was a major factor which frequently determined a captive's fate. Death, servitude or adoption depended upon the whim of the warrior who first touched the captive." In short, there were no certainties. Some women were raped, but many were not.

It seems obvious that we believe what we want to believe about Apaches and their ways. Our unwillingness to change is reflected in these examples from the paperback novels. We are certain that these tribesmen were "as slippery as a snake and twice as treacherous."[33] We are sure that they had superhuman endurance and even without food or water could outtravel a trooper on a horse. We believe that they could hide themselves behind a few blades of grass and become practically invisible. We suspect that they have the power to influence our thoughts from far away, "grasping our feelings and fears and dealing out more of the same to us."[34] But if we give them credit with one hand, we take it back with the other. Here is Captain Maddocks at a frontier post lecturing his class of junior officers, as reported by James Warner Bellah:

> Apaches can make seventy-five miles a day on foot over rough terrain. They can sustain themselves and their ponies on wild mountain grasses, wild onions, cactus fruits, berries, and nuts. . . . All of them have reasoning faculties only slightly superior to instinct. They all

[32] J. Norman Heard, *White into Red*, p. 22.
[33] Martin, *Squawman*, p. 22.
[34] Garland, *Apache Warpath*, p. 60.

enjoy the present and never plan for the future. The gauge of their cultural development is that they cannot carry on abstract conversations. They cannot exchange ideas with each other—only simple facts.[35]

In an atmosphere so full of the mystic and the mythological, minor errors go unnoticed, and even major slips do not seem to embarrass the authors of these tales. W. R. Burnett in *Adobe Walls* has his Apaches living in hogans (p. 68). Jackson Cole portrays the West Texas desert as a land of "primeval forests" where the Apaches wear warbonnets.[36] The wildest misconceptions deal with *tiswin*, the Apaches' corn beer. It is sometimes confused with mescal ("the fiery and revivifying *tiswin*, the mescal wine of the Apaches"). Kirby, one of James Warner Bellah's scouts, decoys the warriors into an ambush by making this concoction, which, according to him, can be smelled far away. The odor "hangs on the wind like, and carries for miles, the stench of it does, and when a 'Pache gets a sniff of that, it's his whole life. Give 'em a sniff of tiswin and God himself can't hold 'em to a fight this time of year."[37]

The limits of confusion seem to have been reached by Wade Everett in his novel *Fort Starke*, in which he appears to identify mescal (an agave) with the mesquite (a shrub that produces seeds in pods).

> "I don't like this, Jim. That rain we had will make the mescal beans ripen. When that happens, the Apaches will be brewin' *tiswin*. Just drinkin'! Diablito knows that and he won't go off to brew *tiswin* without settlin' up here first." [P. 133]

Up to this point most of the books discussed have been "traditional" westerns, supposedly a very stable commodity even in an era of change and transformation. The word "monolithic" has been used to describe them, and they are said to be serenely indifferent to the tides of change. This is a misconception. The western may resist change, but it follows fashion like all things human, though sometimes slowly and afar off. For instance, there are signs that the glorification of our "red" brothers, with emphasis on Indian grievances

[35] Bellah, *Thunder of Drums*, p. 34.
[36] Cole, *Apache Guns*, pp. 6, 53.
[37] James Warner Bellah, *The Apache*, p. 146.

and white injustice, is having its effect on Apache fiction. The evil ways of the "Tucson Ring" of crooked merchants are acknowledged often, and the hero may comment when an Apache butchers a white man's cow, "I'd like to know why the Indian was hungry. Could it be that the agent who was supposed to feed him stole his food?"[38]

The conviction that all employees of the Bureau of Indian Affairs were seedy crooks is universal, and fiction writers share it. Take the case of Joseph Capron Tiffany, agent at San Carlos, Arizona, from 1880 to 1882. Inexperienced and slow-witted, but seemingly a real friend to his Indian charges, he alienated the people of Arizona and was indicted by a hostile grand jury which called him "a disgrace to the civilization of the age and a foul blot on the national escutcheon." The *Arizona Daily Star* (Tucson) quoted the report. Historian John G. Bourke quoted the *Star*. As a result, Tiffany's infamy has become "an article of faith" to later generations.[39] Novelist Hunter Ingram is a believer. In his 1975 novel *Fort Apache* he quotes Captain Emmett Crawford (who never knew Tiffany, having arrived at San Carlos six months after the man's departure):

> "Tiffany is a new low. . . . I know, but can't prove, that the Ring is getting receipts for large amounts of supplies never furnished. Tiffany is getting his kickbacks for those receipts."[40]

As the white man goes down, the Indian goes up—a point previously made. The aboriginal image is improving steadily. It is possible now to read that an old Mescalero woman is "a poetess, a gifting not uncommon among her desert kind" and that her speech is "lyric."[41] The Apache smell is no longer offensive and can be compared to the odor of "rotten bark."[42] The possibility that a white man has his own odor can even be acknowledged ("They would smell the difference in me. I have been eating the white man's food").[43] One author goes so far as to take note of "the ordinary careful grooming" of Apache men.[44]

[38] Bill Gulick, *Showdown in the Sun*, p. 37.

[39] John Bret Harte, "The Strange Case of Joseph C. Tiffany: Indian Agent in Disgrace," *Journal of Arizona History* 16 (Winter, 1975): 384.

[40] Pp. 44–45. Compare Giles Lutz, *The Black Day* (Camp Grant massacre).

[41] Clay Fisher, *Black Apache*, p. 20.

[42] Reuben Bercovitch, *Odette*, p. 186.

[43] Louis L'Amour, *The Lonely Men*, p. 48.

[44] Clay Fisher, *Apache Ransom*, p. 5.

In many, perhaps most, of the popular novels written in the seventies the Apaches are still tough and terrible, but every now and then they turn out to be the good guys. In Clay Fisher's *Black Apache* (1976) they are, in a manner of speaking, on the side of the angels, or at least on the side of the narrator, who is a half-blood Roman Catholic priest. The leading character is a magnificent black man named Robert E. Lee Flicker, the first Negro graduate of West Point (obviously Henry Flipper), who deserted from the Army when falsely charged with attempted rape and went to live with the Apaches in Mexico. His friend and fellow fighter is Kaytennae, a magnificent red man to go with the black. This means that a new set of villains must be found, and the author supplies them in a band of renegade Yaquis led by Santiago Kiefer (read James Kirker), son of an infamous scalp hunter and a scalp hunter himself. His mother is a Yaqui Amazon named Simialita (Monkey Woman). "They're not Indians," says Kaytennae, "they're *barbaros*."[45] When Flicker's party catches up with the band, they have an almost-dead white woman staked out for mass raping—just what the Apaches used to do in earlier novels.

In other ways these stories about the Apache wars have gone with the tide. One way is their response to the demand for shocking violence. It would seem difficult if not impossible to improve on the tortures and mutilations served up in earlier novels, but the writers of the 1970's have done their best. The pattern calls for a man of great strength, cunning, and ruthlessness who undertakes some sort of mission, survives incredible hardships, and slaughters everybody who gets in his way. Lee Kershaw is Gordon D. Shirreffs' contribution to the type. His business is manhunting, but in *The Apache Hunter* (1976) he becomes the hunted. He captures Yanozha, a wild Apache leader, thus spoiling the chief's "medicine" and making a mortal enemy of him. Yanozha escapes and a double manhunt begins. They stalk each other to the end of the book, with the help of Mexican troops and General George Crook. There is much violence—torture, rape, and murder. Here is a sample from Yanozha's attack on the Torcido stage station:

The air was overheated and thick with the greasy smoke and the

[45] Fisher, *Black Apache*, p. 122.

stench was overpowering. He glanced sideways at the kitchen range. Its sides and top were dull red with heat from the great fire that had been stoked within it. Then he heard someone screaming hoarsely at the top of his lung power—himself. The naked girl had been tied down across the red-hot top of the range and the thick, greasy, stinking smoke was rising from her cooking flesh and body fat.[46]

An even better example of the trend is William James's series featuring Cuchillo Oro, so called because of the golden-hilted Spanish knife he carries. This huge and lethal Apache has lost his wife and child in an attack by white soldiers and is out for revenge. At the beginning of *Sonora Slaughter* (1976), number six in the series, he flips out both eyes of a bounty hunter and then castrates him to win the approval of a Mexican bandit leader who has the drop on him. He rapes a captive woman in the presence of the bandit gang. He is capable of good action, however. After escaping from the robbers, he returns to rescue the beautiful Rosita Carlos and reclaim his famous knife. In the final encounter Rosita's mind snaps and she kills herself. "The crimson and gray contents of her head splashed high, then ran down the adobe in a slow ooze toward her crumpled form as if trying to replace itself where it belonged."[47] Her father loses *his* mind, too, when he sees what has happened. Such a carnival of horror and madness could not have been described in the old days of the western, but it has become almost standard fare in these enlightened times. It might be added that Calvera the bandit is a homosexual—another evidence that something new has been added.

A new button, however, does not make a new coat. In Western fiction the Apache is still the Enemy—at least the bad ones are. And the bad ones are at war with the good ones as well as with the white men. It would be safe to say that the bastions of our folk beliefs have been weakened but not breached. To some of us, all Apaches are evil personified, and to others, some Apaches are evil personified. It will probably remain that way in spite of all efforts to upgrade the Indian and make him lovable.

Most consumers of westerns, indeed, do not believe every word they read. John C. Cawelti points out that "the melodramatic imperatives of formula stories tend to call forth more extreme expressions

[46] Gordon D. Shirreffs, *The Apache Hunter*, p. 69.
[47] William James, *Sonora Slaughter*, p. 147.

of political and moral values than either author or audience fully believes in."[48] Even so, it appears that many otherwise sensible people will continue to assume the worst about the Apache—because they want to.

[48] John C. Cawelti, "Myth, Symbol and Formula," *Journal of Popular Culture* 8 (Summer, 1974): 6.

The Two Black Legends

An angry Mexican-American novelist presents this view of "white" California fruit growers:

> So the Anglo growers and guero executives, smiling in their cool, filtered offices, puffing their elegant thin cigars, washed their clean blond bloodless dirtless hands of the whole matter. All they did was hire Roberto Morales. . . . How he got his people down to the pickings was no concern of theirs. . . . They fulfilled their end of the bargain and cheated no one. Their only crime; their only soul grime indeed was that they just didn't give a shit how that migratory scum lived.[1]

The novelist who paints this appalling picture is Raymond Barrio. The novel is *The Plum Plum Pickers* (1969). What you are seeing and hearing is the Black Legend of the United States, corresponding to the Black Legend of Spain, about which there has been a great deal of discussion. The two Black Legends are twins, closely resembling each other, and are best understood together.

The presence of fermenting anti-Americanism south of the Mexican border—a true Black Legend—is common knowledge. The libraries and bookstands are full of evidence—in fact, tons of it. Now, however, the familiar cries are heard on the American side as people of Mexican background, particularly in California and the American Southwest, make wonderful progress in building their own version of the legend, spurred on by sympathetic Anglos.[2] One might say truthfully that the Black Legend of the United States has cleared the border Immigration Service stations, taken out a permit as a resident alien, and come to live among us.

[1] Raymond Barrio, *The Plum Plum Pickers*, p. 61.
[2] David J. Weber, *Foreigners in Their Native Land: Historical Roots of the Mexican Americans*. Weber assembles and discusses the major statements for and against the Latins in the Southwest from earliest times.

Seemingly the movement started recently and explosively. A rash of Chicano publications seemed to spring full grown from the head of the goddess of liberty in the sixties, as if the pickers and diggers, the bricklayers and builders—asleep for a century—had suddenly awakened and come alive. The awakening, however, is not recent. The movement goes back a long way, and the Chicanos did not invent it. It could be argued that they did not understand their own grievances until the gringos opened their eyes, and a good place to watch the awakening is in American fiction. The fictional record goes back fifty years and provides a comparatively untouched resource for the historian of ideas and attitudes.

Novels and stories, particularly stories that are written for "escape" or leisure-time reading, are good reflectors of group attitudes and assumptions. A man who goes to a book for information doesn't know what he thinks yet; he is reading so he can make up his mind. But a man who is reading for relaxation doesn't want his prejudices disturbed. Consciously or unconsciously, the bookmakers accept this fact. They know they have to give him what he wants if they hope to get his money. As Henry Nash Smith puts it in *Virgin Land* (1950): "The individual writer abandons his own personality and identifies himself with the reveries of his readers. It is presumably close fidelity of the Beadle stories to the dream life of a vast, inarticulate public that renders them valuable to the social historian and the historian of ideas" (p. 101). Novels dealing with the Mexican-American background, and they come in all grades of artistry and insight, open a window into the North American mind.

Two cultural historians have tried to look through that window. The first attempt was made in 1961 by Edwin W. Gaston in *The Early Novel of the Southwest: A Critical History of Southwestern Fiction, 1819–1918,* but he could find no better objective for his study than to demonstrate progress from a naïve to a mature romanticism in the forty "major" novels he examined. In the light of what was already happening at the time he made his pioneer attempt, Gaston's approach seems incredibly shallow and academic, but of course it was hard to foretell the deluge when only a few drops of rain had fallen.

Cecil Robinson did better in his important and revealing *With the Ears of Strangers* (1963), which offered ample evidence that people in the United States, who had been listening for over a century "with the ears of strangers" to Latin American voices, were beginning to pay better attention. Professor Robinson used a good many novels to make his point, but he did not get anywhere near the bottom of the great pool of fiction from which he might have learned. Nobody else got near the bottom, either. The reading of fiction has been at a low ebb in our time, and few collectors have tried systematically to gather it all in or understand its broad significance. Not even libraries make the effort. As a result, of the thousand-plus volumes of "serious" or at least semiserious fiction published about the Southwest and its people (including the Mexican-Americans) since 1918, a small percentage by well-known authors have survived. A larger percentage have been forgotten, and a surprising number of the forgotten novels have disappeared so completely that it sometimes takes years to locate a particular book, if it can be found at all. And yet this mass of material is part of the record and tells us something about ourselves and our problems.

Putting all the available evidence together, one learns that the countries to the south of us, particularly Mexico, have fascinated Anglo-Americans since the 1820's. At least one hundred novels have been written in English about Mexico itself, covering all stages of its history from the Aztecs to the Mexican Revolution. Another hundred could be listed dealing with the history of Anglo-Mexican contacts in the Southwest—the Texan revolt, the Santa Fe Trail, the Mexican War, the Mexican Revolution, modern Mexico. Another group deals with Mexican and Mexican-American folk life in the old days and the new—in small communities and great cities, on the ranches and the farms, in the canneries and migratory-labor camps—and continues on down to the handful of Chicano novels which build the Black Legend of the United States with horrifying pictures of abuse and injustice and misery. Much can be learned from these books about the facts of Mexican-American life in the United States, but even more can be found out about the false assumptions, prejudices, guilt feelings, and fantasies of both sides.

To make sense of this mass of fictional material, one starts with the Black Legend of Spain—the assumptions, with about four hundred years of currency behind them, that the Spaniards and all their works (including the conquest of Mexico) are inherently evil. Philip

Wayne Powell reduces the legend to capsule form: "The basic premise of the Black Legend is that Spaniards have shown themselves, historically, to be *uniquely* cruel, bigoted, tyrannical, obscurantist, lazy, fanatical, greedy and treacherous."[3]

This Black Legend, according to its numerous historians, was initiated in Spain by Bartolomé de las Casas, a Spanish friar, and broadcast in the 1550's. Las Casas was outraged by the treatment of the Indian population of the New World, but was not intending to generalize about the universal wickedness of his countrymen. The Dutch and the Portuguese and the English, however, were delighted to hear so much scandal about their enemy and began making sweeping statements about Spaniards everywhere.[4] Novelists and historians, as well as political propagandists, helped to fix the stereotypes in the public mind. Christian reformers like Charles Kingsley (*Westward Ho*, 1855) and romancers like Sir Henry Rider Haggard (*Montezuma's Daughter*, 1893) added fuel to the sacrificial fire. Americans already had their minds made up about what they were looking at when the United States made its first contacts with the outposts of Spain in the early nineteenth century. Their attitudes were passed on down through the generations until very recent times. Professor Powell quotes history textbooks in use only a few years ago which assured impressionable young people that the United States "were settled by homemakers and state builders alive with English ideals of self-government; Mexico was conquered by Spanish adventurers who wanted to go home with their plunder."[5]

The breakaway from Spain of Mexico and the other Latin American countries complicated the situation. These countries believed the Black Legend, too. That was part of their reason for rebelling. But in the eyes of their Yankee neighbors, they were guilty by association—or at least were hopelessly handicapped by centuries of Spanish dominance. In addition to the traditional accusations, the *norteamericanos* believed sincerely that the Mexicans were lazy, dirty, lustful, and cowardly—at least that men of the lower classes

---

[3] *The Tree of Hate: Propaganda and Prejudices Affecting United States Relations with the Hispanic World*, p. 11.

[4] Charles Gibson, *The Black Legend: Anti-Spanish Attitudes in the Old World and the New*, p. 13.

[5] Powell, *Tree of Hate*, pp. 9–11.

were. There was always a wistful persuasion that Mexican women were different—sympathetic, beautiful, and fond of gringo men. How such women could be the mothers and sisters and daughters of the male creatures invented by the writers in the United States remains a mystery.

In Mexico there was naturally a violent reaction. The gringos practically demanded it. Their preconceived ideas of Mexican degeneracy endowed them with corresponding ideas of their own superiority. They even felt a sense of mission which obligated them to wean the wretched Latins from their shiftless and immoral ways and impose upon them (for their own good) the advantages of the American Way. The Mexicans responded by doing for the Americans what the Americans had done for them. They created the Black Legend of the United States.

This "Yankeephobia" has been described as "a witches' brew of truth, half truth, propaganda, prejudice and political expediency"—terms which describe the other Black Legend, the Black Legend of Spain. Prevalent in Mexico for a century, induced and aggravated by the political ineptness and commercial ruthlessness of the United States, it has been gaining a foothold north of the border for the last fifty years. It is not true, however, as Professor Powell says, that hatred of the United States "originated among Latin American intellectuals and is perpetuated by them."[6] Anglo intellectuals were the first to expose the sins and shortcomings of their own countrymen, just as Las Casas pointed the finger at his. Early in the century liberals like John Kenneth Turner attacked the American plutocracy in Mexico along with the Díaz regime, and their shrieks of protest were "enthusiastically received in the United States."[7] Novelists were not far behind the sociologists and political essayists in denouncing our own brand of colonialism.

Stated in Professor Powell's terms, the formula for the American Black Legend would read: "The basic Legend of the United States is that its citizens are *uniquely* acquisitive, aggressive, bigoted, brutal, ignorant, arrogant and self-righteous." The millionaire investors were greedy; the traders and settlers and land hunters were

[6] Ibid., p. 9.
[7] *Barbarous Mexico*, p. xix.

aggressive; the anti-Catholic Protestants were bigoted; the soldiers and the Texas Rangers were brutal; the common settlers were ignorant; and the whole crew of *yanquis* assumed themselves to be better fighters, lovers, and human beings than their neighbors to the south. They believed that their way was the only right way and that it was their mission to educate, uplift, and "ennoble" their brown brothers —to show them how to live.[8]

The situation is obvious in the first real Southwestern novel— Timothy Flint's *Francis Berrian* (1826). Berrian leaves his theological studies at Harvard to look for adventure in the West. He finds it in a Comanche camp in the Rocky Mountains, where a lovely Spanish girl named Martha d'Alvaro is held captive by a red menace named Menko. With the help of The Red Heifer, an Indian girl whose virtue has to be its own reward, Francis rescues Martha and restores her to her distinguished family. The d'Alvaros are rich and conservative, and when Berrian joins the revolutionists under Morelos, they cast him off. They give up, however, when he saves the whole family and their priest from death. Berrian is on his way back to Mexico to claim his bride when he tells his story.

The stereotypes dispensed in this unsophisticated novel became standard fare for almost a century. The manly American, the beautiful Spanish girl, the treacherous and vindictive Spanish lover, the scheming priest—all were accepted and enjoyed by our grandparents.

Closer contacts between the two peoples did not help, mostly because these contacts were the result of war and conquest (the westward expansion). In wartime the Mexicans were the enemy. During the expansion, they were the victims. In neither case could the Americans afford to be tolerant, understanding, and generous. They had too much to lose. On the other hand, the Mexicans, deprived of their territory and their self-respect, could hardly be tolerant, understanding, and generous, either.

In the United States the Mexican War, the Spanish-American War, and the Mexican Revolution fixed the stereotypes more firmly in the minds of both Mexicans and Americans. To begin at the beginning, take the second Southwestern novel, Anthony Ganilh's *Mex-*

[8] Powell, *Tree of Hate*, pp. 132–133.

ico versus Texas (1838). He dedicates his book to Sam Houston and celebrates the Texans as the destined saviors of northern Mexico:

> The Texians may be considered as leading a crusade in behalf of modern civilization, against the antiquated prejudices and narrow policy of the middle ages, which still govern the Mexican Republic. The eyes of the world are upon them [the Texans]. The north of Mexico expects its deliverance at their hands, and if Texas be faithful to the call of providence, power, glory and immense wealth await her among the nations of the earth.[9]

The same tone persists down through the century, and the priesthood often gets credit for the dark night of the intellect which has fallen over the Latin American world. Amelia E. Barr in *Remember the Alamo* (1888) describes "the black-robed monk, gliding about [the] house with downcast eyes and folded hands," creating a breach between Robert Worth, an American physician living in San Antonio, and his Spanish wife—and at the same time inciting the citizens to murder and revenge:

> In every church, the priests—more bitter, fierce and resentful than either the civil or military power—urged on the people an exterminating war. A black flag waved the missions, and fired every heart with unrelenting vengeance and hatred. To slay a heretic was a free pass through the dolorous pains of purgatory. For the priesthood foresaw that the triumph of the American element meant the triumph of freedom and conscience and the abolition of despotism.[10]

The novelists sometimes concentrated on one aspect of the Black Legend and sometimes on another. When Marah Ellis Ryan wrote *The Flute of the Gods* in 1909, she played up the cruelty and inhumanity so often laid at the door of the Spaniard. Tahn-té, who is one-half Spanish, though he does not know it, joins the Coronado expedition of 1540 to find out what can be learned about the invaders. He and another Hopi boy winter with them at Tiguex on the Rio Grande, where the great captain "made his comfort by turning the natives out of their houses":

> . . . there was a season of grievous strife ere the spring came, and the two boys of Te-hua saw things unspeakable as two hundred In-

---

[9] Anthony Ganilh, *Mexico versus Texas, a Descriptive Novel, Most of the Characters of Which Consist of Living Persons*, dedication.

[10] Amelia E. Barr, *Remember the Alamo*, pp. 141–142.

dians of the valley, captured under truce, were burned at the stake by the soldiers of the cross.

Tahn-té learns to read the Bible and reports back to his people at Hopi his impression of the white man's holy book:

> . . . in the talking paper which their god made, there is record of all their men since ancient days. They have never changed. Their gods tell them to go out and kill and take all that which the enemy will not give—to take also the maids for slaves,—that is in their book of laws from the beginning. Since I was a boy I have studied all these laws. It was my work. By the good a man has in his heart we can know the man! Their god is a good god for traders, and a strong god for war. But the watchers of the night must never leave the gate unguarded when they camp under its walls.[11]

Cruelty, materialism, deceitfulness, arrogance—the heart of the Black Legend of Spain! They surface continually. Before the dawn of the twentieth century, however, novelists began to find something to admire in the Mexican character, and the picture started to change. Eager to "establish a cultural tradition in as short a time as possible," Californians in the last quarter of the nineteenth century embraced "all things Spanish." The humble Mexican laborer was ignored, but the Franciscans were "accepted as pious and picturesque," and it was assumed that the Californios were of the best Spanish blood. Helen Hunt Jackson (*Ramona*, 1884) began that trend, and Charles Fletcher Lummis carried it on. Constance Goddard Du Bois (*A Soul in Bronze*, 1898) and Marah Ellis Ryan (*For the Soul of Rafael*, 1906) fell in line and specialized in "hothouse Spaniards" who appealed to romantic readers ignorant of the background.[12]

Twentieth-century writers continued to find something to admire in the Mexican character. Robert Ames Bennet's *A Volunteer with Pike* (1909) is an early example. Dr. John Robinson, young, dashing, and ambitious, meets the beautiful Alisanda Vallois at President Jefferson's dinner table in Washington, falls in love, and crosses the plains and the mountains with Zebulon Pike to find and woo her in her native Chihuahua. The Mexican gentry, yearning for freedom

---

[11] Marah Ellis Ryan, *The Flute of the Gods,* pp. 43, 188.
[12] Franklin Walker, *A Literary History of Southern California*, p. 121–123, 132, 170–171.

from Spanish tyranny, are heroes in the making. The Spanish officials are the villains. Their flag is "a symbol of lust for gold and blood." Alisanda is a descendant of French kings, however, and her pride of race is part of the Black Legend, as is her conviction that American Protestants are not "Christian." And the common people are definitely backward. They live in a "benighted land." They work with "rude ploughs and mattocks." Medicine is "antiquated and barbarous." The love of gambling is "too deeply seated in the natures of these people to be eradicated." They love cockfighting, a passion which causes Dr. Robinson to exclaim condescendingly, "Man has a right to kill for food, but none other than the cruel and brutal enjoys the torment of his fellow creatures."[13] The lovely Spanish heroine is a stereotype, and so is her treacherous lover, who meets Dr. John in a duel and is stabbed by John's second for firing ahead of the count. The Spanish priest, however, is a fine, upstanding fellow who arranges meetings between the lovers and eventually marries them on a British frigate in the Gulf of Mexico.

Two still, small voices were being raised during this period in warmhearted celebration of the virtues of the simple Mexican in California. Mary Austin (*Isidro*, 1905; *The Flock*, 1906; and *Santa Lucia*, 1908) places him in the center of the picture. Kate Douglas Wiggin (*A Summer in the Cañon*, 1889) keeps him on the periphery. Both of these ladies, however, were outside the mainstream, which was carrying forward the image of the noble Californio.

Strangely enough, this appealing if hypothetical personage makes his appearance for some years not in works written for intellectuals, but in popular "westerns" produced for ordinary citizens in search of entertainment. B. M. Bower's *The Gringos: A Story of Old California Days in 1849*, published in 1913, sees the rich Mexican Californios as noble human beings ruling their patrimonies with wisdom and justice: "Till the Gringos came, no watch was put on the cattle. . . . Now they steal the patron's cattle by hundreds, they steal his land" (p. 117). Teresita Picardo—beautiful, willful, and seventeen—is the closest thing to a scheming Spaniard. She causes trouble between Don José Pacheco, her old lover, and Jack Allen,

---

[13] Robert Ames Bennett, *A Volunteer with Pike: The True Narrative of One Dr. John Robinson and of His Love for the Fair Señorita Vallois.* Chicago: A. C. McClurg, 1909, pp. 184, 243, 332, 363.

the handsome young Texan. A duel (with reatas) results. Jack wins and humiliates José, but here the stereotyping stops. Teresita turns against the outsider and goes back to José, while Jack rides off without a backward look.

Obviously B. M. Bower has a high opinion of the California Mexicans and realizes that some of the invaders are scum—a point of view which puts her some fifty years ahead of her time.

William MacLeod Raine, another top writer of westerns, thought up a similar situation for his 1914 novel called *A Daughter of the Dons*. Raine is fascinated by the colonial background of New Mexico, with "its buried yesterdays of history." The Black Legend has left its mark on his basic assumptions, but the bonds of tradition are loosening.

The story concerns Richard Gordon, a figure right out of Timothy Flint. He is a little rough and crude (he says "ain't"), but he can ride and shoot better than anybody in New Mexico, and he "treads the world with the splendor of a young god."[14] His female opposite number is Valencia Valdes, heiress to a huge Spanish grant in the Chama Valley, beautiful as a dream, and a Little Mother to several hundred simple, happy *peones*. Gordon has the papers to prove his ownership of the property and has come to look the place over. He survives repeated assaults and near-fatal accidents and finally succeeds in transferring ownership to the rightful, if not the legal, possessor: Valencia Valdes.

Clichés spring up like mushrooms:

. . . her truant heart was going out to him with the swift, ardent passion of her race. . . .

The young New Mexican was not a savage, though the barbaric strain in his wild, lawless blood was still strong. . . .

It was an indolent, happy life the peons on the estate led, patriarchal in nature, and far removed from the throb of the money-mad world. They had enough to eat and wear. There was a roof over their heads. There were girls to be loved, dances to be danced, and guitars to be strummed. Wherefore, then, should the young men feel the spur of ambition to take this world by the throat and wring success from it? . . .

[14] William MacLeod Raine, *A Daughter of the Dons*, p. 110.

The men of her station that she knew were of one pattern, well-bred aristocrats. . . . But her mother had been an American girl and there was in her blood a strong impulse toward the great nation of which her father's people were not yet in spirit entirely a part. . . .

What this country needs is . . . up-to-date American development . . . the day of the indolent semi-feudal system of occupancy has passed away.[15]

The man who would have been the villain for Timothy Flint—Don Manuel Pesquiera (the proper spelling would have been Pesqueira) seems at first as stereotyped as the hero and heroine. He is a small, intense, proud, resentful man with a sense of personal honor even stronger than his passion for the heroine. For a time it is war to the death between him and Richard Gordon, but the author is not a slave to his assumptions. Instead of dying with bared teeth and a snarl on his lips, Pesquiera proves himself to be a great soul—so much so that at the end the hero shakes his hand and acknowledges that "You're a gamer man than I am, and a better one." The Yankee, however, gets the girl.

Another small step forward was taken with the publication in 1917 of Eugene Manlove Rhodes's *West Is West*. One chapter, called "Peñalosa," tells the tale of the seventeenth-century Spanish governor of that name who ruled New Mexico for a few years, then got into trouble with the Holy Office and was disgraced. Although the historical Don Diego was something less than a sterling character, Rhodes makes him a figure of exalted lineage and tremendous dignity, a man of reason and courage who defies the Church when it demands punishment for a small Indian boy named Popé (later the leader of the Pueblo Revolt of 1680), who is caught worshiping the sun. Poor and in exile, Peñalosa revenges himself by pointing out to La Salle the advantages of claiming Louisiana for France. His defiance of the Dominican friars "changed the tale of history."

"The man I am to speak of now," says Rhodes, "was born to splendor, apprenticed to greatness," and he goes on to roll out the great catalog of Peñalosa's noble forebears:

Peñalosa and Brizeño, Ocampo, Verdugo and Cordova; by the mother's side . . . Davila, Arias de Anaya, Valdivia, Cabrera and

[15] Ibid., pp. 82, 220, 42, 44, 144.

Bobadilla. He was close and doubly kin to the Dukes of Sessa and Escalona, the Counts of Pietro en Rostro and the Marquises of Maya. His wife was granddaughter to Fernan Cortés, "the ever victorious."[16]

Rhodes uses a formal, poetic, mannered style which is impressive, though it may not be as suitable as he meant it to be to the life and personalities of the New Mexican colonists, a turbulent crew who were described by Don Antonio Otermín in 1680 as "a people abandoned by God." The point is that Rhodes was moving counter to the Black Legend in one respect. Some of his Spaniards are black enough, but he refuses to generalize and wants his readers to feel that in 1662 Santa Fe was a more romantic place than Santa Fe in 1917.

A century after the fiction writers began disseminating the Black Legend of Spain, the whole course of writing about the Southwest took a new turn. After World War I the beat quickened; the wheels turned faster. Writing in all departments advanced in both quality and quantity, and new tones began to be heard. Indians and Mexicans were still stereotyped, but they began to be human, more like the people we knew. There was more sympathy and less hostility, more acceptance and less condescension. In 1917 Rhodes tried to set his Spaniards apart from ordinary men. In 1921 Harvey Fergusson made the first attempt to humanize people of Spanish background. His first novel, called *Blood of the Conquerors*, is a story of the changes brought to New Mexico about the turn of the century by the invasion of American businessmen, their wives, and their ways. Ramon Delcasar, scion of an old and influential family, comes home to Albuquerque from St. Louis with a law degree and a firm resolve to defend his people against the gringos who are beginning to take their country away from them. He starts out well, but his fondness for women and his lack of drive and dedication defeat him. Ramon is nothing if not human, as he demonstrates on the first page of his story:

Whenever Ramon Delcasar boarded a train he indulged in a habit, not uncommon among men, of choosing from the women passengers

[16] Eugene Manlove Rhodes, "Peñalosa," in *West Is West*, and reprinted in *Best Novels and Short Stories of Eugene Manlove Rhodes*, ed. Frank V. Dearing, p. 516.

the one whose appearance most pleased him to be the object of his attentions during the journey. If the woman were reserved or well-chaperoned, or if she obviously belonged to another man, this attention might amount to no more than an occasional discreet glance in her direction. He never tried to make her acquaintance unless her eyes and mouth unmistakably invited him to do so.

This conservatism on his part was not due to an innate lack of self confidence.[17]

It might be argued that Ramon is really the lustful Latin of the Black Legend, but Fergusson is not thinking of him as a menace. Rather, he is a victim, and instead of forcing himself on unwilling women, he yields to temptation.

From seeing the Mexican as a human being like everybody else it was a short step to finding something really admirable in him. Robert Herrick took this step in 1924 with the publication of his novel *Waste*, a long and bitter story about "Squalor," by which he means poverty of soul, the worship of things, in the United States. Jarvis Thornton, a lonely architect and engineer, spends his life trying to escape from Squalor and watching "the modern world stumbling blindly down to its fate." The "waste and ugliness of exploitation in America," the "poisonous living" in the big cities, the disregard for the poor and the oppressed, the decadence reflected in "America for Americans," the cult of art "as a substitute for living"—all this oppresses him.[18] As Jarvis see it,

> the American with his Pullmans and bathtubs and sanitary plumbing and concrete sidewalks, prided himself that he had escaped Squalor and looked down upon all "dirty peoples." He had but taken Squalor into his soul and was sick with spiritual corruption.[19]

In the last chapters of the book, Jarvis spends some time in a rural New Mexican village above Santa Fe where Mexicans and Pueblo Indians are at home. His half-Indian, half-Spanish house-keeper, as he describes her to Cynthia (Eastern and rich but close to Squalor herself) "is nearer the mysteries than either you or I." And the little village of Tia is "the most urbane, the most civilized Amer-

---

[17] Harvey Fergusson, *Blood of the Conquerors*, reprinted in *Followers of the Sun*, p. 7.

[18] Robert Herrick, *Waste*, p. 35.

[19] Ibid., p. 151.

ican community in which he had ever lived, poor and primitive as it was by ordinary standards. In sacrificing all the comforts and prestige of life, the Indians had retained their civility, their inner selves."[20] They have no care for material things. The Anglos, on the other hand, seem by comparison spoiled, purse proud, and haughty without cause.

Here is the Black Legend of the United States almost full grown, and as the Americans become blacker, the Latins become whiter.

In the 1930's a good many new trails were broken by American writers who felt a special interest in the Latin population of the Southwest. Frank Applegate (*Native Tales of New Mexico*, 1932) viewed them with kindly humor. Nina Otero Warren (*Old Spain in Our Southwest*, 1936) emphasized their noble ancestry, their traditional courtesy and good manners. Morris Bishop (*The Odyssey of Cabeza de Vaca*, 1933) played up the endurance and piety of three of the earliest Spanish pioneers. The most significant departure from the old stereotypes, however, turned the Mexican-American into a problem—a poor, dispossessed stranger in his native land, subject to disease and discrimination. Haniel Long documented this view in *Piñon Country* (1941), and it became a theme for fiction when Irving Shulman wrote *The Square Trap* (1935), about a Mexican-American boy, Tommy Cantanios, growing up in Los Angeles, trapped in a world he never made and anxious to make something of himself. Boxing seems to offer a way out, but his chances of being beaten into imbecility seem very good at the end of the story. Cantanios shows what was happening to promising young Latins in the United States, and Shulman's book deserves to be called the first Chicano novel, though the Chicanos were twenty-five years in the future.

A year after Shulman opened the door, Paul Horgan examined the problem from another angle in *The Return of the Weed* (1936), a collection of tales about places where people were once at home but which are now deserted and reclaimed by wild nature. "The Hacienda" is such a place. Once a proud New Mexican country mansion, it is now disintegrating while Don Elizario, last of his race, drinks himself to death in the Albuquerque Elks Club.

[20] Ibid., pp. 406, 418.

The aggressive and greedy Anglos are, of course, responsible. They took over the country, and its former possessors are reduced to impotence and despair. The Black Legend of the United States has taken another step forward.

During the thirties political considerations kept Latin America in the public eye. The Good Neighbor Policy, hypocritical and self-seeking as it now seems to many Americans in retrospect, fostered a sense of responsibility toward people of Spanish blood inside the United States as well as outside. In the forties a literature of protest was born, produced almost entirely by Anglos but charged with sympathy for the oppressed and mistreated minority and with resentment against their exploiters. The minority was not yet ready to speak up for itself, but the dominant group was under fire from within, just as the conquering Spaniards had been attacked by Las Casas.

The volume and pitch of these protests were perceptibly higher than the note heard in the thirties. Edwin Corle's *Burro Alley* (1938), for example, was grim enough, portraying the Santa Fe Mexican colony as a sort of decadent subsociety, skirting the brink of degeneracy and preying on the brainless, soulless tourists who frequented the bars and hotels and night clubs of the New Mexican capital city. Nobody got hurt very badly, however, and there were moments of black humor. Seven years later Hart Stilwell's *Border City* got down to serious business. The big man of Border City (which could be Brownsville, Texas, across from Matamoros), is Sheriff Billings. When he rapes his Mexican maid, he seems to be above the law. Stilwell, however, thinks it is just a question of time until the Billingses of the Southwest will have to pay. "The Mestizo," he says, "is a new race, the most interesting since the Anglo-Saxon assimilated the Norman," and new races have new vitality. He feels "the spirit of the Mexican people struggling against its bonds," and wonders what will happen "when the flood is released."[21]

These were urban Mexicans with urban problems. Rural Mexicans and their special difficulties entered the picture with Claude Garner's novel *Wetback* (1947), which tells how Dionisio Molina leaves his home in Guadalajara with one hundred pesos, hoping to

[21] Hart Stilwell, *Border City*, pp. 31, 104.

enter his father's country, the United States. The thirty-five pesos he has left when he gets to Matamoros will not pay his head tax. He crosses the river and enters Texas as a "wetback" looking for work. Repeatedly he is victimized, exploited, and deported. His first boss cheats him out of $1.35 and gets angry when Dionisio objects: "Don't question my settlement. If you don't like my way of doing business, get the hell out of my camp" (p. 39). Others treat the boy worse, but he finds friends, learns English, wins the heart of Rosita, and in spite of everything becomes an American citizen. The Texas Rangers and the American employers are greedy and heartless savages compared with Dionisio—young, intelligent, honest, handsome, and likeable. The gringos go down as the Mexican goes up.

Pauline Kibbee documented the treatment of Dionisio and all the other wetbacks in her important if biased study, *Latin-Americans in Texas* (1947), and Edna Ferber painted the plight of migratory laborers and ranch workers in much more lurid fictional colors in *Giant* (1952). About all either of them could do was stir up a good deal of resentment in Texas. When Estelle Carruth finished *Three Sides to a River* (1963) ten years later—a novel about discrimination in a small Texas town—she had to go to a subsidy press for a publisher.

A different set of writers was organizing, however, and preparing to seize the torch from the Ferbers and the Carruths. In the 1960's the Chicanos and their supporters—many of them academic people—took fire, and an eruption of publication resulted. It was a do-it-yourself kind of writing. Established commercial publishers had little part in it. The Chicanos started their own publishing houses and their own magazines, produced their own poets and short-story writers and essayists and novelists, and proclaimed their dignity and independence and solidarity, mostly for their own consumption, in two languages—sometimes in a mixture of both. At their worst they were wildly fanciful, clamoring for an independent country of Aztlan, supposedly stolen from them by the gringos long before. Beneath all the ranting, however, was a solid basis in fact: the existence of discrimination, injustice, and exploitation perpetrated on some Mexican-Americans by the Anglo majority.

An important segment of the Anglo majority recognized the

truth behind the Chicano accusations—had been recognizing it for forty years—forgave the excesses, and gave the protesters the countenance they needed. The leaders of the movement wished, and still wish, to stand alone against the callous and greedy "whites," making themselves the sons of light and Anglos the agents of darkness, selling the Black Legend of the United States on every page of their propaganda. If they had known more about history, they would have realized that an oppressed minority has its say and mans its barricades only with the consent and encouragement of the dominant group. Las Casas has to accuse his own people. The journalists and lawyers and noblemen have to promote the French Revolution. The "silk-stocking communists," "limousine liberals," *socialistas de Cadillac* have to open the doors to the workers. As Nat Turner said in William Styron's novel about blacks in rebellion: ". . . beat a nigger, starve him . . . and he will be yours for life. Awe him by some unforeseen hint of philanthropy, tickle him with the idea of hope, and he will want to slice your throat."[22]

Even so, the final impetus of Chicano protest has come from the Chicanos themselves. There was something a little unreal about the movement when it was all in the hands of the Anglos, just as there was something that did not ring true about the white people who wanted to join the blacks. But when a true Mexican-American faced the problems of his people, the whole thing came alive. The view was now from the inside out, not from the outside in. The Chicano writers were saying only what the Anglos had been saying since 1924, but they said it louder and better, because they meant it more. It was their ox that had been gored.

José Antonio Villareal started it in fiction with *Pocho* in 1959. He tells the story of Richard Rubio, a California boy caught between two cultures, watching the changes that come with frightening speed to his family, the country, and himself. He becomes involved with the *pachucos*, "truly a lost race" (p. 149), who adopt outlandish clothes and a new polyglot language. From them he learns that the "whites" are the enemy. The police beat him up for no reason. His home falls to pieces, and his father goes away. For a while he ac-

[22] William Styron, *The Confessions of Nat Turner*, pp. 69–70.

cepts his role as the new head of the family and then goes off to war, still unsure of who he is but aware that he will never return to the world he has known.

Pocho was published before the Chicano outburst, and it is by no means a bitter or revolutionary document. It touches the issues but does not grapple with them. It is, however, the first fictional statement by a Mexican-American on the issues and could be called the first Chicano novel, if only because a Mexican-American wrote it.

The pendulum had been set in motion and continued to swing. Ten years later Raymond Barrio's *The Plum Plum Pickers* showed how far it had gone. Barrio gave the Black Legend of the United States the full treatment as he described the "misery, grief and desperation" of the California fruit pickers. The employers were without any trace of soul, and the only human being more despicable than they was the Mexican-American contractor who sold out to them:

> The contratista Roberto Morales stood there.
> His feet straddled. Mexican style. A real robber. A Mexican general. A gentlemanly, friendly, polite, grinning, vicious thieving brute. The worst kind. To his own people. Despite his being a fellow Mexican, despite his torn, old clothing, everyone knew what kind of clever criminal he was. Despite his crude, ignorant manner, showing that he was one of them, that he'd suffered all the sordid deprivations with them, he was actually the shrewdest, smartest, richest cannibal in forty counties around. They sure couldn't blame the gueros for this miscarriage. He was a crew chief. How could anyone know what he did to his own people? And what did the gueros care? . . . It was no concern of theirs. Their religion said it was no concern of theirs. Their wives said it was no concern of theirs. Their aldermen said it was no concern of theirs. Their. . . .[23]

From all this sound and fury one plain fact emerges: a whole set of assumptions cherished by generations of Anglo-Americans has been turned upside down. The Mexican, so long despised, is now a fruit picker in shining armor. The superiority feelings of the white Pharisee, congratulating himself that he is not as other men (particularly Latins), have been replaced by a conviction of sin. Cecil Robinson comments that in the sixties "American writers . . . reflected an increasingly critical attitude toward their own society. In

[23] Barrio, *Plum Plum Pickers*, p. 61.

their growing sense of isolation, their uneasiness at the fragmentation of modern American life, their disgust with materialism and profiteering individualism, their sympathy with the primitive, the passionate and the oppressed, and in their changed attitudes toward sex and death, American writers have tended to find intriguing and salutary the very aspects of Mexican society which had disgusted the early writers."[24]

It is worth noting that while all this action has been taking place in the main tent, a very interesting sideshow has been attracting some of the spectators. As early as 1945 a new note began to be heard in novels about Mexicans. Without the condescension of the Anglo ladies like Dorothy Pillsbury (*No High Adobe*, 1951), who enjoyed the quaint Mexicans and described their delightful eccentricities, a handful of writers managed to keep the enjoyment. Alan Moody's *Sleep in the Sun* is a transitional work, presenting José Mercado and his Mama Chula and "the old one" (grandmother) with humor and tenderness as they go about their business and their pleasures. Frank O'Rourke in *The Springtime Fancy* (1961) shakes off the last traces of traditional sentimentality as he tells the tale of Rosa Sanchez and her red-headed baby. Rosa lives in Rio Arriba, New Mexico, which has become famous for having more illegitimate children born in its confines than any other community in the United States. Reporters descend upon the place to make an investigation. Rosa will not reveal the name of the father of her child. The reporters deduce that she is being coerced and threatened, and they start a crusade for justice.

The book is a good New Mexican farce, and farce can be a healthy thing. If a Jew can laugh at *Fiddler on the Roof*, a New Mexican ought to be able to laugh at Rosa Sanchez. She is worth it. It would be a shame to lose her, just as it was a shame to lose Aunt Jemima and Little Black Sambo, gone for lack of a sense of humor.

The finest and most genial exercise in tolerant laughter came with the publication of *Viva Max* (1966), by James Lehrer. General Maximilian Rodríguez de Santos is ridiculous, heroic, and quite lovable as he leads his hundred soldiers across Texas from Laredo to San Antonio and takes possession of the Alamo for Mexico. The

---

[24] *Mexico and the Hispanic Southwest in American Literature* (originally published as *With the Ears of Strangers*), p. x.

Texan authorities are portrayed with satire a shade less kindly as they vie for the privilege of ousting General Max. The comedy reaches a wonderful climax when "the Chief" comes down from Washington, lands a helicopter in the Alamo courtyard, communes with Max, and reaches a solution. The two appear to the multitude waiting outside the gate of the Alamo. "We," the Chief announces, "have knelt together and sought our God for a solution to this problem" (p. 209), and he goes on from there.

The solution is made manifest when the Chief, his wife, and his daughters appear with much pageantry in Mexico City and unveil a replica of the Alamo to deafening cries of "Viva Max."

A few weeks after the publication of the book, President Lyndon Johnson and his family participated in the unveiling of a statue of Abraham Lincoln in the Mexican capital. Not many people had read the book at that time, however, and the timeliness of the celebration was mostly unappreciated.

We can joke in this fashion only with people whom we love and who know we love them. Another *Viva Max* would be the best sign we could have that both Black Legends are dying, or at least showing signs of debility.

From Hopalong to Hud:
The Unheroic Cowboy in
Western Fiction

"The cowboy," said Owen Wister in his introduction to *The Virginian*, "is the last romantic figure upon our soil." Wister was at least partly right. In American storytelling the cowboy has been a major attraction for almost a century, a focus for public interest on all reading levels. Contrary to the general impression, however, he was never received with unqualified admiration. Writers and readers were ambivalent about him from the start, and a strong undercurrent of disapproval or condescension balanced the fascination felt by the average reader.

In the movies, where leading men demanded and got heroic roles, he did emerge as "the instrument of a just retribution,"[1] a "swaggering, self-confident cowboy standing for law and order,"[2] a "knight-errant of the plains."[3] But even on the screen he was ambivalent. The first cowboy character to emerge on film (*The Bandit Makes Good*, 1908) was a " 'good-bad' man," as Jon Tuska points out, "a Western variation on the Raffles theme."[4] Film historian Jack Nachbar talks about "the rebel-hero's dialectic personality,"[5] and John C. Cawelti (a leading philosopher in the field) notes the "morally ambiguous character" of the horseman-hero.[6] The Western "fable," says James K. Folsom, summing it all up, is "a metaphorical parable of the inconsistencies and contradictions which inhere in the Amer-

[1] Jeni Calder, *There Must Be a Lone Ranger*, p. 110.

[2] Clifford P. Westermeier, *Trailing the Cowboy*, p. 396.

[3] Philip French, *Westerns*, p. 51.

[4] Jon Tuska, *The Filming of the West* (Garden City: Doubleday, 1976), p. 12.

[5] Jack Nachbar, introduction to *Focus on the Western*, p. 5.

[6] John C. Cawelti, "Savagery, Civilization and the Western Hero," in Jack Nachbar, *Focus on the Western*, p. 114.

ican's paradoxical views about himself, his country, and his destiny."[7] In short, the cowboy hero was part angel and part devil.

In discussing movie westerns it is possible to talk about myth and symbolism, the working out of Oedipal complexes, and the six-shooter as a phallic symbol. Since 1960 dozens of articles and twenty-odd books have been written about the movie western, many of them dealing with such abstruse matters. About the cowboy in novels and short stories, however, much less has been said. In this field, which provides a good deal of the raw material for movie and television westerns, the reader finds himself on lower ground. The fictional cowboy hero is not so much a mythical figure as a stereotype. True enough, a solemn Lassiter or a mysterious Shane sometimes springs full grown from the head of a Zane Grey or a Jack Schaefer, but Hopalong Cassidy is closer to the norm.

With Hopalong as a model, the specifications for hero status turn out to be quite simple. It can be demonstrated that the one and only trait which every fictional hero had to have was just plain guts. He did not have to have them at the beginning of the story or all the time or any particular time—just at the right time. He suited us because we don't seem to like perfect heroes. They bore us. We can identify best with someone who has a bad side, or some parts missing, like us. Even so, this flawed human being is still a romantic figure, as Wister said, for romantic heroes are often caught between good and evil, starting low like Lazy Hans and finishing high, changing from frog to prince, achieving wisdom or success only after supreme struggles. The point here, however, is that the negative or unheroic side of the fictional cowboy needs to be examined more closely if the truth about him is to be known.

The negative side is and always has been there. All sorts of surprises may be lurking in the enormous and only partially explored jungle of early Western fiction,[8] but if and when all the cowboy characters of the pretelevision years are counted and classified, there will undoubtedly be more immature, uncurried, drunken, ignorant,

[7] James K. Folsom, *The American Western Novel*, p. 29.

[8] Richard W. Etulain, "Riding Point," in *The Popular Western*, p. 649/7, points out that "many of us are basing generalizations . . . on too little evidence. Few of us have read a hundred popular Westerns when thousands have been published."

timid, ugly, funny, and even repulsive types than true heroes in any reasonable sense of the word.

It can be argued, furthermore, that the misfits and rogues of the sixties and seventies, the focal characters of much of the fiction of recent years, are the direct descendants of these early-day caricatures. The doubts and suspicions which from the first attached themselves to the cowboy hero have not diminished. His course has, indeed, been downward, and now in the third quarter of our century he has found his place among the ineffectual, the defeated, the deluded, and even the debased.

The first question to be answered after this introduction is, "How did this descent begin?" The best explanation seems to be a desire on the part of the authors of the early westerns to tell the truth as they saw it. The nonheroic puncher was indeed the son and heir of the real old-time cowhand, the hired man on horseback who chaperoned his employer's longhorns up the Chisholm Trail and roistered in the saloons and brothels of Abilene. He was not well thought of. Most Easterners and some Westerners assumed that he was like Lord Byron: "mad, bad and dangerous to know," reckless when sober and lethal when drunk. Happy Jack Bates in B. M. Bower's *Chip of the Flying U* (1904) complains:

> I know them Eastern folks down t' the ground. They think cowpunchers wear horns. Yes they do. They think we're holy terrors and eat with our six-guns beside our plates—and the like of that. They make me plum tired.[9]

There was much firsthand testimony to corroborate this view. Joseph G. McCoy, the founder of Abilene, Kansas, tells how these "drovers" habitually imbibed "too much poison whiskey" and indulged in all kinds of "crazy freaks and freaks more villainous than crazy."[10] The real-life cowboy was reputed to be immature, semicivilized, and ignorant of everything but cows, horses, and guns. His fictional counterparts down through the years never managed to free themselves from this stigma of original Western sin. When they began to figure in stories just before the year 1900, they retained some or all of their vices and eccentricities. Andy Adams (*Log of a Cow-*

---

[9] B. M. Bower, *Chip of the Flying U*, p. 38.
[10] Quoted in William W. Savage, *Cowboy Life*, p. 27.

boy, 1903) was about the only one who avoided the wild and woolly aspects of the cowboy's life-style. The urge to pull the puncher off his pedestal was almost as strong as the impulse to put him up there, and this conflict went on until the nonhero, the antihero, and the SOB took over in the 1960's.

It began to happen as early as 1897 with *Wolfville*, Alfred Henry Lewis' fantasy based on life in Tombstone, Arizona. Wolfville is a mining town, but it is set in the middle of a vast expanse of range-land, and the narrator is "the old cattleman." Presumably he speaks the language of the cowboys of his region and embodies their attitudes. Hence, although cowboys are conspicuously absent from the scene, they are just around the corner, and they set the tone for later works of fiction which do feature the life and manners of the cow-puncher.

The first notable peculiarity of the old cattleman is his language. Ever since Henry Nash Smith pointed it out in *Virgin Land* (1950), we have realized that the use of dialect puts a man in an inferior social position. Leatherstocking's speech in Cooper's novels is "a constant reminder of his lowly origin."[11] Even Owen Wister's Virginian, since he is an uneducated man, has to prove to Molly Wood, the schoolteacher, that he is worth her attention and respect. Lewis' old cattleman outdoes both Leatherstocking and the Virginian in his colloquial speech, using a dialect that would have astonished Cooper. It involves the use of rather high-flown language disguised by misspelling, dialect pronunciation, adjectives used in place of adverbs, and far-out metaphors:

> Woman's nacher's that emotional, says Enright to the rest of us, she's oncapable of doin' right. While she's the loveliest of created things, still sech is the infermities of her intellects that gov'ment would bog down in its most important functions if left to women.[12]

At the same time, the old man accepts as normal and natural a standard of behavior which turns civilized notions upside down. "Jack Moore . . . does the rope work for the stranglers,"[13] he says, referring with complete casualness to the activities of the local vigi-

[11] Henry Nash Smith, *Virgin Land*, p. 70.
[12] Alfred Henry Lewis, *Wolfville*, p. 20.
[13] Ibid., p. 19.

lantes. The Code of the West is not mentioned, but one thinks of the Virginian hanging his best friend because the code demands it.

Under these circumstances Lewis is an outsider looking in, and although he enjoys and cultivates the old cattleman, he actually treats him with subtle condescension, listening to him as he would to a friendly Hottentot. The old man knows it, too, and sometimes make slighting remarks about "you-alls back East."

The dialect, the macabre morality, and the quirks of personality exploited in the Wolfville series became part of the equipment of later writers, and some of them equaled Lewis in painting their characters as frontier oddballs. *The Virginian* (1902), for example, is in the tradition, though Wister's book was far more influential than Lewis' work. Jeff, the focal character, is a better man than his fellow cowboys, but he is unlettered and says "haid" for head. When Wister examines Jeff's reactions to the plays of Shakespeare, he is patronizing an inferior, though the point is easy to miss. In *Lin McLean* (1907), the educated Easterner shows his true feelings. Lin, his best friend in Wyoming next to the Virginian, is a young man who never grew up. He has "a boy's soul in a man's body," and Wister remarks, "I looked at him and took an intimate, superior pride in feeling how much more mature I was than he, after all."[14] He probably had a sneaking feeling of superiority to the Virginian, too, but that gentleman, ignorant as he was of Wister's world, did not have a "boy's soul" and demanded courtesy and respect.

The dialect, the eccentric characters, and the image of the cowboy as a perennial adolescent—ignorant but amusing—were standard in the early Western novels. Emerson Hough's Curly in *Heart's Desire* (1905) is Lin's blood brother. Hough, once an extremely popular writer, lived at White Oaks (Heart's Desire), New Mexico, from 1893 to 1898; he knew Pat Garrett well and missed knowing Billy the Kid by just a few years. He loved the newness of the country, enjoyed its good humor in the face of difficulties, and respected its seriousness about serious things (like horse stealing).[15] Curly is his key figure, a delightful, red-headed cowboy who tells Hough about

14 Owen Wister, *Lin McLean*, pp. 44–45.

15 Carol McCool Johnson, "Emerson Hough and the American West: A Biographical and Critical Study," Ph.D. diss., University of Texas at Austin, 1975, pp. 20–45.

his comical experiences just as the old cattleman recounted his to A. H. Lewis, employing a dialect only a little less outrageous than the language of Wolfville and a philosophy only a little less upside-down. He appeared first in a series of stories written for the *Saturday Evening Post* between 1902 and 1905 (put together as a novel in 1905), and Hough loved him so much that he kept him going, transporting him to Wyoming and giving him a place in the "New West," where he encounters businessmen no better than con artists by whom he is continually "suckered again."

Curly is no hero. He is a "character"—a charming and funny character, it is true, but Hough patronizes him and exhibits his peculiarities of speech and attitude with happy condescension:

> "There's a heap of things different already from what they used to be when I first hit the cow range," says Curly. . . . "Look at the lawyers and doctors there is in the Territory now—and this country used to be respectable."[16]

Curly is really a "picaro," says Carol McCool Johnson, Hough's latest biographer, or even "a barbarian and a Yahoo" by the standards of the East,[17] but he had great staying power, and he has lived on down through the years—the engaging adolescent in chaps. As the western grew into its golden age in the teens, twenties and thirties, Zane Grey's unsmiling heroes threatened to submerge that adolescent, but Lin and Curly were always in there defending their claims. They were often drunk and disorderly, but they managed to be amusing, and when a "sagebrush savior" came along and crowded them to the back of the stage, they played Yorick to his Hamlet and sometimes stole the show.

Clarence E. Mulford, in *Bar-20* (1906), was one who opened the doors of the saloons and kept the tradition of the wild cowboy going. When the Bar-20 cowboys (Hopalong Cassidy's outfit) come to town, "nine happy-go-lucky, dare-devil riders" crowd into Cowan's bar. "Laughter issued from the open door and the clink of glasses could be heard. They stood in picturesque groups, strong, self-reliant, humorous, virile." In about five minutes they are involved in a gun battle, but they kill their enemies more in jest than in anger.

[16] Emerson Hough, *Heart's Desire*, p. 203.
[17] Johnson, "Emerson Hough," p. 71.

And when Hopalong does a concealed enemy in, he takes time out to "lower the level of the liquor in his flask."[18]

When the Bar-20 boys are not shooting up the opposition, they find other diversions:

> "From the bottom of my heart I pity you," called the marshal, watching them depart, a broad smile illuminating his face. "I ain't never seen none of that breed what ever left a town without empty pockets an' aching heads. . . . An' I wish I was one of 'em again," he muttered, sauntering on.[19]

Some of Mulford's cowboys are not just wild—they are also ridiculous, and he likes to group them in pairs. Take Skinny and Lanky in *The Coming of Cassidy* (1908): "Both lean as beanpoles, Skinny stood six feet four, while Lanky was fortunate if he topped five feet by many inches."[20] They resemble Wister's Lin and Hough's Curly in their awkwardness and immaturity, though they seem fully grown when the shooting starts.

This "passel of kids" is composed, of course, of run-of-the-mill cowhands—never intended to be heroes. But Mulford does not want even his top men to come out too near the ideal. An example is Nueces (real name Wilcox), the range detective in *On the Trail of the Tumbling T* (1935). He thinks fast and shoots fast, but he is oversized and incredibly homely. With a horse face and "a big ugly mouth,"[21] he is, in fact, so hard to look at that a hotel clerk is "almost fascinated by such an example of human homeliness."[22] Nueces brings the crooks to justice, but his looks would disqualify him in a heroes' sweepstakes.

About the time Mulford was creating Nueces, William Sidney Porter (O. Henry) was writing stories about Texans, including cowboys, which were collected in 1907 under the title *Heart of the West*. His characters are likely to start with two strikes against them. Curly the tramp in "The Higher Abdication" is one of them. He arrives at the Cibolo Ranch fast asleep in the ranch wagon, having chosen it in San Antonio as a good place to sleep off a drunk. Awakened at last,

---

[18] Clarence E. Mulford, *Bar-20*, pp. 16, 25.
[19] Clarence E. Mulford, *Bar-20 Days*, p. 11.
[20] Clarence E. Mulford, *The Coming of Cassidy*, p. 12.
[21] Clarence E. Mulford, *On the Trail of the Tumbling T*, pp. 84–85.
[22] Ibid., p. 29.

"up popped Curly, like some vile worm from its burrow. . . . His face was a bluish red and puffed and seamed as the cheapest round steak of the butcher. His eyes were swollen slits; his nose a pickled beet."[23] Snarling and defiant, this human mistake goes off to sleep in a shed. After three weeks with the cowboys on the roundup, however, a "clear-faced, bronzed, smiling cowpuncher" returns, bearing almost no resemblance to Curly. He turns out to be the long-lost son of the owner.

Curly starts lower than anybody in the field of Western fiction, and at the end he is no hero—just a respectable hired man on horse-back.

An author in the early days of the western who invented a real hero was likely to balance him with a comic or eccentric foil. Ernest Haycox did that in his early novels. W. C. Tuttle did it, especially in the "Henry" series with Sheriff Henry Harrison Conroy at the center (see *Wildhorse Valley*, 1938, in which the comic characters are knee-deep). The amusing sidekick became a fixture in the movies in the era of the singing cowboy. In stories he often had a partner with a different set of peculiarities. For example, look at Slats Kennedy and Rimfire Boggs in *The Bandit of the Paloduro* (1934), by Charles Ballew writing under his pseudonym of Charles H. Snow.

Slats is "six feet four inches tall, and from either front or side he was a trifle thicker than the edge of a soda cracker." His hair is "the color of a jaundiced carrot." Boggs, on the other hand, is "only five feet six, but he had breadth enough to compensate for what he lacked in height. . . . Rimfire's deeply tanned and wrinkled face invariably reflected august dignity, the proportion depending on the amount of whiskey under his belt." Boggs can quote Shakespeare and the English poets, and he makes such illuminating remarks as, "a bar of justice should not be confused with a slab of mahogany across which stimulants are passed."[24] Although they are "the comedians of the outfit," these two do have thoughtful moments. One such instant comes when they call in a bandit named Red O'Malley to deal with the crooked sheriff. O'Malley shows up and takes care of

[23] William Sidney Porter, "The Higher Abdication," in *The Complete Works of O. Henry*, p. 140.

[24] Charles Ballew [Charles H. Snow], *The Bandit of the Paloduro*, pp. 3, 253.

the situation, but he turns out to be Gion Trask, Jr., a city boy with a flair for guns and gallantry. He is a hero but no cowboy. The others are cowboys but not heroes. They play Yorick to his Hamlet.

Looking forward a little, a curious reader will find a similar situation—cowboy hero, comic foil—in W. C. Tuttle's *Tumbling River Range* (1935), in which Tuttle's peripatetic rangeland sleuth Hashknife Hartley comes to the aid of Sheriff Joe Rick, who fails to appear for his own wedding, apparently because of too much whiskey. Actually he has been doped and kidnapped. Hashknife has a comrade nicknamed Sleepy who provides comic relief, but a better one is already on the ground—"Honey" Bee, the sheriff's best friend and confidant. He is a "medium-sized youth of twenty-five, with tow-colored hair, shading to a roan at the ends, blue eyes, tilted nose and a large mouth." Honey is "a top-hand cowboy, even if he was somewhat of a dreamer."[25] Tuttle never does say so, but he might have noted that this puncher was a great big overgrown engaging boy who could just as well have come out of the pages of Wister or Hough.

Sometimes this character is not even engaging. He can be just plain ridiculous (providing he has guts somewhere in reserve). Henry Herbert Knibbs' Sundown Slim from the novel of the same name (1915) is a good sample. Sundown is a six-foot four-inch hobo. He does a little free-lance cooking when he gets the chance (which is not often), and he writes an occasional bit of doggerel verse when he gets a chance (which is too often). Knibbs, his creator, wrote verse himself. This "poor ramblin' lightnin' rod," looking, as one barroom observer puts it, "like crane in a frog-waller," is not just unprepossessing, he is also "childishly egotistical" and a "self-confessed coward."[26] The man who ought to be the hero is John Corliss, who eventually marries the old sheepman's daughter and puts an end to the range war, but Sundown is the viewpoint character and the real "hero" of the novel. He does make a place for himself, earning the respect of the cowboys, learning to be a cowboy himself, and even winning the affections of Anita, a little Mexican girl who notices none of his handicaps and thinks he is wonderful. Sundown, how-

25 W. C. Tuttle, *Tumbling River Range*, p. 16.
26 Henry Herbert Knibbs, *Sundown Slim*, pp. 9, 3, 14, 38.

ever, does not change in any essential way. At the end he is still a ridiculous figure with a heart of gold whose loyalty, sincerity, and honest ignorance make everybody like him—even dogs .

Eugene Manlove Rhodes is another writer of the early period who preferred offbeat types. Known as the most knowledgeable portrayer of the real cowboy of his time, Rhodes saw him as habitually outside the law. Legal matters were in the hands of town dwellers— "God's frozen people," he called them—who didn't understand the conditions of a ranchman's life or the principles by which he lived. So Rhodes's heroes often feel the need to circumvent the law in the interests of justice. Says Pres Lewis in *The Trusty Knaves* (1933):

> Really good men, they never do much of anything—not when it's risky. Always fussing about the rules, stopping for Sunday and advice of counsel. Then, they foster a brutal prejudice against guessing, good men do. Worst of all, they wonder does it pay. That's fatal— that last. What you want is a few trusty knaves.[27]

Rhodes's best-known trusty knave is Ross McEwen of *Pasó por Aqui* (1927), a bank robber who gives up all chance of making a getaway to take care of a Mexican family down with diptheria. His most appealing knave is Aforesaid Andrew Jackson Bates—middle-aged, balding, fiddle-footed, generous, and indomitable, who first appeared in a 1917 short story, "The Bird in the Bush." Bates explains his acquired honorific to J. E. Briscoe, who wants Aforesaid's claim in Bottle Basin.

> I've got a positive genius for bad luck—witness them opprobrious syllables, Aforesaid, wished onto me by acclamation of five States and Territories. . . . I've had all the kinds of trouble a mere single man can have, and most generally got the worst of it; but let me tell you, beloved, none of my victorious and laurel-wreathed antagonists has ever bragged about it any, and that includes the sovereign State of California, the Republic of Mexico, the Espee Railroad, the Diamond-A Cattle Company, Yavapai County, Prescott, Buckey O'Neill and the Arizona House of Reprobates, besides Montana and some few other commonwealths whose memory is now fadin' in the mists that rise down the river of Time.[28]

[27] Eugene Manlove Rhodes, *The Trusty Knaves*, in *Best Novels and Short Stories of Eugene Manlove Rhodes*, p. 253.
[28] W. H. Hutchinson (ed.), *The Rhodes Reader*, p. 180.

Bates is a man much wanted by the authorities, deficient in personal charm, too old to be really interesting to the heroine, and afflicted with a powerful sense of humor which would always keep him from being a really heroic hero. A man who does not take himself with complete seriousness can hardly qualify. All of Rhodes's leading men are something like Bates: nonchalant, wryly funny, fond of misquoting the monuments of English literature, infinitely resourceful, willing to throw life and limb into the balance—"beyond the pale," as W. H. Hutchinson analyzes them, but fulfilling "the frontier's criterion of a man."[29]

The ugly cowboy, the ignorant cowboy, the stupid cowboy, the lawless cowboy—they are familiar figures in Western fiction. Jeni Calder, in her 1974 discussion of Western movies *There Must Be a Lone Ranger*, calls the interest in these shaded characters "a profoundly romantic preoccupation" and quotes actor and director Robbert Redford, who says he wants to make movies about "a guy who is outside society, who is flawed and a loner . . . the kind of guy who appears to be a hero but isn't."[30] Mr. Redford should have a field day looking for plots in these early novels.

Destry of *Destry Rides Again*, perhaps the most famous of all Western heroes, could serve as a model. He is a social liability before he becomes a social asset. "You began as an industrious boy," says the judge who sends him to prison; "you end as a man who scorned any tool other than a Bowie knife or a Colt's six-shooter. You gambled for a living and fought for amusement."

Destry makes no defense: "What you said is plumb true. I been a waster, a lazy loafer, a fighter, a no-good citizen, but what I'm getting the whip for now is a lie! I never robbed the Express!"[31]

Destry does have a useful set of guts, however, and he proves it in a most unusual way: he poses as a spineless weakling, accepting all insults and allowing himself to be branded as a coward, in order to expose the man who framed him, almost losing the girl as well as his character and reputation in bringing the guilty man to justice.

A special kind of negative hero is the rogue—the picaro—a

---

[29] Ibid., p. 38.
[30] Calder, *There Must Be a Lone Ranger*, p. 214.
[31] Max Brand, *Destry Rides Again*, pp. 24, 28.

staple item in the Western bill of fare. He could have come out of the Spanish Renaissance if the writers had ever heard of Gil Blas. Nelson Nye introduced a good example in a 1934 novel called *Wild Horse Shorty*. The scene is just south of Tucson in the Santa Cruz Valley. Shorty, a lover of horses who owns sixteen "bangtails," shows up at a country store, intent on finagling sustenance for himself and his herd on credit. Everybody knows he is a deadbeat, and it looks as if he and his equine relics are at the end of their string. He is not without friends, however. One of them says, "He's a good lad at heart—he don't mean nothin' by it; all this borryin' an' chargin's on account of his horses—he's a natural born horse lover. He jest can't help it." [32]

Besides being a horse lover and a deadbeat, he is a con man whose "line of blarney would move a dead Indian" and something of an actor. Nye mentions "the Bill Hart look which he had taken such pains to cultivate," and he loves to appear in costume:

> He was clean and close shaved, and his five-foot-seven was clothed in rare splendor. . . . His big San Fran hat, white and red-striped shirt and cowhide boots with that dilly of a cactus painted on each were brand new.

And there were "gaudy-gay flowers" on his vest. [33]

Shorty is not easy for his neighbors to love, but he starts a horse ranch by claiming title to land being used by a local horse-and-cattle baron, takes on two eccentric but knowledgeable partners, finds that one of his deceptively ugly horses is a champion racer, and wins all the money, plus the girl, at the end. It is almost as if Mr. Nye had announced at the beginning, "I'll show you that a cowboy doesn't have to be a hero to be interesting and successful."

The con man, of course, cannot exist independently. He has to have somebody to con, and the authors of westerns show considerable ingenuity in digging up victims. Frank X. Tolbert reached a sort of plateau in this respect in 1954 with Bigamy Jones, "tall and red haired and ornery looking" but so irresistible to women that he was married more than thirty times—"He never kept a good tally." In his

---

[32] Nelson Nye, *Wild Horse Shorty*, p. 2.
[33] Ibid., p. 3.

defense it should be said that he never let marrying interfere with his business, "which was making a real hand."[34]

The rangeland Romeo is sometimes a Hero in Spite of Himself. Lee Hoffman conceived such a character in 1966 in *The Legend of Blackjack Sam*. Bo Johnson enters the picture in his underwear, having jumped out of a bedroom window just ahead of a charge of buckshot. He tore the buttons off the rear flap as he departed and is plodding down the road in this unheroic condition when he encounters first a riderless horse and then a man with good clothes, a money belt, and a hole in his head. He puts all the material wealth to good use and is consequently mistaken for Blackjack Sam, a gunman hired by the citizens of the town of Bottleneck to do away with a local menace named Diamond Dick Durston. With good luck and the help of a perceptive and resourceful young woman, Bo carries out the assignment. He is not very bright, and he is anything but brave. He is a hero by accident—a type which reappears again and again in western fiction. Other examples include John Reese's *Sure Shot Shapiro*, about a Jewish drummer who acquires a reputation as a gunman purely by chance, and the same author's *Singalee*, which deals with the adventures of a charming jack-of-all-trades who works magic as an auctioneer in the daytime and performs other miracles at night. A ruthless and determined woman almost gets him shot. He emerges unscathed, however, and about to be married. No hero! Just a lucky man.

It can go the other way. The man can be an anti-Romeo or an un-Romeo, in flight from romance. Take the title character of John and David Shelley's *Hell-for-Leather Jones*, a little fat man who "tops his skinny animal like some bulbous tumor" (p. 5). He has incautiously praised the cooking of the Widow Beeson and is in danger of spending the rest of his life working on her farm. Hence his flight. Booger Jones doesn't look like a hero, and he has shaky knees in ticklish situations, but he doesn't back off from difficulties. He subdues two sets of bad men, brings peace to a feuding village, collects five thousand dollars for finding a missing person, and emerges intact. He is a man with guts, but never—no, never—a hero!

[34] Frank X. Tolbert, *Bigamy Jones*, pp. 2, 4.

Half a dozen more types of unheroic hero could be cut from the herd of early-day novels and stories. One would be the funny cowboy who describes his predicaments and escapades solely for entertainment, as cowboys really did in the bunkhouse and around the campfire. S. Omar Barker sold some thirty stories about a character named Boosty Peckleberry to *All Western* and *Short Story Magazine* back in the thirties, and there were a good many more.[35]

Another category includes the youngsters, all the way from little fellows up to apprentice cowboys, who have filled the role in the years between the publication of Andy Adams' *Wells Brothers* in 1911 and Ben Capps's *True Memoirs of Charley Blankenship* (1972) or Stephen Overholser's *A Hanging at Sweetwater* (1974). Most of them just want to get a job done or be accepted and are not in line for hero status, but they will probably always be with us because readers, remembering their own painful approaches to maturity, identify readily with them. Like their elders, they can even be repulsive, just so they have the requisite quota of guts. Examples are plentiful, but let one suffice: Earl Hardin in Carolyn Lockhart's 1929 story, "No Redeeming Trait." Earl is a chore boy at the Bar B Ranch owned by a female skinflint named Mrs. Rhoda Rice, who is in financial straits. She detests her boy-of-all-work. Earl is "mouthy," a braggart, and a snoop, "lying as easily as he breathes and unabashed when caught." Along with these qualities he has "a rhinoceroslike hide which no amount of sarcasm could penetrate." He steals oats at night for an old cowhorse named Shorty, which he loves, and is suspected of pilfering Bull Durham and socks from the ranch hands. He laughs when accused and replies, "I come by it honestly. . . . Pa done two jolts for rustlin' and I had an uncle made his livin' by selling damp horses till a posse got him."

The showdown comes when Mrs. Rice tries to solve her financial problems by selling her horse herd, including Shorty, to a buyer for a dog-food factory, and Earl lets all the horses out of the corral. When he is caught and brought to trial for horse theft, with the penitentiary just around the corner, he speaks up in his own defense:

> It wasn't right to do Shorty thataway, after all the work he'd done on that ranch. It would 'a' been pure murder and I'd 'a' been yallerer

---

[35] S. Omar Barker, letter to CLS, August 4, 1975.

than she says I am if I hadn't took a chance to save his life. . . . She says I haven't got a redeemin' trait, and maybe I ain't, but . . . I'll set in the Big House till the walls turn green 'fore I'll say I'm sorry fer what I done.[36]

The judge, with an oversize lump in his throat, turns the boy loose. Earl has guts and loyalty, but if he is a hero, the definition will have to be broadened.

Naturally, as the years went by, the world changed, and the western changed with it. The 1950's were pivotal. Television was born, giving the Western myth tremendous acceleration and attempting (unsuccessfully, it turned out) to make epic heroes out of such unlikely specimens as Wyatt Earp. Faith in the American Dream began to fade. The pioneer, once credited with bringing "civilization" to a savage land, was downgraded in the sixties, and his Indian foe was transformed into a noble being outraged by brutal whites. Conventional standards of decency went overboard, and permissiveness about sex and violence neutralized the old taboos. Cowboys talked with less restraint. Finger bones cracked, and eyeballs popped, and Apache tortures were described in great detail. The writing of westerns began to be a new ball game, and the cowboy hero was naturally affected.

The change did not come at once, and it did not go all the way. The continual reprinting of thirty-year-old westerns—for example, the stories about Ranger Jim Hatfield—kept the old traditions alive, and reader interest on the paperback level remained more or less constant. But more and more nonformula, unconventional Western stories were published, and at the same time, academic critics and historians of culture began to take a passionate interest in fictional accounts of the early West. Psychologists, sociologists, and popular culturists followed suit, and for the first time in its history the western was taken seriously. In fact, the shoot-em-up or horse opera was in danger of being analyzed to death. Most of the commentators were talking about movie westerns, but the stories on which the movies were based could not be left out. What was true for the Western moving picture was at least partly true for the Western novel.

[36] Carolyn Lockhart, "Not a Redeeming Trait," in *Western Stories*, ed. William MacLeod Raine, pp. 139, 140, 149.

A good sample of the kind of discussion that has become familiar is found in a well-known essay by the Swedish movie historian Harry Schein. The Western hero, he observes, has become "an omnipotent father symbol," always "alone in the little community" and often "one of those exceptional human beings who seem never to have had a mother."[37] An American political scientist adds, "The Western hero is rarely a Sir Galahad in chaps; he is instead what might be termed a Madisonian hero. . . . reaffirming our deep political skepticism."[38] Today's directors, says another motion picture specialist, are reacting to "a deadening mass society and a dehumanized technology,"[39] pitting their central characters against the establishment.

It would be difficult to think seriously of Hopalong Cassidy or Sundown Slim as "omnipotent father symbols" or "Madisonian heroes." As examples of "the predominant figure in American mythology,"[40] Shane and a few others might qualify, but only a few. These generalizations do show, however, how seriously the cowboy is being taken, especially as he appears in the movies. What they do not show is how low the fictional cowboy has fallen, still paying his debt to his flesh-and-blood cowboy ancestor and still less than a hero in public opinion.

Skeptics there have always been who insisted that he was only a hired man on horseback. Eugene Manlove Rhodes resented these doubters and in a famous poem pictured him at the end of his earthly career riding into heaven with head held high to the welcoming shouts of the "gentlemen adventurers" of all the ages.[41] Today's skeptics will not allow him even this much dignity. William Savage, Jr., their latest spokesman, warns that a distinction must be made between an intelligent, aggressive, and successful cattleman and the cowboy, a rangeland dropout who worked for wages and died poor because he lacked the ability to own and operate a ranch of his own.

[37] Philip Durham and Everett L. Jones, *The Western Story: Fact, Fiction and Myth*, p. 329.

[38] Walter S. Karp, "What Westerns Are All About," *Horizon* 17 (Summer, 1975): 39.

[39] French, *Westerns*, p. 110.

[40] Savage, *Cowboy Life*, p. 3.

[41] Eugene Manlove Rhodes, "The Hired Man on Horseback," in *Best Novels and Short Stories*, p. 551.

His life, says Mr. Savage, was "dull," and he himself was "an individual of little or no significance"—definitely "not the stuff of which legends are made."

How, then, did he become a legend? Easily answered, says Savage. In order to make him interesting, the fiction writers gave him a six-shooter and transformed him "from ranch hand to gun hand." The gun made the difference, and very soon the cowboy became a symbol of "courage, honor, and individualism."[42] So he did, if Lassiter and Shane are the models. But what about Curly and Lin McLean and Sundown Slim and Wild Horse Shorty and the rest who are, at best, hired men on horseback with guts? Mr. Savage is ignoring the unheroic cowboy of the early novels, a man who had courage and sometimes nothing else. His descendants are still here, still not quite making it with other people.

These bedeviled characters are particularly prevalent in the hardback novels with some pretensions to literary merit—books which have only a nodding acquaintance with the Hopalong Cassidy tradition, still represented by soft-cover westerns on the newsstand racks. It is on this upper or hardback level that most of the changes are taking place. In such books the nominal heroes fall into fairly obvious categories. The main ones would be misfits, failures, and SOB's.

It is an ironic coincidence that one of the best of the cowboy-as-misfit novels was published in 1956, the very year in which television began to apply hothouse treatment to the Western myth. This book was Edward Abbey's much-admired *The Brave Cowboy*. Critics hailed it as "highly original," meaning that Mr. Abbey had thrown the cowboy-hero formula, as generally understood, into reverse.

Jack Burns, the cowboy, is an anachronism when he rides his mare Whisky into contemporary Albuquerque. He is still young, crowding thirty, but he belongs back in the eighties. There is no place for his kind of rugged independence anymore.

He has come on an impossible mission. His friend Paul Bondi is in the Albuquerque jail, on his way to prison, for refusing to cooperate with the provisions of the Selective Service Act. Jack gets himself into the jail in order to get Paul out. They are both rebels

---

[42] Savage, *Cowboy Life*, pp. 3, 6.

against the rule of "law," but in different ways. Jack wants to take Paul back to the wilds where civilization has not arrived—the West of frontier times. He knows it can be done, because he has been doing it, though he has had to descend to herding sheep in order to put distance between himself and the things he despises. The proof of his success is the absence among his scanty possessions of a social security number and a draft card. "Come with me," he pleads:

> We'll go high up in the Rockies—maybe the Shoshone forest in Wyoming. I know where there's a cabin, a good tight windproof cabin, at the foot of a glacier. . . . We'll lay in a good supply of venison and elk and pine logs and just sit tight while the snow falls. I'll write songs and you can work on your treatise or whatever you're working on now.[43]

Paul won't go. He wants to make his protest where he is, and Jack has to escape without him. Once outside, Jack heads for the mountains and touches off one of the great pursuits in Western fiction as the forces of the law, reinforced by the United States Army, follow him and Whisky up the cliffs of the Sandia Mountains east of Albuquerque, where only eagles and the cable car should go, all the way to the top and down on the other side with the Manzanos just ahead and Mexico beyond. Whisky hates pavement, however, and the end comes on Highway 66 when the horse and rider go down before a truck loaded with plumbing fixtures intended for the comfort of civilized Americans with draft registrations and social security cards.

Jack is no hero. He overcomes nothing and rights no wrongs. His appearance is enough to keep him outside the boundaries of heroism. He has a "long scrawny neck" and a nose "like the broken beak of a falcon," and his skin, "bristling with a week's growth of black whiskers," has "the texture of a cholla and the hue of an old gunstock."[44] He does have guts and a horse, but they are not enough to save him from futility. It is not fate which opposes him. He has no real tragic flaw. He is just born at the wrong time. In his Quixotism and recklessness he reminds us of something we learned from Sig-

[43] Edward Abbey, *The Brave Cowboy*, pp. 87–88. A good discussion of Abbey's ideas and significance is Tom Pilkington, "Edward Abbey: Western Philosopher," in *Western American Literature* 9 (May, 1974): 17–31.
[44] Abbey, *Brave Cowboy*, pp. 9, 10.

mund Freud: there is no such thing as a hero, anyway. The man who appears to be one is just compensating for something. We can admire Jack Burns. We can pity him. But we can't identify with him. He is not one of us. And we can't let him win, because nobody does.

He does throw some of our assumptions into reverse. We are often told that the quest for law and order is the backbone of the Western story—a "republican law and order" which will not tolerate "usurpation" of the functions of society by the rich rancher or the sheriff or anybody else.[45] In novels like *The Brave Cowboy*, society is the usurper. "The old heroes used to protect society from its enemies," Paul Newman says. "Now it's society that is the enemy."[46]

It is easier to find such crypto-revolutionary commentaries in the movies than in novels, but Abbey is by no means the only one to paint the cowboy hero as a victim. In Jack Schaefer's *Monte Walsh* (1963) the aging punchers are exploited by the faceless money merchants of Wall Street. In J. P. S. Brown's *The Outfit* (1971) the working cowboys are pawns in the plans of a Hollywood character who uses the ranch as a hobby. Most of the time the man in the foreground, as Savage argued, does not have sense enough or luck enough to get ahead. He is ineffectual, frustrated, or unlucky. No matter how hard he climbs, he winds up back in the ditch.

We may miss the point because he is funny, as in Max Evans' *The Rounders* (1960). The book was made into an "engaging" movie in 1965, and readers may miss the underlying pessimism because Dusty Jones and Wrangler Lewis, the men under the gun, are funny in speech and hilarious in action. What we laugh at, however, are broken bones, irrational behavior, and exploitation of the weak by the strong.

The boys work for a predatory cattleman named Jim Ed Love and are breaking wild horses for him when the story opens. It is brutal work, and they show it:

> [Wrangler] looked just like a ground hog coming up for air when he crawled out of his bedroll in the morning, and he didn't look a hell of a lot better now except that I stood so far above him I couldn't see much but the brim of his hat and his potbelly hanging out over his droopy britches. What his britches was hanging on I don't know.

---

[45] Karp, "What Westerns Are All About," p. 38.
[46] Quoted in Calder, *There Must Be a Lone Ranger*, p. 215.

They looked like they would droop right down around his knees any minute, but that was as far as they would have gone. His legs was bowed so bad that if you was to straighten them up, he would have been twice as tall.[47]

Dusty doesn't describe himself, but the pair resemble the funny cowboy combinations of forty years before. The difference is, these two can't win.

Deceived by Jim Ed's persuasive tongue, they settle down for the winter at a camp out in the wilds where they are to gather wild cattle at five dollars per head for themselves. They are accompanied by an equine demon known as Old Fooler because of his deceptively meek demeanor just before he starts bucking. They are about one hundred miles from anywhere, have not been to town for a year, and are in for everything unpleasant, unforeseen, or crippling that could possibly happen. A branding scene is typical:

> Those were big calves—wild and mean. We were shorthanded and had only a bunch of raw broncs and an outlawed roan son of a bitch to rope off of. Wrangler said the irons were ready. He went out and fit a loop on a big white-face calf. Then he fought his bronc around and started dragging him to the fire. I went down that rope and reached over his back with one hand in his flank and the other on the rope. The calf jumped straight up and kicked me in the belly with both feet. While he was up I heaved and down he went.
>
> Wrangler bailed off his horse and came to help. In the meantime the calf had got one foot in my boot top and tore the bark off my shin. Then he kicked me in the mouth with the other foot. I had only one tooth in front that hadn't been broke, and now I didn't have that.[48]

This is one of the milder episodes in the epic of Dusty and Wrangler. In the spring when three of Jim Ed Love's hands ride in to help get the reclaimed livestock out, Dusty says, "It's a good thing you boys showed up when you did because me and old Wrangler had just one catch rope left between us, and we would have had one hell of a fight to see which one got to use it to hang himself with."[49]

Again the cowboy hero has nothing going for him but guts. We know because they are frequently showing. The point of view could

[47] Max Evans, *The Rounders*, pp. 5–6.
[48] Ibid., pp. 44–45.
[49] Ibid., p. 290.

be called realistic if his luck were not so consistently bad. His trail goes back to Andy Adams' *Log of a Cowboy* (1903), Ross Santee's *Cowboy* (1928), and on down to Ben Capp's *The Trail to Ogallala* (1964). It reaches a sort of plateau with William Decker's highly praised *To Be a Man* (1967), the life story of Roscoe Banks, who doesn't lose as much blood as Dusty and Wrangler but has all he can do to survive.

Roscoe is left an orphan when his father is killed by a party of resentful Wyoming ranchers who suspect him of cattle theft. The father's partner gives the boy a good start before sending him off at sixteen to become a wandering puncher and rodeo performer. In his old age he settles down at Coconino, Arizona, and is mourned by the entire population of perhaps four hundred people when he is killed by a young punk who is robbing the post office.

Roscoe learns to be master of his job and master of himself, but his life is commonplace if not, in Mr. Savage's term, "dull." Skeptical as we are about our fellow men, we can admit that something may be said for people in former times, and that fact gives the book a nostalgic appeal. Roscoe makes the point when a dissatisfied puncher is trying to promote a strike:

> We've got a lot of holes in us. Me and the men on that crew, we'll never amount to a damn and likely we'll all die broke. We're easy to fault. But I'll tell you this: there isn't one I can't count on. They may look like dumb dirty hillbillies to the likes of you, but they'll go out alone and get the job done knowing that they won't get thanked or paid extra for it. Maybe nobody would ever know he did the job or if it was tough or if he hurt doing it. We could all soldier on the job. Easy. . . . But we don't and, like I said, if you have to ask why, you'll never know.[50]

When Roscoe is in his coffin, the preacher says, "Here was a man whose like few of us will ever see again." He is a nonhero, an ordinary man whose virtues are "integrity, responsibility, and an abiding code of personal honor"[51]—not enough to make him a hero, but too much to make him anything else.

J. P. S. Brown's *Jim Kane* (1970) is one of the many more which expose the somber side of the cowboy hero's life and portray him as

---

[50] William Decker, *To Be a Man*, p. 152.
[51] Ibid., p. 239.

a man with more guts than luck. Jim is a cattle buyer operating in Sonora, Mexico, who survives incredible difficulties getting his cattle to Chihuahua only to find at the end of the trail that his employer won't give him a square deal. Like the cowboys in *The Rounders*, he heads for the wilds to start over.

Then there is C. W. Smith's prize-winning novel of West Texas called with some preciosity *Thin Men of Haddam* (1973), with a Chicano in the leading role. Rafael Mendez is foreman of a ranch owned by a rich man who is city bred and unmindful of others. Mendez dreams of acquiring the spread and making a cooperative Chicano Utopia out of it where all his stagnating, outraged, hopeless compatriots, personified by his cousin Manuelo, can be useful and happy. The Mexicans can't realize, of course, that he has this vision, and they call him "Tio Taco" because he won't find jobs for them on the ranch. He can't tell them that he is only a "glorified flunkey" (p. 30). The plight of these people who can't get work and must endure the insults of the egregious gringos is harrowing, and the climax, a manhunt, leaves Mendez crucified and defeated.

Perhaps the best of these novels about men who can't make it is Elmer Kelton's Spur Award winner, *The Time It Never Rained* (1973). It tells the story of Charley Flagg of Rio Seco in West Texas —too old to be a cowboy and more sheepman than cattleman anyway—who won't accept government help or subsidies for anything, but manages, with the help of the local banker, to survive a seven-year drouth that sweeps men of less principle away. Ironically, the rain, when it finally comes, brings Charley's ultimate defeat, but he goes down fighting, his head bloody but unbowed. The book is not a western, but it is a fine novel of the West which reveals much about the life and the people of its region.

Among the defeated are a small group who feed on their illusions and refuse to live in the present. Jack Nachbar calls their stories "anti-Westerns" and says that "the central tension is invariably between a cynical contemporary knowledge of the horrors of the westward movement and past idealism about the glories of the great Western migration." The theme is central in Richard Gardner's *Scandalous John* (1963), which is about a demented old ranchman named John McCanless, a sagebrush Don Quixote with a long, skinny body, a leathery face, a scraggly mustache, and a complete set of illusions about who, when, and where he is. With the help of a Mexican Sancho Panza named Francisco Jimenez Xumen, he drives a single cow (his "herd") north to market. After incredible adventures, including some time spent at a Western Days celebration at Warbag, Colorado, he dies in a battle with police on the streets of Chicago.

In the estimation of almost everybody who knows him, he is a "nut," and even his daughter Amanda, who loves him, wails that she is tired of being his "keeper." Only one man sees the truth. Billy, his future son-in-law, says, "He's a hero, and we haven't got many of those left . . . part of the great American myth, an as yet unheroed Nibelung."[52]

Scandalous John is more than a satire on the mythical West. It is a lament for an age which exploits the violence of the frontier without understanding the solid qualities on which the Western myth is built. It raises the question: Does a man in our time have to be crazy to be a hero?

Robert Flynn's *North to Yesterday* (1967) tells a similar tale without the thunder and lightning. Lampassas, "a little man, wrinkled, dried up and soured . . . old and frail" (p. 1), has dreamed all his life of being part of a trail drive, and he finally does gather a herd of wild cattle and harries them all the way to Trail Town. He arrives ten years too late, however. The trail is closed and nobody wants his cows. A number of similar stories have appeared on the screen and in nonfiction.

The disillusion which produced these chronicles of wasted time gathered momentum in the fifties and produced the antihero or SOB. He appeared as an isolated example as early as 1944 in the person of Lewt McCanles in Niven Busch's *Duel in the Sun*. Lewt has no conscience and no scruples about anything, and eventually he has to be shot for his own good by the girl who loves him. He is not a real cowboy since his father is rich and powerful and a U.S. senator, but as an SOB he could not be more authentic.

He reappears in 1960 in Larry McMurtry's *Horseman, Pass By*, which was made into the movie *Hud* (the name of the central character, a complete SOB). The time is the 1930's. Children ride to school in yellow buses, and Grandma has a radio. Granddad, once

---

[52] Richard Gardner, *Scandalous John*, pp. 11, 22, 151.

known as Wild Horse Homer Bannon, is old and out of place. Hud, in his red suede boots, pursues blondes and booze in the nearby town of Thalia and personifies the New Day on the Texas range. He gets anything he wants, and he wants Granddad's ranch. When the hoof-and-mouth disease is detected in the Bannon herd, Hud tells his stepfather, "Some day I'm gonna have your land, Mr. Bannon, and right here may be where I get it. You're an old senile bastard who bought them Mexican cows, and you're the one who better get us out of this jam, if you don't want to end up workin' from the shoulders down yourself."[53]

Just to show his true colors, Hud rapes the negro cook Halmea before the eyes of Lonnie, the fifteen-year-old narrator, and when Granddad, half crazy over his losses, falls off the porch and breaks his hip, Hud puts a bullet in him. "He was just an old worn-out bastard," he explains. "He couldn't a made it no way in the world. He couldn't a made it another hour."[54]

Nobody calls him to account.

There is some question about what Mr. McMurtry means by such a display of heartlessness. Philip French, analyzing the movie version, thinks this "unattractive Texan" represents a "perversion of Western ideals, the decadent fag end of a tradition."[55] The publishers believe that the book "paints a picture of ranching Texas as it exists today." Either way, Hud brings seventy years of doubt about the cowboy hero to final disillusion.

In 1975 the novelists continued to deny that there was anything heroic about the cowboy. George L. Voss did it with a minimum of subtlety in *The Man Who Believed in the Code of the West*, which follows the fortunes of Thaddeus Baldwin of Chicago, educated at Harvard, who establishes a ranch at Flat Butte, Montana, under the illusion that in the West there is honor even among thieves. In the first chapter he encounters Steve Hurd's collection of hard cases on the porch of Hochler's store. "In the course of reading many books on the frontier," he says,

> I have often encountered allusion to the Code of the West, one apparently as rigid in its way as the code of chivalry was in an earlier

[53] Larry McMurtry, *Horseman, Pass By*, p. 79.
[54] Ibid., p. 159.
[55] French, *Westerns*, p. 142.

time. Therefore I was in no real danger from five over-armed men when it could be plainly seen that I carried no weapon of any kind, neither pistol, rifle nor knife. The code would obviously protect me. [P. 7]

His perception of the truth is delayed for a while, but when it comes, he develops into a true Westerner and fights lead with lead. Fortunately, he learned to shoot before he left Chicago. Furthermore, he learns to speak in "the local patois" and wins so much money at blackjack that he comes to be known as "Bet a Bundle Baldwin." And he stops talking about the Code of the West. He is a cowboy only by adoption, but he is useful in making the point that the cattle country was not a haunt of heroes.

A funnier and less labored attempt to downgrade the cowboy hero and put the western in its place is Gary Jennings' *The Terrible Teague Bunch*. The man to watch is L. R. Foyt, a broken-down old cowpuncher who organizes a train robbery in 1905, driving a herd of stolen culls from Shreveport to Teague, Texas, where the holdup is to take place. Trail-driving days were never like what Foyt and his assortment of odd characters (an oil-field rigger, a Cajun lumberjack, and a former soldier with half a mind) encounter on their month-long odyssey. The story is a good takeoff on the epics of the trail, and Foyt adds a finishing touch. He wears bib overalls and implies that all sensible cowboys do so too on account of the extra pockets. He carries his six-shooter in the bib and has surprised more than one opponent who was not expecting a fast draw from such a place of concealment. The tone of events is forecast as the conspirators make their plans and the whiskey begins to take effect:

> It was getting to all of them. Karnes's normally brick-red face was now darkened to puce. Boudreaux was slumped so low in his chair that he seemed to be hanging on the edge of the table by his mustache, and Foyt's ordinarily pale gray eyes now looked like the ends of two severed veins. None of them probably, could have stood up and walked very gracefully, but their thinking and speaking functions seemed relatively unimpaired.[56]

Not a hero among them. And the leading man in bib overalls! That really removes the cowboy from his pedestal.

---

[56] Garry Jennings, *The Terrible Teague Bunch*, p. 65.

This discussion has penetrated only a little way into the mighty forest of Western fiction, but what has been said should discourage easy generalizations about the cowboy hero. He is not always heroic. A sizable number of examples paint him in shades of gray and sometimes black, and as we approach the present, the shades deepen.

The Private World of
Miss Sue Pinckney

Susan Shubrick Pinckney of Hempstead, Texas, is probably the least known of Southwestern novelists. She may have written as many as five or six book-length stories, but only four were published (one in 1892 and the rest in 1906), and the collectors and the literary historians have never heard of her. Yet Miss Sue's romances open the door to an unusual human-interest story and throw light on a number of interesting matters—the effect of the Civil War on sensitive Southern women, for example; the survival of the literature of the sentimental era in the Southwest; and the strange things that can go on in the mind of a repressed and talented girl born into the world half a century too soon.

All four of her tales are wildly romantic narratives of the school of Augusta Evans Wilson, Bertha M. Clay, and similar chroniclers of tears, heartthrobs, and melodrama. Her characters have names like Muriel Dacre, Guy Walsingham, and Lady Maud Villiers, and their adventures and misunderstandings are followed in confusing detail. Miss Sue had no sense of structure and never worried about the probabilities, but she did succeed in creating for herself a private world as a solace for a cramped soul—a world of English lords and Italian countesses, of children exchanged in their cradles, of Southern aristocrats of fine family and great wealth, of love stronger than death and death more beautiful than life. In the flesh Miss Sue lived in a small frame house in a little, unexciting Texas town. In spirit she moved freely in a romantic realm where all the glass was crystal, all the tables had marble tops, and all the clocks were ormolu.

Douglas; Tender and True (1892), her first novel, is a Civil War story involving the crushed hearts of Godfrey Dacre and Cecile Clare. Godfrey is a typical Pinckney hero: 'Tall, well-proportioned, a strongly built, firmly knit frame, a regal head crowned with sunny curls, face fair as a woman's, eyes of the soft pansy hue so lovely in a woman, more lovely in the stronger sex." Cecile is just as luscious. In addition to her "dainty loveliness," she has the appeal of being alone and friendless. She cannot resist Godfrey's "winning tones"—who could?—and they are married.[1]

For a few weeks they live out their dream of love in a vine-covered cottage. Then the blow falls. A lady calls to tell Cecile that her beloved already has a wife and a crippled child. Cecile does not wait to find out that he is divorced from this woman. At once she puts on a "small, close bonnet and thick veil" and goes forth alone into the world.[2] Of course she finds loyal friends, and of course Godfrey searches for her in vain for years. Finally he goes back to the family he left in Mississippi, closes his former wife's dead eyes, and comforts his little crippled Muriel. Then comes the Civil War. He enlists as a private in the army of the South but soon rises to a colonelcy (most of Miss Sue's favorite characters become colonels). When he is wounded, his lost love turns up as a nurse in a Richmond military hospital and tends him devotedly, leaving just before he is well enough to recognize her.

Meanwhile, back in Mississippi the Yankees have camped on Godfrey's plantation, and all the officers have fallen in love with little crippled Muriel, though her favorite is Lieutenant Douglas Grant —Douglas, tender and true. Later, Douglas saves Godfrey's life on the field of battle. After the war he returns and marries Muriel.

By this time Colonel Dacre has finally located his long-lost Cecile, now an heiress. He finds that she has borne him a child who was too delicate to survive in this wicked world. They are reunited, after some debate, at the grave of their dead infant in a scene which Grandmother would have loved but which an irreverent granddaughter would be unable to take seriously.

And now Miss Sue pulls a final surprise out of her small, close bonnet. Douglas takes his Muriel to Paris for her health, and when she is sufficiently improved, he tells her that for years he has been studying surgery in order to help her to walk. He proposes to operate on her; she consents; and with a distinguished surgeon at his elbow

---

[1] Susan Shubrick Pinckney [Miss McPherson], *Douglas; Tender and True,* pp. 5, 6, 9.
    [2] Ibid., p. 29.

to see that all is done properly, he successfully completes the opera-
tion. At last his little wife is able to run to the door to greet him
when he comes home.

In the Southland (1906) is composed of two novelettes: "Disinherited" and "White Violets." Both involve attempts to use native
material, indicating that Miss Sue was aware that there might be
good stories in Texas. The Civil War is again the backdrop for the
action. In the first story Philip Delmont of Kentucky turns his son
out of doors for becoming a Confederate soldier. Vance, the son,
rides across Texas on his way home in the course of the struggle and
rescues beautiful brunette Inez Watson from a herd of buffalo, a
band of Comanches, and a Mexican bandit—all at the same time. He
is much attracted to her, but her lovely blonde sister Ligeia impresses
him almost as much, and he rides away without making a choice.
After the war is over Vance (now a colonel) returns to Inez but has
to get through a jungle of misunderstandings before they can be
married.

One of the most interesting chapters in the book deals with an
old-time Texas ring tournament with all its knightly trappings. Miss
Sue adds a masked rider, a mix-up in the favors worn by the con-
testants, and an attempted stabbing to put spice into the racing and
chasing.

"White Violets" comes closest of all to being a Texas novel. It
deals, in a way remotely suggesting Jane Austen, with three Texas
sisters and their love affairs. Miss Sue ranges far as usual, however,
and scenes are laid in New York, the Latin Quarter in Paris, and
England. The most important relationship is between Hilda Rivers
and Geoffrey Clifford, whom she marries in order to save him from
alcoholism. When he strikes her in a drunken frenzy, she droops and
nearly dies, but he watches by her bedside and "love was the potent
charm that snatched her from the grave."

Darcy Pinckney (1906) is almost impossible to summarize. It is
the longest, least logical, most fantastic of the four stories. As a sample of what happens we may take the case of Eugenia Hartly of New
Orleans, who appears in the opening scene dressed for a ball "with
her usual *recherche* taste as the acknowledged leader of the *ton*
should be" (p. 8). Before many pages she finds that she is not Mr.
Hartly's daughter at all and that there is a terrible secret in her fam-

ily. She flees to France, later becomes a governess in England, and is recognized as she sits in a box at the theatre by her mother, who is (the shame of it!) an actress. In no time at all the actress-mother turns out to be an Italian countess whose husband has been spirited away by the Spanish Inquisition. Mother and daughter live in Italy until the American Civil War breaks out, when Eugenia (call her Nina Mendoza now) becomes a nurse in a Confederate hospital. There she cares for her supposedly faithless lover. Eventually she marries him after she finds that he was estranged from her through the machinations of a female villain. The most sensational scene is the suicide of this abandoned creature before the altar during a marriage ceremony.

What these four tales show about Miss Pinckney and her time is perhaps more interesting than the stories themselves. Given the materials which life placed ready to her hand, it is hard to see how she could have written differently, if she wrote at all, or how she could ever have sought or attained popular success. These materials included first of all her pride of family, then her sentimental reading, and finally her personal frustration as a result of the Civil War.

Family pride came to her through her father, Thomas Shubrick Pinckney of Charleston, South Carolina, who made his first trip to Texas in 1836 to escape the consequences of a once famous duel.[3] Later he went to Texas to live, this time because his family opposed his romantic marriage to a delicate, convent-bred Catholic girl who had been reared in Boston. To his children, growing up in a log cabin in primitive surroundings near Fields's Store in Waller County, the Pinckney traditions seemed like a wonderful dream.

The dream became a brief reality for Sue when in 1848, at the age of five, she went back to the Pinckney mansion in Charleston for her education. She was thirteen when she returned to a family whose faces she did not recognize and whose ways were strange. Having grown up in Texas, her brothers were rough-and-ready country boys who seemed crude and ignorant. Of course she was homesick for what she had left, and her brother Dick hinted broadly that if she liked the Charleston people better than her own family, perhaps she should go back there. Only John, two years her junior, petted

[3] Miss Sue's scrapbooks, left by her to her niece, Mrs. George Scott, contain a full account of this episode, written by Thomas S. Pinckney himself.

her while she was making her readjustment, and she was eternally grateful to him.[4]

She found her refuge in reading and writing. From her girlhood she was a scribbler, writing in old ledgers because of the shortage of paper, lying on her stomach in front of the fire when candles were scarce. Her reading was what an adolescent girl in the 1850's would choose—tales in what Poe called "the Laura-Matilda romantic manner." Her taste and style were formed by such stories, and her favorite reading later on was in the same vein. Ouida was her first choice (she had a complete set of Ouida), but passages in her novels indicate that she was almost as fond of *St. Elmo* and *Beulah* as she was of *Under Two Flags.*[5] Among the poets she read were Campbell, Byron, and her "favorite," Tennyson. She speaks highly of *Adam Bede* and *Romola*, but she obviously preferred August Jane Evans to Mary Ann Evans. A good deal about her tastes may be learned from newspaper stories she pasted in her voluminous scrapbooks. One typical anecdote is about the young Earl of March, who was said to have been betrothed and married to a "dowdy" just out of pigtails. Immediately after the ceremony he left to go on his travels and was away for several years. Returning, he went to the theatre one night and saw a ravishing creature sitting in one of the boxes. "Who is she?" he asked. "The beautiful Lady March," they told him. That was the kind of story Miss Sue preferred in furnishing her private world of illusion.

Stronger even than her books in its influence on Miss Sue's mind was the War Between the States. It caught her in a pitifully vulnerable position. A few years after her return from Charleston she fell seriously in love with a young man named Groce Lawrence. Her father objected to him because he drank too much. Before he marched away to fight for the South, he pleaded with her to marry him, but she would not defy her parents. He was killed in battle, and Miss Sue never mentioned his name to her father and mother again, but neither did she forget him or get over his loss.[6] In three of her four stories she described an episode in the Battle of the Wilderness

---

[4] Mr. and Mrs. George Scott interview with CLS, Houston, Texas, July 2, 1943.

[5] For example, *Douglas; Tender and True*, p. 144; *Darcy Pinckney*, p. 378.

[6] Mr. and Mrs. George Scott interview.

when Lee ordered Hood's Brigade to assault a position. A young Texas soldier, "an eager look in his dark eyes, a flush on his handsome face," took Lee's bridle rein and said: "General, you must not risk your life. We will take the position." The boy was killed in the assault, but *"always* will the name of that young Texas soldier, Groce Lawrence, live with the memories of the Wilderness fight and shine, side by side, with that of Robert E. Lee."[7]

Miss Sue risked more than a lover in those battles. Her brother Robert was fourteen and John sixteen when they entered military service. No wonder Miss Sue pictures the Confederate soldier as a mere boy with an eager face and a manly desire to go home after the war and take care of his widowed mother. She was remembering that Lee himself arranged to have Robert transferred out of Hood's Brigade, remarking, "I did not know that I had babies in this army."

In three stories out of four she relives her memories of the war: the men marching away, the heroism of the Texas regiments, Lee's surrender, Jefferson Davis' imprisonment. The same phrases rise in her mind as she goes over the familiar ground; the same anecdotes reappear. Quite obviously the deepest groove in her brain was worn by the War Between the States.

The war was over in 1865, but poverty and struggle remained, and Miss Sue had her full share. Her father became a hopeless invalid as a result of the wounds received in his youthful duel. Her mother died. Sue had to take over the responsibility for the whole family, and she did it without hesitation or complaint.

She was determined, however, to find some method of breaking the mold—of finding a way out of the dead end in which she and her brothers found themselves. She could not do much herself, not in those days, but she had four brothers to work with. She talked to them about the Pinckney name and the Pinckney blood. They were as good as their relatives in Charleston even if they were poor. Blood would tell. A Pinckney could always be somebody. Why not read law? A lawyer could rise high, make a fortune, enjoy high social

---

[7] *Douglas; Tender and True*, p. 118; *In the Southland*, p. 139; *Darcy Pinckney*, p. 29. There is some question about who turned Lee's horse back. See B. F. Chilton (comp.), *Unveiling and Dedication of Monument to Hood's Texas Brigade on the Capitol Grounds at Austin, Texas, Thursday, October Twenty-seven Nineteen Hundred and Ten.*

position, go to Washington perhaps. To everybody, including themselves, the brothers appeared to be plain, ordinary country boys, but
Sue struck a spark somehow. John was working full time as a cotton
weigher, but he began reading Coke and Blackstone in his off moments, sitting on a cotton bale. When the father died, John succeeded him as justice of the peace, and ambition burned higher. He
moved the family to Hempstead,[8] got himself appointed district attorney, and in 1875 was admitted to the Texas bar.[9]

Still, Sue was not satisfied. She urged John to run for the office
of county judge. He had no political ambitions, he said, and anyway,
he did not know enough civil law. But he ran. And he was elected.

All this meant a larger life for "Sukey," as John called her. She
was no longer a country woman, though her new home was a plain,
small, Texas county-seat town so given to violence that it is still
called Six-Shooter Junction. She and John (who never married) lived
in a modest white "cottage," as Sue liked to call it, two blocks from
the courthouse, and there she began her serious writing. She lived
very much to herself, though she had many devoted friends and was
known to everybody in town. They were all familiar with her slight-
ly stooped figure, her plain black dress, the white sunbonnet she
wore to shade her weak eyes. They all spoke to her with respect and
affection as they saw her among her flowers or walking with a sort
of deliberate daintiness across the street to see her niece, Mrs. George
Scott, but they all recognized that Miss Sue was different.

It was partly that she never went out. Though she was a convinced Episcopalian, she never attended church, and while she loved
to receive her friends at her home, she never returned their visits.[10]
Then there was her rigid reserve and her immense personal dignity
which discouraged all familiarity and, to cap it all, the rumor that
she had written books. Only a few members of her family ever saw
a line of what she wrote, and up to the time she was forty-nine years
old, she had printed nothing but a few stories in Texas newspapers,
mostly in the *Navasota Tablet*. Then John, who was fond of his sis-

[8] "Stories of Pinckney," *Galveston News*, April 26, 1905.

[9] *John McPherson Pinckney Memorial Addresses, Fifty-ninth Congress,
First Session, Houston of Representatives, April 29, 1906*, p. 23.

[10] Mr. and Mrs. George Scott interview; Mrs. R. E. Tompkins, Mrs. M. T.
Crook, Miss Barbara Groce interviews with CLS, Hempstead, Texas, June 29,
30, 1943.

ter and appreciative of her talents, took matters in hand. In 1892 he paid the Nixon-Jones Printing Company of St. Louis three hundred dollars to print one thousand copies of a little book—two hundred pages—bound in Sue's favorite shade of purple and called *Douglas; Tender and True*. Seven hundred copies were sold at a dollar each, and the author used to say, "The book paid for itself." It made her some reputation and probably stimulated her to write more, but she waited fourteen years to publish again, and then with disastrous results.

Today we wonder why she did not try harder for success. Part of the explanation must lie in her time and place. In the 1880's, when she was most active as an author, ladies were expected to shun competition. It might mean appearing before the public, and that was cheapening. Her mother had convinced her long before that any girl who went to more than one dance a month was "common," and perhaps writing for money and fame was common, too. She told herself that authorship was really the only outlet possible for a woman of any breeding, but she had qualms about it. "Not that ladies should compete with gentlemen," she makes one her characters say. "Ah, no, woman must fill a humbler, holier sphere—that of the home. Yet it was her right to embark on the sea of literature."[11]

Some distinctions must be made, of course. "Light literature," she said, "is not injurious in its place," but "history, both modern and ancient . . . will help you much more than novel reading."[12] Since novels were "light literature" and she felt compelled to write them, she was uneasy about what she was doing, concealed the product from everybody (except John), and recoiled at the thought of looking for a publisher.

So the years passed, and Sue lived her placid life among people who thought they knew her. They would have been astonished if they could have looked into her mind and seen what went on there.

She never rebelled outwardly against the conventions which confined her. While her father was alive, she behaved as he wished; after his death she listened to John, who had similar ideas. It must have been hard sometimes. There was the day, for example (it would have been in 1892 after the publication of *Douglas; Tender and*

[11] *Darcy Pinckney*, p. 112.
[12] Ibid., p. 284.

True), when she learned that she had been elected to membership in the Texas Press Club and was invited to come as guest of honor to a convention in Fort Worth. John said, "Oh, Sukey, you don't want to go up there. It isn't right for a woman to appear before the public that way."[13] She didn't go, of course. For sixty years she didn't go anywhere. Hempstead was in some ways a prison. But when she opened the little door in her mind and stepped through it into the world she had made to suit herself, things were very different and quite wonderful. Perhaps Sue asked no more of life than the right to spend part of her time in that special world.

Then in 1903 Tom Ball resigned from the national Congress, thereby creating a vacancy which had to be filled by special election. The last thing in the world that would have occurred to John Pinckney was to run for that office. It occurred to Sister Sue, however, and she went to work on him and on everybody else—urging, persuading, and writing endless streams of letters. John was elected, mostly because of a feud between his opponents, but he gave full credit to his sister.[14]

And so it was that when she was over sixty, Miss Sue had her chance to see a little of the world she knew so well in fantasy. John insisted that she travel to Washington with him. She was nervous about going, but she went, and she saw it all—the Smithsonian and the White House and the Capitol. She attended the inaugural ball. She bought souvenirs for everybody back home. For the first time she could compare her world of dreams with the world of reality. Was she disappointed? It is hard to say. Possibly Washington seemed a bit commonplace in comparison with the European capitals where she was so much at home in reverie.

In one way her mind and heart were enlarged. Some of her friends had been shocked when she allowed a Southern girl to marry a Northern soldier in *Douglas; Tender and True*. They need not have worried about her loyalty to the Lost Cause, for she remained unreconstructed for over forty years. When she went to Washington, she was not pleased to hear John joke and compare notes with Union veterans who had fought on the same battlefields. She changed her mind about Northerners only when her youngest brother, Tucker

[13] Mr. and Mrs. George Scott interview.
[14] *Pinckney Memorial Addresses* (Mr. Beall of Texas), p. 90.

Pinckney, was killed by a gang of Negroes in 1904 and she was called home to his funeral.[15] The people in her Washington hotel were so kind to her that she could not hate the Yankees any more.

On her return to the East after Tucker's death, she found that her star as an author was rising again. In 1905 John Pinckney, who was now serving his second term in Congress, made contact in Washington with a publisher named Neale. This man offered great inducements for permission to publish Sue's books, though John neglected to have the proposals reduced to writing.[16] Sue was happy about the renewal of her prospects, but her joy was brief. On April 24, 1905, her world came to an end in a brief blaze of gunfire back in Texas.

The campaign that year had been a bitter one in Waller County over the prohibition issue. The drys, with John as a leader, had gone all out to purify their town and county. The WCTU had buttonholed and admonished every voter. Hysterical audiences had cheered the dry speakers imported to whip up prohibition sentiment.[17] John Pinckney had been returned to Congress on an anti-rum ticket, and although the wets were white-hot about their defeat, the election had gone off quietly and nobody expected further trouble—the Pinckneys least of all. John and Sue stayed home that spring without an inkling of what was ahead. But Hempstead had some very rough citizens along with the good ones and was famous as a six-shooter town. There were men with guns at the final meeting of the Prohibition League in the courthouse, and when the smoke cleared away, four men lay dead on the courtroom floor, including John and Tom Pinckney.[18] Sue was left alone except for one brother and a devoted niece in Houston, with whom she spent the brief remainder of her life.

And now, of all times, Fame came knocking. While she was in Austin attending the trial of the young man accused of killing her

[15] Mrs. R. E. Tompkins interviews. Mr. Tompkins was Congressman Pinckney's secretary, and Mrs. Tompkins went along on this trip.

[16] *Galveston News*, April 12, 13, 15, 1904.

[17] For the Prohibition movement in Texas, see Glynn Austin Brooks, "A Political Survey of the Prohibition Movement in Texas," M.A. thesis, University of Texas at Austin, 1920; *Galveston News*, April 25, 1905; *Hempstead News*, April 21, 1905.

[18] *Houston Post*, April 25, 26, 1905. The "courthouse tragedy," as it is locally known, is discussed in some detail in C. L. Sonnichsen, *Ten Texas Feuds*, pp. 167–184.

brothers, who should appear but Mr. Neale, the publisher. He wore a frock coat and a top hat, and he had a bundle of contracts under his arm. He seemed the soul of integrity, and in her distress Miss Sue was an easy mark. Without consulting anybody, she signed the papers, hoping to make thousands of dollars and take her shattered heart abroad, as a character in one of her novels would have done. She paid Neale two thousand dollars to publish *In the Southland* and *Darcy Pinckney*. Neale himself chose the title for the latter in order to capitalize on the publicity attending the congressman's death. All Sue ever gained from the bargain was fifty copies of each book. Two thousand were contracted for, but what happened to the other thirty-nine hundred (if they were printed at all) has never been revealed.[19] They are almost impossible to find now, and only a few had been sold in 1909 when Miss Sue died.

That was Miss Sue Pinckney's life, and her literary career was determined by it. She was poor, so she dreamed of wealth and luxury. She was deprived of her lover, so she dreamed of immortal love. The Civil War dominated her early years, and naturally she came back to it again and again. She inhabited a microcosm of scrubbing, baking, mending, and mothering in which a woman was expected to stay behind the scenes, so she imagined ladies who left home, went abroad, nursed in military hospitals, and met English aristocrats as a matter of course. In her private world she had things her own way.

It was a world of beauty, for Miss Sue loved beautiful things. The ladies had small, sweet faces with soft eyes and delicate complexions. The men had manly forms, loving hearts, and large landed interests. Love was the central consideration in everybody's life, causing rapture when returned and decline when unrequited. Miss Sue understood perfectly how an ideal love operated. One always knew, for example, whom one loved, but one had to be careful about revealing the secret. The worst fate that could happen was to "give one's love unsought,"[20] in which case the only course of conduct possible was to go to bed and become desperately ill. There were rules that had to be followed, too. Suppose a lady had lost her lover, only

[19] Mr. and Mrs. George Scott interview.
[20] *In the Southland*, p. 156.

to find him lying wounded in an army hospital. Should she wait for his recovery and discuss the situation with him when he showed signs of becoming rational? Good heavens, no! Miss Sue comments on one such case: "Delicacy forbade. He who had ignored her existence must be forever dead to her."[21]

Widows had a code of their own. If your husband had been a soldier, as of course he had, your heart was buried in "a soldier's grave." You might form a friendship with an English lord, but you must be shocked if he should offer marriage—at least the first time he did it. Of course if your little boy sickened and the lord nursed him devotedly, you might weaken, particularly if the little boy pleaded for him.

The worst danger to the human heart in Miss Sue's special world was the jilt, male or female. A rejected lover was a public menace, for he unavoidably became "a true nobleman or a very demon," with odds in favor of the latter.[22] When the demon in him appeared, he would tempt young men to the gaming tables, fight duels, kidnap innocent ladies, and mutter to himself: "Ah, Inez, Inez! If you had been true to me, sin would never have stained my soul; but I, stern Phil Walker, must not grow weak and womanish now."[23]

These ladies and gentlemen, good and bad, sometimes appeared at home in modest cottages with "white straw matting on the floor, chairs of willow . . . curtains of white muslin to the low French windows,"[24] but they usually inhabited more sumptuous quarters. Miss Sue knew exactly how their mansions looked, inside and out, and she loved to describe in detail the "vases of Persian glass," mirrors with "festoons of thread lace about the massive gilt frames," "curtains of rose-colored silk," "tables, chairs, lounges and settees of rosewood," and other artistic objects to match.[25]

When her characters came to the table, they enjoyed a "light repast" of wafers and tea cakes, orange marmalade and strawberries and cream; or "a tray of dainties"; or a "sumptuous collation" of fruit, cake, wine, sherbet, lemonade, tea, coffee, fish, pheasant and

[21] *Darcy Pinckney*, p. 300.
[22] Ibid., p. 227.
[23] Ibid.
[24] *In the Southland*, p. 91.
[25] Ibid., pp. 26, 92; *Darcy Pinckney*, pp. 159, 352, 374; *Douglas; Tender and True*, p. 203.

"light and spongy bread."[26] People in the Pinckney world were never allowed to eat heavy food.

Usually they spoke a special language. A man did not just put an engagement ring on his beloved's hand. He slipped a "broad band of gold" on one of her "slender fingers."[27] He did not take her for a walk at dusk. They went for "an evening ramble."[28] And a group of ladies was "a bright parterre of breathing flowers."[29] Naturally in such a world a person would not remark, "How odd!" He would exclaim in well-bred accents, "Strange, passing strange!"[30]

Even the children that Miss Sue imagined were not in the least like her very masculine little brothers. They had "fairylike forms," "angelic expressions," and "birdlike laughs," and they were usually very delicate. Often such a child was "too precious a bud long to adorn her earthly home,"[31] and in such cases Miss Sue would say farewell in a touching deathbed scene. The precarious health of these infants, together with the tendency of her young men to succumb to tuberculosis or die on the field of battle, give a romantically tearful atmosphere to much of Miss Pinckney's work.

The most interesting feature of it all, however, is the delightful uncertainty which hovers over every character. Picture yourself as a young husband, rapturously married and apparently settled for life. You can never be sure that your bride will be there to greet you when you come home from work. Quite probably someone has called during your absence and betrayed your secret (of course you have one), and the poor, delicate little creature has fled. If you have really lost her, you may be sure that years of search will not run her to earth, even though she may be living only a few miles away with dear friends of yours. But suppose you should give up and go to England to forget—you will undoubtedly encounter her on a runaway horse about to plunge over a cliff unless you save her (as you naturally do).

Furthermore, you can never be sure who anyone really is, even yourself. Your father is probably keeping from you the fact that you

[26] *Darcy Pinckney*, pp. 146, 246.
[27] Ibid., p. 149.
[28] *Douglas; Tender and True*, p. 203.
[29] *In the Southland*, p. 54.
[30] *Darcy Pinckney*, pp. 10, 133.
[31] Ibid., pp. 100, 149, 156, 395.

were left on his doorstep many years ago with a locket, a jeweled dagger, and a book of photographs. To relieve your mind, in case this sort of thing depresses you, there is always the chance that you are a nobleman's lost child, that you will unexpectedly come into vast estates, or that you may marry a member of the aristocracy of England or Italy (not France—Miss Sue was suspicious of France).

It is really a quaint and charming world which Miss Sue created, and it is our loss that we have become too sophisticated to enjoy it. It is probably our loss also that she had to make her world out of second-hand materials. If she could have lived in a place more like her imaginings; if her lover had lived; if she had found a niche in a freer society; if she had had more education; if anybody had been interested in her work; if she had had better luck with her publishers—there are any number of "ifs"! But if some of the ifs had been removed, Texas might have had another Ouida—if not a Jane Austen or a Fanny Burney—instead of a forgotten little Southern lady asleep in the Hempstead cemetery.

The Sharecropper in
Western Fiction

IN 1940 a Texan named Edward Everett Davis published a novel, called *The White Scourge*, about sharecroppers and tenant farmers. In his preface Mr. Davis expressed himself as follows:

> Before us lies a cotton field, the great open air slum of the South, a perennial Hades of poverty, ignorance, and social depravity. Between the long rows, crawling on their knees in the terrible Southern sun, are men, women, and children gathering the staple. For each hardwon pound a heavy toll of pride, intelligence, and hope is exacted. This is the toll of the white scourge.
>
> Poverty and ignorance have always clung to the cotton stalk like iron filings to a magnet. Too much of America's worthless human silt has filtered into the cotton belt. Cotton culture is simple, an elemental means of subsistence for that portion of the South's rural proletariat composed of lowly blacks, peonized Mexicans, and moronic whites numbering into several millions.
>
> The southern cotton fields have a greater affinity for illiteracy and thriftlessness than the corn fields and wheat fields of the great Middle West. It doesn't require as much intelligence to raise cotton in Texas as it does to raise corn and feed livestock in Iowa. The most serious rural problem in the South is not that of soil conservation, crop production, co-operative marketing, or race relationships, but that of the biologically impoverished tribes of marginal humanity—black, white, and Mexican—subsisting on cotton. . . . The human creature of weak body and moronic mentality who would perish without reproducing his hideous kind amid the blizzards and wheat fields of the Dakotas can survive successfully and populate half a schoolroom in the mild cotton regions of Texas.

The author of this extraordinary utterance was none other than the dean of the North Texas Agricultural and Mechanical College, now the University of Texas at Arlington. He says he is stating only what he has seen with his own eyes during the preceding half century.

Actually, he is saying only what everybody, including the novelists who are the subject of this essay, took for granted: that cotton does terrible things to the land and to the people on it. The difference between Dean Davis and other writers, both fictional and documentary, is that he views the situation with pity but with very little hope. The sharecropper novels of the twenties and thirties, on the other hand, look for the exceptions—the men and women who are able to defeat the White Scourge.

Every single one of these writers has an axe to grind and intends to inform or to persuade. Unlike authors of our time, who know that nonfiction far outsells fiction, they believe that they can best attract an audience by telling a story. What we have in these novels, then, is a partial record of what was being said and believed during the time of the Great Depression and the New Deal about the most depressed segment of American society. Such a record must be of interest to students of the period. In fact, historians of this era can hardly afford not to know something about its propaganda novels.

The sharecropper had his day in fiction in the years between 1920 and 1940. He had been with us since the slaves were freed— suffering, scrambling, always in debt, always at the mercy of the owner and the storekeeper[1]—but the novelists did not notice his plight and demand justice for him until after the agricultural depression of 1921–1922. When the men at the bottom of the pile became aware of "the awesome gap between the prices for which they sold their crops and the prices they paid for the products of industry,"[2] everybody began to take notice.

At this moment a new school of writers, capable of understanding and presenting rural problems, was about to go into action. Caroline B. Sherman of the United States Department of Agriculture noted in 1938 that beginning in the 1920's, "not only were farm novels published in rapidly increasing numbers but the stories began to show individual worth."[3]

[1] Problems of the sharecropper in Texas before World War I are discussed by Raymond Elliott White in "The History of the Texas Cotton Ginning Industry, 1822–1957," M.A. thesis, University of Texas, Austin, 1957.

[2] James H. Shideler, "The Development of the Parity Price Formula for Agriculture, 1919–1923," *Agricultural History* 27 (July, 1953): 78.

[3] Caroline B. Sherman, "The Development of American Rural Fiction," *Agricultural History* 12 (January, 1938): 67.

Two East Texas women who dominated the field of sharecropper fiction during the 1920's were Dorothy Scarborough and Ruth Cross. Miss Scarborough, a Texas University Ph.D. who taught writing at Columbia University until her death in 1935, led off in 1923 with *In the Land of Cotton*. Reprinted in 1925 and reissued in 1936, the book had many readers and must have had considerable influence. Two later novels—*Can't Get A Redbird* (1929) and *The Stretch-Berry Smile* (1932)—dealt with the same material.

In the Land of Cotton is the story of Ben Wilson, son of a struggling tenant farmer. The landlord is Mr. Jerry Llewellyn, one of the few owners in sharecropper fiction with a heart and a conscience. He helps Ben to take a degree at Baylor University. Even with an education, however, life is never easy for Ben. His greatest frustration is his inability to get ahead far enough to propose to Serena Llewellyn, the owner's daughter. His final defeat occurs when cotton prices slump and night riders take to the roads, scaring the hands out of the fields and forcing the gin owners to shut down. Ben takes charge of the Llewellyn gin and is killed by the masked terrorists. His life is not completely wasted, however. He has convinced others who will carry on his ideas about farmers' unions and cooperative enterprises.

A good many stereotypes emerge in this novel: the father who can't get ahead, the mother who was meant for better things and passes her ideals on to her children, the boy who has the intelligence to profit by an education if he can only get one, the little children out in the fields, the poor boy in love with the rich girl. The scene is the rural slum depicted by Dean Davis, but emphasis is on the exception, not on the rule. Jerry Llewellyn says of Ben Wilson, "He's poor and he's white, but he's not trash."[4]

Some of Miss Scarborough's material is indeed conventional, but she does her best to go beyond the ordinary. She wants, in fact, to make her book a prose *Epic of Cotton* in which all aspects of the business and all the people connected with it will have a place. "There's a lot of poetry about cotton," Llewellyn says, "so much drama there, pathos and comedy and tragedy . . . somebody ought to put them in a book." The cotton boll itself seems to Miss Scarborough a thing of beauty, "a five-pointed star that has ensnared a snowy

[4] Dorothy Scarborough, *In the Land of Cotton*, p. 17.

cloud . . . with human hopes and dreams interwoven with it." At the same time, it is a cruel and merciless thing—a White Scourge, in fact. Ben himself, aware of the beauty in the long files of cotton plants, "thought with bitterness of a crop that was raised largely by the toil of women and children."[5]

The black people get special attention from Miss Scarborough. "Cotton-picking time is the negroes' carnival." They are "children of the sun, lovers of light and heat," who enter the cotton fields "with shout and song and wild, barbaric mirth."[6] She did not, of course, realize her confident condescension as she wrote those lines.

Miss Scarborough was looking for a way out in 1923, and in 1929 she thought she had found it. *Can't Get a Redbird* is about the cooperative movement. Johnny Carr, the viewpoint character, has to give up school at the age of eleven and take charge of the farm when his father's health fails. He seems condemned to a life of ignorance and hopeless toil with all the other slaves of cotton, but again we have the exception which Dean Davis did not allow for. Johnny diversifies his crops, plans shrewdly, marries a girl who encourages him to make progress, and moves into a new house with Delco lights and a bathroom.

On a cattle-buying trip to Michigan, Johnny hears of the Farm Bureau and helps to establish a state unit called the Texas Council of Agriculture and Home Economics. Under the management of a fine organizer named Adam Aronson, this organization becomes the American Cotton Planters' Exchange, with ramifications throughout the South. Then comes the bumper crop of 1926 and the ruinous break in cotton prices. Johnny and his co-leaders meet President Coolidge and Secretaries Jardine and Mellon in Washington and try to persuade them to take four million bales off the market. Their cooperative, they say, can take care of the storage. Their offer is refused as the novel ends.

Much of what happens seems to be a transcript of history, and some, at least, of the characters are real people. Adam Aronson, for example, can be no one but Aaron Sapiro, whom Professor Theodore Saloutos vividly portrays in *Farmer Movements in the South*. Johnny's interview in Washington may be the very one which Mr. Salou-

---

[5] Ibid., pp. 315, 316.
[6] Ibid., p. ix.

tos describes as taking place in October, 1926, when "a committee consisting of Andrew Mellon, Secretary of the Treasury, Herbert Hoover, Secretary of Commerce, William M. Jardine, Secretary of Agriculture, and Eugene Meyer, the chairman of the War Finance Corporation, met and discussed means of financing the storage of four million bales of cotton. . . ."[7] Earl Williams, spokesman for the co-op, could be Johnny Carr.

Last and weakest of Miss Scarborough's novels about the cotton country is *The Stretch-Berry Smile*. Perla Flippen, a girl with "asking eyes and stretch-berry smile," at the age of six is already a slave of cotton. "She puts her feet under the table to eat three times a day, don't she?" her father remarks. "Well, then, she's got to do her share of the work. Hit the grit, Perly."[8]

Perla's difficulties mount as she grows older. She is a bright and sensitive child—another exception—but her chances of getting an education are remote. Besides, she is devoted to Britt Hefferline, a neighbor boy who has eyes only for Carita Fairfield, daughter of the plantation owner. Britt actually marries Perla when Carita throws him over. Immediately thereafter Perla throws Britt over when he proves to be less than a husband. After a number of incredible adventures, Perla finds her place in New York as a writer and publisher's reader. In the final chapter she learns that she can have Britt on her own terms, but she gives him to Carita, whose need is greater than her own.

Quite obviously the first part of the book is standard-model sharecropper fiction. The last part sounds like Ouida or Mrs. E. D. E. N. Southworth or Augusta Jane Evans. Perla is a sympathetic character, but the story is not really worthy of her.

A less impressive writer than Miss Scarborough, but as deeply serious about the plight of the sharecropper, is Ruth Cross, who lived and wrote at Palestine, Texas, but had a national audience. She is at home in a village which she calls Laws Chapel, the locus of action in *The Golden Cocoon* (1924) and *The Big Road* (1931). The heroine of the first is Molly Shannon, poor but precocious, who gets a scholarship to the university and goes to live in Austin. There she falls in love with the wrong man, and when he leaves her to marry a

[7] Theodore Saloutos, *Farmer Movements in the South, 1865–1933*, p. 269.
[8] Dorothy Scarborough, *The Stretch-Berry Smile*, p. 9.

rich girl, she attempts suicide. Judge Stephen Renfro, a noble character, rescues her and befriends her. Eventually Stephen becomes
governor of Texas and makes Molly his lady.

We recognize the real Ruth Cross when she says of Molly,
"Sometimes in the midst of a merry group she would catch sight of
her finger tips, browned and roughened by cotton-picking, or there
would come a searing vision of the wretched, tumble-down shack
that was her home, and she knew herself hopelessly alien."[9] Unfortunately, Miss Cross does not spend much time with the sharecroppers, where her touch is sure. When she ventures out among the
governors and millionaires, she is obviously out of her depth. The
only nonrural group which she seems able to evaluate convincingly
is the faculty of the University of Texas. She calls them "a backwash
of incompetents whom life had rejected."[10]

David Strawn, the hero of Miss Cross's second sharecropper
novel, *The Big Road* (1931), is the son of a man who owns his own
cotton fields, but his problem is the standard one in sharecropper
fiction. He has a great musical talent, but his brutal father will not
listen to any talk of a musical education. The old man is about to
take him out of school at cotton-picking time, but David's gentle
mother pulls a pistol and David goes back to the classroom. At the
end of the story he is about to leave for Europe and a musical career,
thanks to a legacy from the man his mother should have married.

Although most of the story is the wildest kind of romantic non-
sense, Miss Cross does bring some new touches into her picture of
life in the cotton country. She introduces a family of German immi-
grants whose thrift and kindliness and flair for living are in pleasant
contrast to the barrenness and bitterness of life in the Strawn home.
She likes to think also that in the sixteen years since the opening of
her story in 1895, life has become much better at Laws Chapel. The
Big Road reaching westward to the Panhandle and the Rio Grande
is paved now. The little towns have become "shining clean cities."
And no child now can "be kept out of school to hoe or chop cotton."[11]
On this note Miss Cross leaves the sharecropper and turns her attention elsewhere.

[9] Ruth Cross, *The Golden Cocoon*, p. 25.
[10] Ibid., p. 71.
[11] Ruth Cross, *The Big Road*, p. 313.

Miss Cross abandoned the White Scourge theme in this final utterance, but other writers of the thirties reached new heights of indignation in depicting the backwardness of the sharecropper and the hopelessness of his struggle to find a way out.[12] By then, of course, the exploitation of voiceless and defenseless farm workers had become a matter of national concern. Norman Thomas and his socialists, the Civil Liberties Union, and Senators Bankhead and Jones, among other influentials, were reacting vigorously against the failure of the Agricultural Adjustment Administration to help the people at the bottom of the agricultural pile. The novelists dramatized the situation and used their own tools to build public indignation and demand reform. Cotton was still the White Scourge, but the novelists were not looking for bright boys who could break the pattern by working their way through Baylor University. They were hunting for a hero who could structure a sharecroppers' union and make a real weapon of it.

The search took them first to eastern Arkansas, where desperate tenant farmers and socialist organizers in the mid-thirties put together an organization which got national headlines and spread to other states. Close to this situation was Charlie May Simon, a sincere and successful Arkansas writer whose indignant novel *The Sharecropper* appeared in 1937.

Bill Bradley, Simon's main character, is young and anxious to become independent, but he can never get ahead though he works like a demon and tries every means he can think of to beat the system. "Ain't you never heard of relief?" his neighbor Newt Goins asks him (Newt is one of Dean Davis' "moronic whites"). "I'm on relief, killin' time on the road, and bein' paid twelve dollars a week for it."[13] Bill's family is hungry, and he tries to qualify for relief, but his landlord won't recommend him. He is not in debt to the commissary, and the landlord won't get a cut of the relief money, so he is not interested.

Desperate to find some means of bettering his situation, Bill

---

[12] Backwardness is the theme of "A Saturday in Town" from Roxylea Melas' collection *Revival and Other Stories*. Elvira's father is an illiterate preacher-farmer whose antics make her "bite her lips to keep from crying in shame" (p. 212).

[13] Charlie May Simon, *The Sharecropper*, p. 176.

joins a young lawyer named Abner Young in organizing the first unit of the Sharecroppers' Union. The results are frightening. The big owners fight back with violence and boycott. Their hired bullies try to "run these reds and anarchists out."[14] When the tenant farmers strike and refuse to chop cotton, they are arrested for vagrancy and forced to work out their fines in the fields. These things actually happened.

We leave Bill and his family squatting in a flimsy, homemade shack in the river bottom, still poor, but still not crushed and hopeless. He looks forward to a better day for his children—a time when they will live in good houses, have schools for everybody, and not have to pay 10 percent interest at the commissary.[15]

There is a strong feeling of authenticity about Mrs. Simon's rambling chronicle. The material, she says, was gathered by her father, Charles Wayman Hogue, who may well have been a participant in the events of that crucial summer of 1936. She certainly throws light on what happened. As an example we may take an act of violence mentioned by M. S. Venkataramani in his excellent study of Norman Thomas's involvement in the Arkansas troubles: "On March 25 a band of about forty masked 'night riders' fired upon the house of C. T. Carpenter, a respected citizen who had incurred the wrath of the extremists by serving as attorney for the union."[16] C. T. Carpenter has to be the young lawyer Abner Young in Mrs. Simon's novel, and her account of Young's heroic stand against the lynch mob is probably authentic history.

The Sharecropper's Union spread to other states, including Oklahoma, where Edwin Lanham picks it up in his novel *The Stricklands* (1939). He follows the misfortunes of two brothers, Jay and Pat Strickland, natives of the hill country where the hard life can produce conscientious moonshiners like their father and popular desperadoes like Pretty Boy Floyd. On the flatlands below them the farmers raise spinach, lettuce, and cotton and wring the last drop of

[14] Ibid., p. 203.

[15] Ibid., pp. 246–247.

[16] M. S. Venkataramani, "Norman Thomas, Arkansas Sharecropper, and the Roosevelt Agricultural Policies, 1933–1937," *Agricultural History* 34 (September, 1960): 234.

blood out of their tenants. Hillbillies or flatlanders, "poor people ain't got no chance" in Oklahoma.

Each brother in his own way tries to break the grip of his environment. Pat tries to do it with a pistol, staging a holdup in Texas and becoming a fugitive. Jay tries to help his fellow man by organizing a Tenant Farmers' Union.

Jay gives his all to the cause. "Nothing ain't going to stop us," he says, "and the Southern Tenant Farmer's Union will git to be a power in this here state."[17] He is defeated, of course. White farmers hesitate to join a union open to Negroes, and the big owners move in with clubs and guns. Jay's black helper Rock Island Jones loses his life, and Jay barely escapes with his own. At the same time, Pat and his wife Belle are being shot to pieces by a posse, and the novel closes with the biggest funeral the hill country has ever seen for Pat, Belle, and Rocky Jones.

"We got to have a day of reckoning," Jay tells the assembly. "You got to change the whole God damned set-up that can bring about three people killed and all that blood and only because they was poor people in a rich man's world."[18]

The Stricklands is the best of the sharecropper novels—a powerful and moving book written with pity and indignation. It comes to no real conclusion since the fight for social justice will never be finished, but Mr. Lanham does end on a cautious note of hope for the future.

Sigman Byrd's *The Redlander*, likewise published in 1939, is a moderately good novel, but not in the same class with Lanham's book. It deals with the rise of John David Huntsman, an orphan from the Redlands district of northeast Texas, from barefoot country boy to United States Senator. John David appears on the streets of Fraternia (Nacogdoches) leading a cow and carrying a portrait in oils of his unknown ancestor. He has nothing else in the world. The Daughters of the Fraternian (read Fredonian) Republic take him over as a civic enterprise and give him shelter in exchange for what they can get out of him. He becomes a lawyer, and in the course of his legal activities he finds that the first Fraternians were actually a

[17] Edwin Lanham, *The Stricklands*, p. 65.
[18] Ibid., p. 284.

gang of pirates who managed to palm themselves off as patriots by suppressing everybody who might have told the truth, including Storm Haggard, John David's "unknown ancestor." In gratitude for what the Daughters have done for him, however, he destroys the evidence, marries the deserving sharecropper's daughter, and begins his march toward the Senate and possibly the presidency. Mr. Byrd, a Houston newspaperman, takes his hero out of the cotton patch as soon as he conveniently can, goes back to the rags-to-riches formula of Dorothy Scarborough and Ruth Cross, and makes his best contribution in his deft satirical handling of the Fraternian Daughters and the Lamb of God Church.

In 1940 Edward Everett Davis published the curious outburst which we have used as a point of reference in this essay. His emphasis on the defeat and degeneracy of the sharecroppers has been a basic element in almost every one of the novels under consideration. He is unique only in his belief that all tenant farmers are snaggletoothed and oversexed weaklings—in his failure to allow for exceptions. His story tells how Isaac Hobson comes to Texas in 1865 and establishes the Clear Creek Ranch. The land is rich, nesters and farmers come crowding in, and eventually Hobson breaks his ranch up into farm-sized units. Milton LaGrone gets more acres than Hobson wants him to have and imports tenant farmers to work the land. Silas Green is typical. He has nine squint-eyed children with toe itch. He himself has flat feet, prematurely hardened arteries, and a calcified spine. His wife is a repulsive creature with a flabby bosom, stooped shoulders, and a protruding lower lip (from lining it with snuff). It is obvious that Texas is being ruined by the White Scourge and the sharecropper. "All the sandy Cross Timber counties . . . are ruined. Ellis, Hunt, and Collin Counties in the rich black lands are slipping. Some day," says Hobson's son, "they too will fall."[19]

Dean Davis brings the crusading period of the sharecropper novel to an end. George Sessions Perry's *Hold Autumn in Your Hand* (1941), a prize-winning book which was made into a successful motion picture, sees the whole problem from a new angle. Sam Tucker, the central character, has been a poor sandy-land farmer, but he figures he is not "sand caliber" (p. 13). He persuades Mr. Ruston, a

---

[19] Edward Everett Davis, *The White Scourge*, p. 192.

big owner, to let him take over sixty-eight acres of black land and Johnson grass at day wages, moves his family into a really fragmentary shack, and pits his strength against the explosive power of the black soil. Everything bad and unexpected happens to him, but Sam is nothing if not resourceful, and he survives triumphantly. At the end he has just about what he started with, but that is really an achievement. His wife Nona remarks with satisfaction, "It don't differ so long as we're gettin somewhere."[20]

Perry accepts the poverty and ignorance of the sharecropper. He accepts the hopelessness of his situation. But he sees also a heroic element in the Sam Tuckers of the cotton country. Dean Davis' serfs and helots are in the background, and Sam knows about them, but he places himself above them. He theorizes: "Land catches the culls that can't do no good in cities"—the ones that don't have "that little old shirttailfull of hold-your-head-up."[21] Sam insists that he is no cull, and he proves his point over and over. Furthermore, he is satisfied with his place in the universe. Thinking of the two weeks he once spent in the Ford factory in Houston, he has "almost a feeling of shame for the richness of his own way of life.[22]

An even more unusual treatment of the sharecropper theme appeared in 1948 in John W. Wilson's *High John the Conqueror,* the only novel in this category to offer a Negro as the central character. Cleveland and his wife Ruby Lee are renting from Mr. John Chaney in the Brazos Bottom and raising good cotton, but Cleveland is deeply troubled. He has guilt feelings over having left his family fifteen miles away on the Navasota. He has brought his mules with him, and his father has no way to make a crop. A bigger difficulty, however, is Mr. John's habit of coming by the house when Cleveland is in the field. Mr. John has been in trouble before over black women. When Ruby Lee tells Cleveland there is going to be a baby, he wants to know, "Whose baby it goin' to be?" Ruby Lee is quite innocent, but the situation drives Cleveland from the farm.

Wilson writes well. He is sensitive to nature and to what goes on inside tormented and disinherited human beings. His great contribution, however, is bringing the black sharecropper to the front of

[20] George Sessions Perry, *Hold Autumn in Your Hand,* p. 239.
[21] Ibid., p. 134.
[22] Ibid., p. 180.

the stage. We are no longer talking about happy darkies dragging their cotton sacks along the rows with laughter and song. We get inside the skin of a poor tenant farmer who happens to be black, and we share his trouble: "Nothing was his own, not even the mules that he had bought and paid for. He had to take them and go wherever he was sent. And his wife? Not even Ruby Lee. You couldn't make trouble with the white man. . . . It all belonged to Mr. John, everything. . . ."[23]

The last of the true sharecropper novels, John Watson's *The Red Dress*, appeared in 1949. It combines cotton farming with a murder mystery and dissertations on the Good Earth. The sharecroppers themselves are a new breed. Aunt Dode and Uncle Deck Cherry have been cropping for thirty-five years for Elmer Doolittle, mostly because they have never got around to making a down payment on the land. They are not starving. They are not degenerate. They don't hate anybody. In fact, they are the finest kind of rural people. Even their landlord is an excellent gentleman and treats them with the utmost consideration. They do have a cross to bear, however: their daughter Pearl, who gets herself a red dress which starts her on a selfish and sinful life. She is the Scarlet O'Hara of the Brazos Bottom. Her wickedness reaches a climax when she takes her pregnant sister Belle's husband away and marries him herself.

A strange hunchbacked character with the impossible name of Fermin Mole is anxious to comfort Belle. She repulses him, and he murders her, making it look as if one of her black friends named Roy Washington was the killer. In the end Pearl drops a hint that Fermin did it, and Fermin kills her, too. He goes to jail, and the Cherrys look forward to better times. They may even make the down payment on the farm.

Like Sam Tucker's family, the Cherrys are poor but self-respecting and glad to be what they are. The repulsive Mole family and Aunt Dode's Negro-hating brother-in-law belong in *The White Scourge*, but they are outweighed by the Cherrys and their kind. These good people have an admirably simple religion, treat the blacks who deserve it as valued personal friends, and are kind and conscientious toward everybody. There is no hint that they are abused or need to be defended.

[23] John W. Wilson, *High John the Conqueror*, p. 139.

A good illustration is the reaction of Elmer Doolittle when Uncle Deck is about ready to buy the farm. "I'm goin ahead and make out the deed to you. The money you spent on the fertilizer will go in as the down payment."[24] Nothing like that could possibly have appeared in the earlier sharecropper novels.

In the fifties and sixties a good many novels and short stories deal with the cotton country, but the emphasis is off the cropper and his way of life.[25] A book which at first glance seems not to be fiction at all—William Owens' *This Stubborn Soil*, which won the Carr P. Collins Award of the Texas Institute of Letters in 1967 and had a good reception nationally—indicates where we stand on these matters at the present time. Owens himself admits that it is "fictionized autobiography," which is another way of saying that it is a novel in disguise. It is the story of his growing up in the neighborhood of the hamlet of Pinhook, Texas, in the midst of second-rate cotton country. The family had a hard time to live decently and educate the children. Young Bill yearned hopelessly, like the children in the novels of the twenties, to go to college. When he finally made it, he did not stop till he had his Ph.D. and was on his way to becoming an associate professor at Columbia University. In living flesh he is the ambitious country boy of the early sharecropper novels—the fulfillment of the dreams of Dorothy Scarborough and Ruth Cross.

It may be noted in conclusion that our novelists picked up the sharecropper at a time when other depressed minorities were getting attention. We remember *Gentlemen's Agreement* and *Strange Fruit* and the writers of the forties in the Southwest who asked us to do

[24] John Watson, *The Red Dress*, p. 177.
[25] An exception is a story by Harry Kidd, Jr., called "Low Road Go Down," which appeared in the *Southwest Review* for the autumn of 1948, and was anthologized by William Peery in *21 Texas Short Stories*. Herb, a white boy, learns that Mr. Jere Thomas is giving his top Negro picker short weight and realizes that he can't fight the system. Other works dealing with the cotton country but not with the sharecropper's problems include Oren Arnold, *The Golden Chair*; Bonner McMillion, *The Lot of Her Neighbors*; William Humphrey, *Home from the Hill*; William A. Owens, *Look to the River*. A good example from the seventies is Darby Foote's *Baby Love and Casey Blue*. Nine-year-old Leah Ann Blue and her father Casey are stranded in the West Texas town of Sisterville, where Boss Henson controls the cotton fields and the lives of all the people. The emphasis, however, is not on social justice but on some rural bad boys, a revivalist preacher, and the adventures of Amy Sunshine—no better than she should be but impossible to overlook.

something about Mexican wetbacks and migratory workers. For a time it looked as if we had a powerful literature of protest going. Then the war came on. We grew prosperous, and jobs were easy to find. And we forgot. The books are in the libraries, however, and the record is there to read—the record of a time which, we hope, will never come again, a time when a father could say of his six-year-old daughter: "She puts her feet under the table three times a day, don't she? Well, then, she's got to do her share of the work. Hit the grit, Perly."

Sex on the Lone Prairee

WESTERN fiction has traditionally been clean. Where the coyotes howl and the wind blows free was never a place for promiscuous sex, kinky sex, or perversion. Since the early sixties, however, all this has changed. Western novelists have not gone as far out on the pornographic limb as some of their counterparts in the East and in California, but they have done their best and are still doing it in the times we live in, although there are signs that the urge to show all and tell all is slowing down—in the Great Open Spaces as well as nationally.

Sex has always been a commodity, and sometimes a literary commodity, and its appearance in works of fiction has provoked intermittent controversy for at least a century. It is only in recent times, however, that it has been put into a book like chile or oregano into a *sopa*, and with just about as much emotional involvement. This cold, commercial use of sex began even before the courts decided that *Lady Chatterley's Lover* was not obscene and might be fruitfully perused by precocious babes in arms. It achieved status with *Portnoy's Complaint*, which recognized masturbation as a normal adolescent activity, like brushing one's teeth. The result in American fiction is that adultery is what everyone is living in, and rape is a spectator sport, like boxing or basketball.

We who live west of the Mississippi are not surprised that such things exist in the blasé East or among the porno sheets and underground newspapers of Los Angeles, but who would look for them in Texas or Arizona or Montana? There can be no doubt, however, that Santa Fe and San Antonio are following New York and Philadelphia in this respect, though without much hope of catching up. Larry McMurtry and a sedulous company of younger novelists have gone just about as far as they can in the pursuit of "realism," and lovely ladies from Austin, Texas, and Tucson, Arizona, are tiptoeing into what used to be forbidden territory—and are doing it for money. Westerns, gothics, murder mysteries, antiestablishment blasts, rural epics, family sagas—whatever the category, the doors are open, and the obscure corners of human sexuality are on view. An ordinary unsophisticated reader (a few still exist) who picks up a modern novel about the American West may feel like Kipling's color sergeant at the hanging of Danny Deever: "I'm dreadin' what I've got to watch."

As a result, people with a respect for Literature (with a capital L)—and many of them do indeed survive—are thrown into convulsions by the books that come to hand. The editor of a book-review department in a Southwestern daily newspaper, a Southern Lady from Dallas, sent me a copy of David Helton's *King Jude* (1969) with this comment: "I don't want *any* review of this loathsome book. I give it to you for your Texas collection."

Perhaps it is good for Southern Ladies to be jolted out of their complacency by Mr. Helton's portrait of a brawling singer of "down-home music" with "king-size sexual prowess." Perhaps not. Whether this opening of doors is good or bad will have to be decided by posterity. The point is that the doors are open in Western fiction, as elsewhere, and the way they have been opened can be noted and described. A few preliminary points must be made, however, before the matter can be intelligently discussed.

First of all, it should be noted that the revolution of the sixties and seventies was not just the result of a number of court decisions recognizing the freedom of the press. It followed the disintegration of a once-powerful set of taboos. The whole structure of the unmentionable, the unnamable, and the unthinkable has crumbled, and the sewage of centuries appears to be assaulting our ears, noses, and imaginations. The sewage is of our own creation, of course. Nothing is unclean unless we agree that it is. If most of us believed that it was clean and permitted, it would be clean and permitted. Southern Ladies and their equivalents forget that it is all in our minds.

Two basic human activities cause most of the trouble—elimination and copulation. The simple, sturdy monosyllables by which our ancestors referred to them became indecent as "civilization" progressed, and they were replaced in polite conversation by circumlocutions, euphemisms, Latin equivalents, and the language of the nursery. These "quadriliterals," as *Time* magazine once described them, were surprisingly few in number, but their strength was as the strength of ten, and they were taboo for centuries—familiar in the barnyard and the brothel but carefully avoided in other circles. "Gentlemen, there are ladies present!" and the vulgarians quieted down.

Now all is changed. Young people use the words as casually as they say "sugar" and without any feeling of barriers broken, but it took a long time for this freedom to come about, and one wonders why. One reason may be that elimination and copulation are exceptionally personal and private matters. A man engaged in either one of them is defenseless—with his pants down—and if any publicity is attached to the interruption of either pursuit, he is at the very least ridiculous. So our ancestors agreed that under ordinary circumstances they would not talk in plain terms about these two important aspects of human experience.

The breaking of verbal taboos is part of the enlarged liberty which we now enjoy—or deplore—but even more awesome is the elimination of the visual taboo, the restriction on what can be shown or described. This is where "explicit" sex comes in. Earlier novelists took us to the bedroom door. Their successors have removed the door, and sometimes they walk right through the bedroom into the barn.

Look, for example, at Larry McMurtry's much-admired and much-imitated novel *The Last Picture Show*, published in 1966 and transformed into a popular motion picture. It is set in the small Texas town of Thalia, where all the inhabitants—small boys, adolescent girls, housewives, civic officials—are sex-ridden and doing something about it. I grew up in a small town about the size of Thalia and went to the picture shows and the high-school entertainments. All of us were discovering sex, but we were not in the same league with McMurtry's adolescents. Take the matter of zoophily—intercourse with animals. We sometimes told stories about sexually deprived sheepherders, but we never thought of these situations as being absolutely for real. Nobody that I knew, and many of us were country boys, engaged in such practices. Yet McMurtry makes a sort of specialty of zoophily and implies that when you say "Boys will be boys," this is one of the things you mean.

The implication is always that McMurtry and his tribe are telling it truly—at last. The publishers call *The Last Picture Show* "a sensitive, poignant and powerful work of fiction" which portrays accurately "the wild, heartbreaking condition called adolescence" as experienced in Texas. I believe the publishers are wrong. I do not agree that McMurtry's primary object is to describe Things As They Are. I wonder sometimes if he may not have been outside his peer group in high school and is out for revenge, but probably his aim is simply to shock the reader. He knows that people over fifty and some not over twenty are often scandalized by what he talks about and uncomfortable with the language he uses but keep on reading to see what he will come up with next—like a bird fascinated by a snake. It amuses him to think up a new sexual irregularity, a new obscenity, as if he were saying to himself, "This will panic them!" And of course it does. If it did not, he would lose much of his reason for writing and might even be out of business.

In their hearts his admirers know that this is true. When Mc-Murtry won his second Carr P. Collins Award from the Texas Institute of Letters in 1968, he was introduced, with a sort of shy pride, by a Houston matron as "our *enfant terrible*"—as if to say, "our *enfant terrible* is more terrible than your *enfant terrible*." The reviewers and the critics know he is trying to shock, but they seldom say so. They ignore his seamy side and concentrate on his real gifts as a narrative artist. Thus, he and his imitators are left with the conviction that the field is theirs and what they are writing is what everybody wants to read.

Having proclaimed these truths to be self-evident, one can look with increased understanding at the sexual side of the Western novel and proceed to a few generalizations. First, it is obvious that since the early sixties "explicit" sex has been permitted and even encouraged. What the Victorians barely suggested is now described in detail. As a result, we are much better informed than our forebears were, but not necessarily better served. Whether they know it or not, people like to have something left to their imaginations. Suggestion plus imagination is a better stimulant than revelation—something the inventor of the bikini failed to realize.

Western novelists, by and large, do not realize the power of suggestion either, and it is hard to think of a single recent writer, aside from the begetters of assembly-line westerns, who does not feel obliged to make a public display of the mating ritual somewhere in his work. And the commercial western is not as pure as it was.

There used to be stopping places. Now there are none. Seventeen-year-old Eli Russell elopes with twenty-year-old Ginny Harris in Lucas Webb's 1971 novel *Eli's Road*. They camp for the night. Ginny says, "A man has rights offen a woman who goes off with him," and she starts to "shuck." This would be a good place to leave them, but Mr. Webb moves right on. In Jack Bickham's *A Boat Named Death* (1975), Faith Socumbe offers herself to the murderer Shed if he will try to get her and her two boys out of their wilderness cabin and back to the settlements down the flooded Buttermilk River. "You can't give a man what he's already made up his mind to take," says Shed, but Faith has fully committed herself, and "her fingers reached the top button of her dress." There really is no need to describe what happens next, but Mr. Bickham insists, and the reader has to watch, like it or not. Gabe Wyld and Kala Fields in Jesse Bier's pleasant novel *The Year of the Cougar* (1976) are a Montana Romeo and Juliet who fall in love in spite of serious rivalry between their fathers. They have their meeting in her father's barn. "Just hold me first," she says, and Gabe does so. This would once have been the end of the chapter, but not now.

Any number of examples come to mind. Look at Edward Abbey's *The Monkey Wrench Gang* (1975), a sumptuous satire on American "civilization," with special emphasis on the havoc wrought by road and dam builders, in which explicit sex is hardly needed to make the point. Look at William Eastlake's *Dancers in the Scalp House* (1975), aimed in the same direction; at Matt Braun's *The Kinkaids*; at Evan Hunter's *The Chisholms*; even at Colin Stuart's Indian novel *Walks Far Woman*—all published in 1976 and each one intent on taking the reader to bed. The problem, obviously, is not to find a novel with explicit sex, but to find one without it.

Since the fiction writer is charged with depicting life as viewed in his time, and since the country is obsessed with sex, it must be admitted that Western novelists have risen nobly to meet their great challenge. If any aspect of the subject remains unexplored, it is probably because the writers have never become aware of the resourcefulness of human beings in finding ways to improve and extend their carnal comforts. In some cases, however, Western writers with unusual endowments of instinct or experience have been able to venture out beyond the bounds of the conventional and "normal" and rival Barbara Rogers or Erica Jong in putting novelty and adventure into the bedroom.

For openers, consider the matter of adolescent sex. People respond emotionally to Romeo and Juliet, to Holden Caulfield and Alex Portnoy and Lolita. Young people, beautiful and unused, are always sexually interesting. We are told that the potentates enthroned in the Alhambra during Moorish times stocked their harems with ladies no more than twelve years old, and that when these ladies reached the age of fifteen, they were considered superannuated and were retired to housekeeping duties. Men in Granada—or in Great Falls, Montana, or Guthrie, Oklahoma—would probably do as the Moors did if they could, but since they live in an age too late, they are obliged to settle for looking, dreaming, and reading.

Western novelists have done their best to help them. J. P. Miller in his 1968 novel *The Race for Home* is one who gave his all for these voyeurs. Laddy, his viewpoint character, is a fifteen-year-old sexually precocious waif who comes to the Texas Gulf Coast town of Espada and becomes part of the family of well-to-do farmer Tom Calvin. Laddy has developed "an amazing monodexterity" from keeping one hand constantly in his pocket to conceal his unremitting sexual excitement. He is a Texas Portnoy. His opposite number is Tom's adolescent daughter Polly, a bombshell primed to go off at any moment. Masturbation is a way of life with her, as it is with Laddy, but she is eager for more meaningful experience. Laddy offers a way out, but she considers him beneath her and uses him only on an experimental basis until her father dies, leaving her under the thumb of her domineering Aunt Caroline. It occurs to her then that if she can become pregnant, she can escape from her legal dependency. Taking refuge in the barn, she does her best with Laddy's assistance to avail herself of this avenue of escape. The reader has no need to take any part of her campaign on faith.

The blurb calls the book "a Rabelaisian portrait of an era"—the Depression. Rabelaisian it is, but it is more than a portrait. It is a symptom.

Western novels spotlighting the sexual experiences of the young are easy to find. They came along with some regularity in the sixties and multiplied during the seventies. One could start with Patricia Gallagher's *The Sons and the Daughters* (1961), showing what goes on in Shady Bend, Texas, or with Tom Mayer's *Bubble Gum and Kipling* (1964), a collection of short stories which does the same for Santa Fe, New Mexico. The list would include *The Last Picture Show* (1966) and *The Race for Home* (1968). In the seventies stories of adolescent love continued to be written, but the best of them were not blatantly carnal. David Wagoner's amusing *The Road to Many a Wonder* (1974) is a sample. Ike Bender is a twenty-year-old innocent who starts out for the Colorado gold fields in 1859 with all his worldly possessions in a wheelbarrow. Fifteen-year-old Millie Slaughter, a determined but conventional heroine, runs him down and marries him en route.

In another 1974 novel, Barbara Moore's *Hard on the Road*, Pepper Fairchild has to leave his Louisiana home in post–Civil War days and travels through the West with his eccentric Cousin Calvin, an itinerant photographer. His temperature is raised by Emma Prosser, a red-headed crusading female journalist whom Pepper rescues from molasses-and-feathering by townspeople outraged by her efforts at reform. Emma is too old for him, however, and Mrs. Moore keeps it clean. John Reese's *Blacksnake Man* (1976) features another fifteen-year-old heroine named Wanda Archambo, who falls in love with Ike Hazen, "a young Eastern dude" who joins forces with her crude and violent family of moonshiners in western Nebraska. Ike is an expert with a blacksnake whip and uses it effectively instead of a six-shooter. Wanda is not wicked or wanton. She just knows what she wants and goes after it. In such novels as these, there is little to alarm a sensitive reader. The norm, however, seems to be the kind of brush-and-cotton-patch Lolita found in Darby Foote's *Baby Love and Casey Blue* (1975), in which the most interesting character is a young girl named Amy Sunshine. "If Amy Sunshine was a whore," says nine-year-old Leah Ann ("Baby Love") Blue, the viewpoint character, "then a whore was exactly what I wanted to be when I grew up. I thought she was beautiful." C. W. Smith's *Country Music* (1975) raises the pitch considerably as he follows the fortunes of Bobby Joe Gilbert, "out of high school and hanging around," who has "a '57 Ford with full skirts and duals and a girlfriend in penny loafers who goes all the way." It hardly needs to be pointed out that Smith has learned a great deal from Larry McMurtry.

One promising aspect of juvenile sex which has been more or less neglected involves rape, including parental abuse, of little girls. It has been tried. John Irsfeld tried it in his 1975 novel *Coming Through* (also "evoking comparison with . . . Larry McMurtry," according to the dust jacket), in which LaWanda Lutts, fourteen years old, enters the story as a fugitive from molestation by her father. It turns out that Tudor Lutts, a brute in most other ways, is innocent of this particular charge. LaWanda, however, is ready to take an advanced degree in sexology.

A bona fide victim is Jansie, the little Texas heroine of R. G. Vliet's *Rockspring* (1974). Jansie is captured in the year 1830 by three Mexican bandits when she wanders too far from home. She is forced to spend the winter with them in their hideout far back in the hills. They use her and abuse her, and she suffers all the torture they can inflict on a sensitive child. She lives and learns, however, and finally comes to love the youngest of the outlaws, who is only a boy himself. They escape, and she takes him back to her home, but one of her neighbors, not understanding the situation, kills him on sight and leaves Jansie doubly desolate.

Vliet is no pornographer. Even the rape scene is transmuted into poetry, and the story is told with such simplicity, sensitivity, and refinement that Malcolm Cowley calls it "a lovely novella." The field is open for less sensitive writers, however, and at least one of them has used the rape of an adolescent to rise to new heights of the unspeakable. He is Forrest Carter, the part-Indian creator of Josey Wales, the outlaw hero of *Gone to Texas* (1973) and *The Vengeance Trail of Josey Wales* (1976). Wales is a Missouri farmer who lost his wife and baby when the Kansas Redlegs burned his log house in 1858. He gets his revenge by making a career of banditry, robbing banks and dodging the Yankee cavalry during the Civil War years. At the beginning of the second novel, Josie learns that two of his friends have been done in by a renegade Mexican general named Escobedo, and he invades Mexico in search of revenge.

A climactic moment comes when Escobedo rapes the captured Apache girl En-lo-e, still a child, but a wise one. He lets her know that he is going to strangle her because the final convulsions of a dying woman give the rapist his supreme pleasure. She counterfeits the ultimate paroxysm just before she is about to experience the real thing, empties her bowels to show that she is dead, deceives the sadistic general, and escapes to join Josie and help him attain his revenge. It would be hard to equal the sheer horror of this revolting scene, which seems to have achieved the ultimate in indecency, but Western writers are resourceful and may find ways to add new shudders to a promising subject.

Rape and attempted rape of mature women, often presented in graphic detail, are common enough. An example is David Case's *Plumb Drillin'* (1975) about a hunt for a lost gold mine near Mexican Hat, Utah. Jane Turner has been raped by Turk Strange in the presence of her blind husband. Turk is a gunslinger and the nastiest kind of a villain, but he joins the treasure hunt, and Jane has to put up with him and her memories until Luke Adam DeCaire takes care of the situation. A white woman raped by Indians has been a favorite subject of Western fictioneers for years. It has remained for contemporary novelists, however, to enable the reader to watch it happen.

It may be a comfort to concerned individuals that the Western novel has not yet gone in for much really "kinky" sex. It has not even paid much attention to lesbianism and homosexuality. Leslie Fiedler in *The Return of the Vanishing American* (1968) tried to redefine the western to include a possibly homosexual relationship between a white man in search of freedom and a darker companion who humanizes him and leads him into larger life. On his list of "new westerns," along with *One Flew Over the Cuckoo's Nest*, was J. L. Herlihy's *Midnight Cowboy* (1965), in which a Houston dishwasher moves to New York, dresses up in Western garb, and becomes a male prostitute—a hustler. He forms a friendship with a consumptive black who gives him some new perspectives. The story is not a western by anybody's definition but Fiedler's, but it does open a door.

It might be worth mentioning that John Rechy, the novelist laureate of the male hustler in the big city, grew up in El Paso but doesn't bring his business home to Texas. Edwin Shrake of Fort Worth, however, takes his readers on a guided tour of the gay world which will be hard to equal for savage satire and bitter laughter. The narrator of *Peter Arbiter* (1973) is a bisexual interior decorator (named with an eye cocked toward Petronius) who moves about among Texas millionaires and their ample, amorous wives. His companions are an old poet who cons his greedy friends for millions and a fifteen-year-old runaway youth who likes to live with men. Early in the story two ambidextrous lesbians tie Peter up at the point of a pistol and try to rape him. Many bizarre scenes follow, but probably the most bizarre of all is set in a "clinic" where two strange women try to restore Peter's potency and enable him to resume his abnormal life. The men have names like Guy-Guy and Poo Poo Roote and Dr. Scrodmuir, and the life they lead is something no "normal" person would believe. The blurb writer for the Encino Press calls the book "a hilarious romp as power and money, in the form of some devilish caricatures of well-known Texas personalities, try to cope with the exuberance and energy of these three cavalier interlopers."

Whatever else a reader may have to say about *Peter Arbiter*, it stands pretty much alone in Western fiction—at least up to the time of its publication—in its intense concentration on peripheral or far-out sex. When these irregularities come up in most novels, they are incidental—a sort of fringe benefit. For an illustration, take Richard Martin Stern's *Power* (1975), a novel about third-generation heirs of a big ranch in New Mexico. Will, the weak brother, is married to Sue, a beautiful creature who can go either way and frequently does. She has a lesbian relationship with Ethel Wilding, and we catch a glimpse of them in a huge bathtub, once a fixture in a Denver bawdy house, soaping each other's bodies. A glimpse, however, is all we get.

Without getting deeply involved in the gay community, a fair proportion of recent Western novelists have experimented with what might be called unorthodox sex as public tolerance has grown and authors have probed deeper into the Formerly Forbidden. Take the matter of what has come to be termed "oral sex." A pioneer venture into this once undiscussable area is Marilyn Harris' *In the Midst of Earth* (1969). Myra Cinrus comes as a foundling to the house of "Mr. Jack" Cinrus somewhere on the parched Southwestern prairies. At first this intelligent, disillusioned, highly educated outcast ignores her—then decides to bring her up in his own image. They come to value and finally to love each other, but dark forces are at work in both of them. At night Myra is swept away in the "floodwaters of perverted sexuality," even in her girlhood. Mr. Jack is having experiences of his own in the cottage he keeps for his pleasures away from the big house. The truth comes out in their last encounter, which involves oral sex. When it is over, Mr. Jack goes back to his study and shoots himself.

Seven years later this indulgence is no longer scandalous, but is taken as a matter of course. To Shelby Hearon of Austin, Texas, it is a natural part of human relations and a potential refreshment, like water on a thirsty land. In Mrs. Hearon's family chronicle *Now and Another Time* (1976), Louisa follows Sam Tabour to his house after a party for her father and takes part in a scene of animal passion which goes on for "hours and hours," most of the time "with her begging" before she gets what she wants. Mrs. Hearon observes it all with the detached interest of one watching a snake shed its skin or a banker foreclosing on a mortgage.

Jeanne Williams in *A Lady Bought with Rifles* (1976), a novel of the revolution in northern Mexico, brings young Miranda Greenleaf from school in England to the hacienda of Las Coronas. Before she is forced into marriage with the depraved and sadistic Court Sanders, she meets Trace Winslade, who gives her lessons in love. He leaves her a virgin, but makes considerable contributions to her education and her pleasure, sending "liquid fire" through her until she bursts into "lovely, pulsating explosions." It would seem that this particular indulgence is now a creature comfort, much like a fire in the fireplace when one is cold or a good, hot bath when one is tired. Sexual eccentricities have become tolerable, almost respectable. Nobody shoots himself now.

It might even be demonstrated that a quiet competition is going on to see who can go farthest in discovering and exploiting new quirks of human sexuality. An example comes to mind in Kathryn Marshall's 1977 novel *Desert Places*, conceived in the spirit of the Larry McMurtry school of realism. Beatrice Lawrence is a rich, self-centered Texas woman whose roughneck husband Quinn chases every female in sight. She gets even by making herself available to a traveling salesman whom she despises, charging him two hundred dollars, and making sure the whole town knows about it. Her victim is partially compensated for the humiliation he endures, however, by a trick with a knotted scarf which multiples his pleasure. The device is a plus for Marshall, who must have spent some time in the field finding out about it. It remains to be seen whether any of her fellow craftsmen do better. It is worth remarking, however, that she is a teacher of writing, and some bright student may be expected to go beyond his teacher, as bright students do.

It is perhaps not fair to leave Marshall without some mention of her tragic view of life and her picture of Texas as a wasteland in which sick, sadistic, sex-driven characters pass their frustrations on to their children. In such a desert place erotic aberrations might be expected. The point here, however, is that Marshall seems to be trying to outdo her competitors.

Not many Western novelists drift this far in the direction of sexual experiment, but they do introduce new male-female relationships to make sure of the reader's interest. Sex between members of different racial groups has been useful to some of them. Richard Martin Stern, who got his start writing literate and successful whodunits with Santa Fe as a locale, beginning with *Murder in the Walls* in 1971, features Johnny Ortiz of the San Cristo police department. Johnny is part Mexican and part Apache, with the "gifts," as James Fenimore Cooper called them, of both racial groups. He is emotionally attached to Cassie Enright, black, beautiful, and beguiling, with a Ph.D. in anthropology. Stern does not play up their sexual relations, but he makes sure the reader knows they have them.

Indian men have been falling in love with white girls, and sometimes vice versa, ever since Marah Ellis Ryan's *Indian Love Letters* (1907), Harold Bell Wright's *The Mine with the Iron Door* (1923), Zane Grey's *The Vanishing American* (1925), and Edgar Rice Burroughs' *The War Chief* (1927). Elliott Arnold imagined Tom Jeffords into a sexual relationship with Sonseeahray, the beautiful Apache girl, in *Blood Brother* (1947), and Dorothy Johnson's nameless Bostonian in *A Man Called Horse* (1953) becomes the husband of Pretty Calf and functions successfully as a member of the Crow tribe. A new twist was given to an Indian-white marriage in Jane Barry's *A Time in the Sun* (1962) when Joaquin, half Apache and half Mexican, became the husband of Anna Stillman, a white captive, with her full consent. The hero of *Little Big Man* (1964) is the enthusiastic spouse of a Cheyenne woman, though author Thomas Berger plays his sex life mostly for laughs. Jay Grobart in Marilyn Durham's *The Man Who Loved Cat Dancing* (1972) has two children by his Shoshone wife. Walks Far Woman in Colin Stuart's novel of that name (1976) marries a white man and lives in both worlds.

Most of these earlier authors were untroubled by demands for explicit sex, but later novelists could not escape. In Jean Rikhoff's *The Sweetwater* (1976), Benjie Klomp becomes the wife of the Sioux Bone Hand and bears him two children. We learn a good deal about how they were conceived. With William Eastlake's *Dancers in the Scalp House* (1975) there is more to see as red-headed Mary-Forge teaches Navajo children to be proud of themselves and spends her off-duty hours making love with Tom Charles at his place (which he calls the Scalp House) and dancing with him naked afterward. Tom Charlie has gone to the university and learned about science and spends *his* leisure hours making an atomic bomb with which to blow up the Atlas (read Glen Canyon) Dam. The couple's lovemaking is subjected to close scrutiny.

Perhaps the most sensational of all these racially integrated recent novels is Paul King's *Hermana Sam* (1977) about an attractive little Irish nun from Boston who has received a medical education and comes out to Santa Fe in 1847 to start a hospital. Once the reader accepts this obvious impossibility, he is called on for even greater acts of faith as Sister Samantha (Hermana Sam to her Mexicans) meets with the Apache leader Mangus out on the plains, where he has been chasing Comanches. Mangus is immobilized by a bullet lodged near his spine, and Sister Samantha has to cut it out or die. She cuts it out. The result is an attachment between the Indian and the white girl which leads to their living together as man and wife after the Apaches rescue her during the Taos Rebellion of 1847. She even has a child by Mangus and is content to be an Apache mother, but he appreciates her gift for healing, sends her back to her people, and arranges for his own death because he can't go on without her. Their union strains credulity, but the idea of a sexual attachment between an Apache chief and a Roman Catholic nun is bound to arouse interest, and King makes sure it is interesting by giving a play-by-play account of their encounters—the first one taking place chest deep in a stream of water.

Neil Claremon, in his poetic novel *Borderland*, finds still another way to deal with a mixed marriage. J. P., an American hydrologist brought to northern Mexico to start an irrigation project for the benefit of a community of Opata Indians, is half of the equation. He falls in love with Tsari, a *curandera* (healer) with all sorts of other-worldly gifts and powers. Claremon not only offers the reader a clear view of their lovemaking—he also makes J. P. violate tribal taboos and assist at the birth of their twin sons. Explicit sex is one thing. Explicit birth goes a step farther.

Nothing has been said up to this point about the traditional or "commercial" western, with a small *w*. A number of examples have been cited from Doubleday's Double D list of westerns, but these are a step ahead of the multitude of soft-cover examples which carry on more or less in the tradition of the twenties and thirties. One might guess that nothing needs to be said and that the most unlikely place to look for explicit sex would be in the shoot-em-up, hayburner, or oater. The printed horse opera used to be satisfied with the most modest suggestion that the cowboy wanted more than friendship from the schoolteacher, or that the teacher had more than friendship to offer. It is not satisfied with such meager fare any more.

The change came on gradually. Nelson Nye, with a hundred tales to his credit, says the first "sexy" western was Homer Croy's *West of the Water Tower* (1923), which was about a seduction. He claims credit for number two himself—*Riders by Night* (1950). The idea of "sexy," of course, has to be considered relatively. What was sexy in 1920, or even 1951, may seem timidly reserved twenty or thirty years later, and it is true that the growing tolerance—or numbness—of the reading public has spurred ambitious writers on to new levels of explicitness and specificity. In the old days when the frontiersman headed into the wilderness in search of the lost mine or the lost relative, or whatever was lost, he went by himself or with a small company of males. Now the female lead insists on coming along, unprepared as she is for what lies ahead, and the author lets her go with just one thing in mind. After a week or two on the trail, transformed and humanized by dangers and hardships, she yields to passion beside a mountain stream, sometimes with death just around the bend, and it is suggested that a good and beautiful thing has taken place.

T. V. Olsen's *Savage Sierra* (1962) used this formula. Will Angsman is the tough frontiersman. James and Judith Amberley from Boston are the tenderfeet who wish to go into dangerous Indian country to look for their brother Douglas, who disappeared a year before while searching for a lost Spanish mine. Bonito, the great Apache leader, is tired of fighting and has retired to his mountain fastness, but he has warned the white man to stay away or take the consequences. Angsman, against his better judgment, agrees to guide the Easterners. Wicked white men, as well as hostile Indians, pursue them, and much blood is shed before they get out, but love does come beside the mountain stream.

John Benteen's *Apache Raiders* (1970) follows the fortunes of Neal Fargo, a supertough frontiersman who is looking for a treasure hidden in the Big Bend of Texas. Nola Shane, a Pennsylvania schoolteacher, has come to El Paso on the trail of her brother, a mining engineer held for ransom south of the border. She tags along when Fargo leaves. Nola turns out to be a seductive and voluptuous woman who can't wait to get in bed with the hero, and she gets him back in at every opportunity. He is not hers to keep, however. Mr. Benteen's motto, where Fargo is concerned, is "He who makes love and runs away. . . ."

Westerns featuring raw sex and violence keep on coming. William James is the instigator of a series called "Apache," spotlighting a mighty warrior named Cuchillo Oro from his favorite weapon, a golden Spanish knife. Number seven in the series, titled *Blood Line* (1976), begins its action in 1864 as the lone Apache watches six Indian renegades gang-rape a white woman. The action, including some abnormal sex, is described in detail. After giving the reader time enough to get his money's worth, Cuchillo Oro shoots one of the gang and sends the others on their way. He is not particularly shocked by what has taken place, since he is no lover of white people himself, Captain Cyrus Pinner of the United States Cavalry having killed his wife and child. He does not war on white women, however, and he saves Linda Daughton before moving on to more bloody encounters in the town of Angus Wells.

Many more examples of this sort of sex-with-violence could be cited from the 150-plus novels which have been written about the Apache wars in the Southwest, and sexual frankness is not hard to find in other types of westerns. The majority of them, however, avoid heavy sex. Steve Overholser's Spur Award–winning *A Hanging in Sweetwater* (1974) is about a former soldier and a saloon girl who preempt some rich Wyoming bottomland in 1879 in defiance of a big cattleman. They are obviously in love, but Boomer Jones, the narrator, is only fifteen years old and is not in a position to describe their intimacies in detail. Will Bryant in *Blue Russell* (1976) does not get all the mileage he can out of young Blue's first sexual ex-experience. John Reese, in his series about the adventures of Jefferson Hewitt, a private detective in the turn-of-the-century West (*Sequoia Shootout*, 1977, for example), takes pains to keep Jeff out of the bedroom. Milton Bass brings his adolescent leading man (*Mist'r Jory*, 1976) into contact with aggressive women, but keeps him from getting seriously involved. It would seem that the western preserves its heart intact though the forces of change have crumbled its outer works. What the future holds for the traditional horse opera remains unrevealed, but its readers have always been conservative and may discourage further experimentation.

It should be noted that some writers of superior or upper-case Western novels have refused to be pressured into excessive frankness about sex. Dorothy M. Johnson, a very competent and highly respected Montana novelist, is one of them. Her prize-winning *Buffalo Woman* (1977) has all the sex it needs to make it convincing, but no more. The same can be said for the work of Jane Gilmore Rushing, a superior writer who is at home in the Texas Panhandle. *The Rain Crow* (1977) traces the mistakes of the fathers through three generations without using explicit sex for its own sake.

There are, in truth, signs that the wave of permissiveness on all fictional and nonfictional levels has begun to recede. In 1977 the verdict of guilty against Larry Flynt and his *Hustler* magazine, controversial though it was, indicated that the tide might be turning. Syndicated newspaper columnists, who represent in some degree the conscience of the country, are unhappy about the smog that blankets the land. Jon-Michael Reed, for example, is outraged because TV serial writers "get away with murder, not to mention abortion, incest, child abuse, prostitution, rape, interracial relationships, sexual promiscuity, sibling and parental rivalry, illegitimacy, insanity, as well as more mundane staples, infidelity and divorce" (*Arizona Daily Star*, February 21, 1977). Mike Royko (*Star*, July 27, 1976) regrets that "In order to preserve the right of Walter Cronkite to report the news, we must defend the right of Strange Oscar, who likes to dial the phone numbers of young ladies and pant."

The reaction may be beginning, but it has a long way to go. People will have to get fed up with pornography, or lose interest, before any significant slowdown in production may be expected. Time may be on the side of purity, however, as two forces work together for good for those who hate smut.

The first of those forces is the natural and normal tendency of any movement to go too far. The purveyors of heavy sex assume that since their books have sold, the way to sell more books is to make the sex heavier. Thus, they hasten their own downfall, and the way to get rid of them entirely is to spur them on to new efforts. Apparently they do not need much urging and are, in fact, eager to get on with it. *Time* magazine, in a review of Rosemary Rogers' 1976 novel *Wicked Loving Lies* (January 17, 1977), reports that the heroine is raped on page 62, on page 86, on page 192, and on page 277. She is "violated twelve times on three continents by five men." On page 654 she announces, "I am tired of being raped." This sort of thing will bring the cleanup a good deal nearer. Readers get tired of being raped, too.

The second Force for Fumigation of Fiction is the fact that anything overdone becomes ridiculous, and ridicule is the best weapon against it. People kept insisting, when the Portnoy craze was at its height, that that performance was hilarious. Perhaps it was, in a sad way, but in other novels, even Western novels, sex began to be played in the 1960's for heartier laughs. As early as 1965 David Markson did it in *The Ballad of Dingus Magee*. On page 66 Dingus completes a seduction which we learn about from the broken utterances of both parties as they pretend they don't know what they are doing. A passage like that is a big help in the fumigation campaign.

Even Larry McMurtry, after sixteen years of trying to outdo himself, seems to have come to the end of the trail. His 1972 novel *All My Friends Are Going to Be Strangers* is a sort of *ne plus ultra*. In a chapter regarded by some connoisseurs as particularly funny, Danny Deck pays a visit to his uncle, who lives in a decayed Victorian mansion out in the desert fifty miles south of Van Horn, Texas. Among his uncle's retainers is a Mexican named Antonio who goes farther than any other McMurtry character in sexual eclecticism. He finds zoophily a welcome diversion, but ranges much farther afield. Anything with a visible opening is a challenge to him—he even goes for postholes and the intake to a gasoline tank. It is almost as if McMurtry has thrown up his hands and admitted that he has done all he can—there are no more sexual oddities to explore. A little of this sort of thing may go a long way toward restoring sanity to fiction.

Once the break is made, anything can happen. It has long been axiomatic among religious people that the worst sinners make the best evangelists, and it is not beyond the bounds of possibility that McMurtry and his disciples may become the spearhead of a new reform effort. The movement seems to have begun and may need only a few enthusiastic converts to become a crusade. Consider Barbara Cartland, who in 1975 wrote nineteen novels *without* explicit sex for a public demanding more. "BRITISH AUTHORESS BARBARA CARTLAND FINDS PUBLIC CLAMORS FOR CHASTITY," says the headline in the *Wall Street Journal* (September 1, 1976). "My heroines are all virgins," Mrs. Cartland told the reporter. "Many publishers thought that Cartland innocence wouldn't sell. Many publishers were wrong."

If the word gets out that she is making it big with such material, and sooner or later it will, a revolution may be expected, maybe overnight. And if virginity does well at the cash register and the box office in the East, it will have its day in the West. Southern Ladies from Dallas will be happy again, and purity will return to the Lone Prairee.

Gus Lenniger of the Lenniger Literary Agency in New York says it has already returned. In a letter dated March 8, 1977, he comments:

> The "sex & violence" western was really used only by the shyster paperback original publishers . . . who tried to become legitimate by introducing "category" lines like mystery and westerns when hardcore pornography killed their sales of silly bed-hopping soft-core porno! . . . All are out of business . . . only one still continuing a couple of sex-and-violence type *series* they started during the era when "spaghetti westerns" flooded the movie and TV shows and practically ruined public acceptance of westerns. . . .
>
> In a serious, believable western historical or family saga set in the

West, sex may rear its lovely head if integral part of story line, necessary to motivation, honest realism, as it does in all types of novels today. But I fully agree with you that the *cheap* sex-and-violence western is not only on way out, but *out*. We would not attempt to market such a manuscript at present; would wish the author luck in peddling it himself.

Gail Gardner, cowboy sage and singer of Prescott, Arizona, encountered the phrase "oral sex" for the first time as he read a newspaper in the lobby of the headquarters hotel at Billings, Montana, during a recent convention of Western Writers of America. "What in the hell does that mean?" he was heard to inquire. "Does it mean they are just going to talk about it?" If Gus Lenniger is right, Gail may never have to know.

Doors to Open: A Conclusion

"But where," says the skeptical reader who has come this far, "are the great novelists? How can you write about the Western novel and ignore, completely ignore, Vardis Fisher and Frederick Manfred? Are you telling us that H. L. Davis is not a part of Western literature—or Oliver La Farge or Jack London or John Steinbeck?"

"Sir," I answer, "this is not a book about Western literature. It looks at the Western novel, much of it on the popular level and much of it contemporary, in an effort to reach some valid conclusions about where we the people have been, where we are, and where we are going as revealed in our fiction. It avoids literary criticism and ignores the Great Names unless they make personal appearances in the areas under consideration." If there had been world enough and time for an essay on the Donner Party in fiction, Vardis Fisher would have had his share of attention along with the rest. Much has already been said about Oliver La Farge as man and artist, but it would have been useful to set him alongside some of the many others who have written fiction about the Navajo from Zane Grey's *Vanishing American* (1925) to Shepard Rifkin's *The Snow Rattlers* (1977) and the Gordons' *Ordeal* (1977). I just did not get around to him.

The book about great Western writers will be written. The members of the Western Literature Association are working on it, and they will give Frank Waters and Paul Horgan their due. Meanwhile, many doors remain to be opened in the pattern of the chapters in this book. Somebody should put together an essay called "The Mirrors of Waco; or, Who is Prowling in My Graveyard?" It will start with Madison Cooper's once-sensational two-volume novel *Sironia, Texas*, published in 1952, which supposedly tells many painful truths about the founding fathers of Waco, Texas. Since that date almost any place in the West which can call itself a town has had its acid chronicler. A bumper crop of these novels comes from Texas. William Humphrey (*Home from the Hill*, 1958, and later novels) uses the Clarksville cemetery as a peephole into the lives of several generations of prominent but peculiar townspeople. Al Dewlen (*The Bone Pickers*, 1958) and Jamie Mandelkau (*The Leo Wyoming Caper*, 1977) have paid their respects to Amarillo. Jack Guinn (*The Caperberry Bush*, 1954) and Jan de Hartog (*The Hospital*, 1964) are two among several who have done it for Houston. There are Dallas novels and Austin novels and Santa Fe novels and Tucson novels, not to mention novels about West Coast towns and cities—all rearranging our notions about the early settlers and citizens.

Why this disillusion about the first comers? The social historian working in Western fiction wants to know, and this is only one of many types of Western novel waiting for the analyst. Let's look at a few of them.

Historical novels, hundreds of them (and this is no exaggeration), need to be read, classified, and talked about. All our wars and feuds from Canada to Mexico have been fictionalized, exposing our secret thoughts about ourselves and our friends and enemies. There are some good recent realistic novels about the Indian, showing him warts and all, and the sentimentalists are not having it all their own way. Starting, perhaps, with James Warner Bellah's *Sergeant Rutledge*, novels about black people in the West have multiplied, and the Chicanos continue to provide new angles for looking at the Mexican. Other minor groups—Germans, Czechs, Norwegians—are part of the scene. Frontier farmers need to be looked at, along with buffalo hunters and miners. Perhaps two dozen novels have been written about the impact of oil. Somebody should read them and add them up.

Humorous novels, dozens of them, are begging for attention. From *Wolfville* to *Sure Shot Shapiro*, Western fiction has displayed a vein of priceless wry humor—funny cowboys and amusing backcountry philosophers, picaros and preachers, photographers and medicine-show con men, youngsters on their own and girls on the make. Nobody has put it all together.

Neither has anyone gathered up the novels about religion, about

178 From Hopalong to Hud

politics, about horses and grizzly bears and mountain lions. There
are more than a nonspecialist might think. And a hundred Miss Sue
Pinckneys—minor, forgotten, but full of the juices of life—are waiting to be discovered.

Probably the best writing in the West today deals with the contemporary scene. Tough, hard-nosed novels about life in Western
small towns and big cities have impressed critics, especially in recent
years. Writers of murder mysteries, some of them very competent,
choose Western settings. The Western Gothic is a presence in the
bookstores, and more and more writers are turning out three-
generation family chronicles which end in the present no matter how
far back they start.

There is not much point in trying to analyze this lively and vital
writing on the basis of literary quality—to talk, as some academic
essayists do, about "literature" and "trash." The longer the student
works in Western fiction, the more he realizes that a clear-cut divi-
sion between "commercial" and "serious" fiction is impossible. So
many novels fall into the gray area between, so much that is said of
one applies to the other, so necessary is the understanding of one to
the comprehension of the other that the student finally gives up and
works both sides of the street simultaneously. He who wishes to explore the fiction shelf as a key to American attitudes toward the
Mexican will read Harvey Fergusson and Richard Bradford, Neal
Claremon's *Borderland*, and Raymond Barrio's *The Plum Plum Pickers*, but he will skip an important segment of his subject if he misses
Will Bryant's *Escape from Sonora* or Forrest Carter's *Vengeance
Trail of Josey Wales*. All the paperbacks about miners and treasure
hunters, gunrunners and bounty hunters—these have their place and
meaning, too.

The least significant potboiler may be studied now without loss
of face or dignity. Gunfire has echoed even in the groves of Academe,
and today it is respectable to have opinions about westerns, not as
literature, but as popular culture. The Popular Culture Association
has now grown so large that it is breaking up into regional divisions
and staging monumental conventions. It helps young people discover
who they are by looking at the modes of expression which their generation favors. The program of the 1976 convention, held in Chicago,
included such papers as "The Western Hero in an Anti-Western

World," "The Western—a Filmic Reflection of America," and "Western Movies and Modern Social Criticism."

As usual, major attention goes to movie westerns, but the novel is not ignored. Pulp magazines, now relics of the past, have become collector's items and are being studied just as the dime novel has been. More than one doctoral dissertation has been written on a popular Western writer. Richard Etulain did one on Ernest Haycox, for example (University of Oregon, 1966), and Lambert E. Neal followed suit with "The Western Writing of Owen Wister: The Conflict of East and West" (University of Utah, 1966). Even the historians are interested. The prestigious Organization of American Historians, meeting in Dallas in 1968, swung into line with a paper on "Mack Sennet's America," illustrated with film clips, and *The American West*, organ of the Western History Association, carried in the issue of March, 1968, an article by sociologist John C. Cawelti, "The Gunfighter and Society," which took a long step toward recognition of the western as an important part of our popular culture. Looking for a "relation between the individual and society" in movie westerns, Cawelti concludes: "These patterns of action suggest that the new adult western seeks to resolve in fantasy some of the major social dilemmas of our time: the sense that human society is doomed to terrible outbursts of violence; the fear of social conflict; the recognition that society both protects and threatens the individual; the increasing awareness of the chaotic violence, crime and brutality that lie just below the peaceful surface of American life." Cawelti and a new generation of social and cultural historians have continued down this road, coming up every now and then with new ideas and new information.

We tend to define the Western novel in terms of the frontier, the formula and the legendary Wild West, but it is much, much bigger than that, and it needs to be plumbed and measured. It is not enough to be a literary specialist when one deals with Western fiction. The serious student needs to turn social historian and find out, if he can, what it all means. He will be in for some surprises if he follows the trail all the way from Hopalong to Hud.

Bibliography

BOOKS AND ARTICLES

Abbey, Edward. *The Brave Cowboy.* New York: Pocket Books, 1957 (copyright, 1956).

————. *The Monkey Wrench Gang.* Philadelphia: Lippincott, 1975.

Adams, Andy. *Log of a Cowboy.* Boston: Houghton Mifflin, 1903.

Alberts, Marvin H. *Apache Rising.* New York: Gold Medal, 1957.

Arnold, Elliott. *Blood Brother.* New York: Duell, Sloan & Pearce, 1947.

Arnold, Oren. *The Golden Chair.* Houston: Elzevir, 1954.

Ballard, Todhunter. *The Sheriff of Tombstone.* Garden City, N.Y.: Doubleday, 1977.

Ballew, Charles [C. M. Snow]. *The Bandit of the Paloduro.* New York: Morrow, 1934.

Barr, Amelia E. *Remember the Alamo.* New York: Dodd, Mead, 1888.

Barrio, Raymond. *The Plum Plum Pickers.* Sunnyvale, Calif.: Ventura Press, 1969.

Barry, Jane. *A Time in the Sun.* Garden City, N.Y.: Doubleday, 1962.

Bartholomew, Ed. *Wyatt Earp, 1848 to 1880: The Untold Story.* Toyahvale, Tex.: Frontier Book Co., 1963.

————. *Wyatt Earp, 1879 to 1882: The Man and the Myth.* Toyahvale, Tex.: Frontier Book Co., 1964.

Bass, Milton. *Mist'r Jory.* New York: Putnam's, 1976.

Bellah, James Warner. *The Apache.* New York: Gold Medal, 1951.

————. *Massacre.* New York: Lion Books, 1950.

————. *A Thunder of Drums.* New York: Bantam, 1961.

Bennett, Robert Ames. *A Volunteer with Pike: The True Narrative of One Dr. John Robinson and of His Love for the Fair Señorita Vallois.* Chicago: A. C. McClurg, 1909.

Benteen, John. *Apache Raiders.* New York: Belmont, 1971.

Bercovitch, Reuben. *Odette.* Port Washington, N.Y.: Ashley Books, 1973.

Berger, Thomas. *Little Big Man.* New York: Dial, 1964.

Bickham, Jack. *A Boat Named Death.* Garden City, N.Y.: Doubleday, 1975.

Bower, B. M. *Chip of the Flying U.* New York: G. W. Dillingham, 1906.

————. *The Gringos.* Boston: Little, Brown, 1913.

Boyer, Glenn G. *I Married Wyatt Earp*. Tucson: University of Arizona Press, 1977.

Brand, Max. *Destry Rides Again*. New York: Triangle, 1941 (copyright, 1930).

Braun, Matthew. *The Kinkaids*. New York: Putnam's, 1976.

Brent, Lynton Wright. *Apache Massacre*. Reseda, Calif.: Powell Publications, 1969.

————. *The Bird Cage*. Philadelphia: Dorrance, 1945.

Bret Harte, John. "The Strange Case of Joseph C. Tiffany: Indian Agent in Disgrace," *Journal of Arizona History* 16 (Winter, 1975).

Brooks, Glyn Austin. "A Political Survey of the Prohibition Movement in Texas," M.A. thesis, University of Texas at Austin, 1920.

Brown, J. P. S. *Jim Kane*. New York: Dial, 1970.

Bryant, Will. *Blue Russell*. New York: Random House, 1976.

————. *Escape from Sonora*. New York: Random House, 1973.

Burnett, W. R. *Adobe Walls*. New York: Knopf, 1953.

————. *Saint Johnson*. New York: Dial, 1930.

Burns, Walter Noble. *Tombstone*. New York: Doubleday, 1927.

Burroughs, Edgar Rice. *Apache Devil*. New York: Ballentine, 1964 (copyright, 1933).

————. *The War Chief*. Chicago: A. C. McClurg, 1927.

Bush, Niven. *Duel in the Sun*. New York: Hampton Publishing Company and William R. Morrow, 1944.

Calder, Jeni. *There Must Be a Lone Ranger*. New York: Taplinger, 1975.

Cameron, Lou. *Guns of Durango*. New York: Dell, 1976.

Capps, Benjamin. *The True Memoirs of Charley Blankenship*. Philadelphia: Lippincott, 1972.

Carter, Forrest. *Gone to Texas*. New York: Delacorte/Eleanor Friede, 1973.

————. *The Vengeance Trail of Josey Wales*. New York: Delacorte/Eleanor Friede, 1976.

Case, David. *Plumb Drillin'*. New York: Stein & Day, 1975.

Castle, Frank. *Guns to Sonora*. New York: Berkley, 1962.

Catlin, Don. *Desert Crucible*. Derby, Conn.: Monarch Books, 1965.

Cawelti, John C. "The Gunfighter and Society," *American West* 5 (March, 1968).

————. "Myth, Symbol and Formula," *Journal of Popular Culture* 8 (Summer, 1974).

————. *The Six-Gun Mystique*. Bowling Green, Ohio: Bowling Green University Popular Press [1971].

Chilton, B. F., comp. *Unveiling and Dedication of Monument to Hood's Texas Brigade on the Capitol Grounds at Austin, Texas, Thursday, October Twenty-seven Nineteen Hundred and Ten*. Houston: privately published, 1911.

Claremon, Neal. *Borderland*. New York: Knopf, 1975.

Clum, John P. *It All Happened in Tombstone*. Flagstaff: Northland Press, 1965 (originally published in the *Arizona Historical Review* 1 [April, 1929]).

Cole, Jackson. *Apache Guns*. New York: Popular Library, 1958.

Cook, Will. *Ambush at Antlers Spring*. New York: Award Books, 1962.

————. *Apache Fighter*. New York: Bantam, 1967.

Cross, Ruth. *The Big Road*. New York: Longmans, Green, 1931.

————. *The Golden Cocoon*. New York: Harper, 1924.

Croy, Homer. *West of the Water Tower*. New York: Harper, 1923.

Davis, Edward Everett. *The White Scourge*. San Antonio: Naylor, 1940.

Decker, William. *To Be a Man*. Boston: Little, Brown, 1967.

Durham, Marilyn. *The Man Who Loved Cat Dancing*. New York: Harcourt Brace Jovanovich, 1972.

Durham, Phillip, and Everett L. Jones. *The Western Story: Fact, Fiction and Myth*. New York, Harcourt Brace Jovanovich, 1975.

Eastlake, William. *Dancers in the Scalp House*. New York: Viking, 1975.

Ellis, Edward S. *Trailing Geronimo*. Philadelphia: John Winston, 1908.

Etulain, Richard W. "Riding Point," in *The Popular Western*, ed. Richard W. Etulain and Michael T. Marsden. Bowling Green, Ohio: Bowling Green University Popular Press, 1974.

Evans, Max. *The Rounders*. New York: Macmillan, 1960.

Evarts, Hal G. *The Blazing Land*. New York: Dell, 1960.

Everett, Wade. *Fort Starke*. New York: Ballantine, 1959.

Falke, Ann. "Clay Fisher or Will Henry?" in *The Popular Western*, ed. Richard W. Etulain and Michael T. Marsden. Bowling Green, Ohio: Bowling Green University Popular Press, 1974.

Fergusson, Harvey, *Blood of the Conquerors*, reprinted in *Followers of the Sun*. New York: Knopf, 1936 (original issue, 1921).

Fiedler, Leslie. *The Return of the Vanishing American*. New York: Stein & Day, 1968.

Fink, Julian. *Major Dundee*. New York: Gold Medal, 1965.

Fisher, Clay. *Apache Ransom*. New York: Bantam, 1974.

————. *Black Apache*. New York: Bantam, 1976.

Flynn, Robert. *North to Yesterday*. New York: Knopf, 1967.

Folsom, James K. *The American Western Novel*. New Haven: College & University Press, 1966.

Foote, Darby. *Baby Love and Casey Blue*. New York: Putnam's, 1975.

Forster, Logan. *Proud Land*. New York: Random House, 1954.

French, Philip. *Westerns*. New York: Viking, 1974.

Gallagher, Patricia. *The Sons and the Daughters*. New York: Julian Messner, 1961.

Ganilh, Anthony. *Mexico versus Texas, a Descriptive Novel, Most of the Characters of Which Consist of Living Persons*. Philadelphia: N. Siegfried, 1838 (facsimile reproduction of the 1842 edition, Austin, Tex.: The Steck Company, 1967).

Gardner, Richard. *Scandalous John.* New York: Popular Library, 1963.

Garfield, Brian. *Death Wish.* New York: David McKay, 1972.

Garland, George. *Apache Warpath.* New York: Signet, 1959.

Garner, Claude. *Wetback.* New York: Coward, McCann, 1947.

Gibson, Charles. *The Black Legend: Anti-Spanish Attitudes in the Old World and the New.* New York: Knopf, 1971.

Gilman, George. *The Bounty Hunter.* New York: Pinnacle, 1974.

————. *Edge: The Loner.* New York: Pinnacle, 1971.

————. *The Valley of Blood.* New York: Pinnacle, 1976.

Grey, Zane. *The Vanishing American.* New York: Harper, 1925.

Gulick, Bill. *Showdown in the Sun.* New York: Popular Library, 1958.

Hall, Oakley. *The Adelita.* Garden City, N.Y.: Doubleday, 1975.

————. *Warlock.* New York: Viking, 1958.

Hamill, Pete. *Doc.* New York: Paperback Library, 1971.

Harris, Marilyn. *In the Midst of Earth.* Garden City, N.Y.: Doubleday, 1969.

Heard, J. Norman. *White into Red.* Metuchen, N.J.: Scarecrow Press, 1973.

Hearon, Shelby. *Now and Another Time.* Garden City, N.Y.: Doubleday, 1976.

Helton, David. *King Jude.* New York: Simon & Schuster, 1969.

Henry, Will. *Chiricahua.* Philadelphia: Lippincott, 1972.

————. "Let's Tell It Like It Was," Western Writers of America *Round-up* 24 (December, 1976).

————. *The Seven Men at Mimbres Springs.* New York: Bantam, 1960.

Herlihy, James Leo. *Midnight Cowboy.* New York: Simon & Schuster, 1965.

Herrick, Robert. *Waste.* New York: Harcourt, Brace, 1924.

Hoffman, Lee. *The Legend of Blackjack Sam.* New York: Ace, 1966.

Hopkins, Tom J. *Trouble in Tombstone.* New York: Signet, 1951.

Hopson, William. *The Tombstone Stage.* New York: Phoenix Press, 1948.

Hough, Emerson. *Heart's Desire.* New York: Grosset & Dunlap, 1905.

Humphrey, William. *Home from the Hill.* New York: Knopf, 1958.

Hunter, Evan. *The Chisholms.* New York: Harper & Row, 1976.

Hunter, J. Marvin. *Lottie Deno,* new ed. Bandera, Tex.: *Frontier Times,* 1959.

Hunter, John. *Lost Valley.* New York: Ballentine, 1971.

Hutchinson, W. H. *The Rhodes Reader.* Norman: University of Oklahoma Press, 1957.

Ingram, Hunter. *Fort Apache.* New York: Ballentine, 1975.

Irsfeld, John. *Coming Through.* New York: Putnam's, 1975.

James, William. *Bloodline.* New York: Pinnacle, 1976.

————. *Sonora Slaughter.* New York: Pinnacle, 1976.

Jennings, Gary. *The Terrible Teague Bunch.* New York: Norton, 1975.

Johnson, Carol McCool. "Emerson Hough and the American West: A

Biographical and Critical Study," Ph.D. diss., University of Texas at Austin, 1975.

Johnson, Dorothy M. *Buffalo Woman.* New York: Dodd, Mead, 1977.

———. *A Man Called Horse.* New York: Ballentine, 1953.

Kelland, Clarence Budington. *Tombstone.* New York: Harper, 1952.

Kelton, Elmer. *The Time It Never Rained.* New York: Ace, 1973.

Ketchum, Philip. *Apache Dawn.* New York: Avon, 1960.

Kidd, Harry, Jr. "Low Road Go Down," in *21 Texas Short Stories,* ed. William Peery. Austin: University of Texas Press, 1954.

King, Paul. *Hermana Sam.* New York: Coward, McCann & Geoghegan, 1977.

Knibbs, Henry Herbert. *Sundown Slim.* New York: Grossett & Dunlap, 1915.

Kreps, Robert. *The Hour of the Gun.* New York: Fawcett, 1967.

Lake, Stuart. *Wyatt Earp: Frontier Marshal.* Boston: Houghton Mifflin, 1931.

L'Amour, Louis. *The Lonely Men.* New York: Bantam, 1969.

Lanham, Edwin. *The Stricklands.* Boston: Little, Brown, 1939.

Leach, Joseph. *The Typical Texan.* Dallas: Southern Methodist University Press, 1952.

Lewis, Alfred Henry. *The Boss.* New York: A. S. Barnes, 1903.

———. *Wolfville.* Chicago: A. L. Burt, 1897.

Lockhart, Carolyn. "Not a Redeeming Trait," in *Western Stories,* ed. William MacLeod Raine. New York: Dell, 1949.

Lummis, Charles Fletcher. *General Crook and the Apache Wars.* Flagstaff, Ariz.: Northland Press, 1966.

Lutz, Giles. *The Black Day.* New York: Ace, 1974.

Lyon, Peter. "The Wild Wild West," *American Heritage* 11 (August, 1960).

———. *The Wild Wild West.* New York: Funk & Wagnalls, 1969.

McGaw, Bill. "Deming Woman 'Took' Holliday for $70,000," *Southwesterner* 1 (May, 1962).

McMillion, Bonner. *The Lot of Her Neighbors.* Philadelphia: Lippincott, 1953.

McMurtry, Larry. *All My Friends Are Going to Be Strangers.* New York: Simon & Schuster, 1972.

———. *Horseman, Pass By.* New York: Harper, 1960.

———. *The Last Picture Show.* New York: Dial, 1966.

Manzo, Flournoy D. "Alfred Henry Lewis, Western Storyteller," *Arizona and the West* 10 (Spring, 1968).

Markson, David. *The Ballad of Dingus Magee.* Indianapolis: Bobbs-Merrill, 1965.

Marshall, Kathryn. *Desert Places.* New York: Harper & Row, 1977.

Martin, Gil. *Squawman.* New York: Berkley, 1972.

Mayer, Tom. *Bubble Gum and Kipling.* New York: Viking, 1964.

Melas, Roxylea. *Revival and Other Stories*. San Antonio: Naylor, 1934.

Michaels, Dale. *The Warring Breed*. New York: Gold Medal, 1961.

Miller, J. P. *The Race for Home*. New York: Dial, 1968.

Miller, Nyle H., and Joseph Snell. *Why the West Was Wild*. Topeka: Kansas State Historical Society, 1963.

Moore, Barbara. *Hard on the Road*. Garden City, N.Y.: Doubleday, 1974.

Mulford, Clarence E. *Bar-20*. New York: A. L. Burt, 1907.

————. *Bar-20 Days*. New York: A. L. Burt, 1911.

————. *The Coming of Cassidy*. New York: Grosset & Dunlap, 1908.

————. *On the Trail of the Tumbling T*. New York: Doubleday, Doran, 1935.

Nachbar, Jack. *Focus on the Western*. Englewood Cliffs, N.J.: Prentice-Hall, 1974.

Nelson, Bobby Jack. *Brothers*. New York: Macmillan, 1975.

Nye, Nelson. *Riders by Night*. New York: Macmillan, 1950.

————. *Wild Horse Shorty*. New York: Macmillan, 1934.

————. "What's the Matter with Westerns?" WWA *Roundup* 11 (June, 1963).

Nye, Russell B. *The Unembarrassed Muse: The Popular Arts in America*. New York: Dial, 1970.

O'Connor, Jack. *Boom Town*. New York: Knopf, 1938.

Olsen, T. V. *Savage Sierra*. New York: Fawcett, 1962.

Olson, James R. *Ulzana*. Boston: Houghton Mifflin, 1973.

Overholser, Stephen. *A Hanging at Sweetwater*. Garden City, N.Y.: Doubleday, 1974.

Owens, William A. *Look to the River*. New York: Atheneum, 1963.

Patten, Lewis B. *Apache Hostage*. New York: New American Library, 1970.

Perry, George Sessions. *Hold Autumn in Your Hand*. New York: Viking, 1931.

Pilkington, Tom. "Edward Abbey: Western Philosopher," *Western American Literature* 9 (May, 1974).

Pinckney, Susan Shubrick [Miss McPherson]. *Darcy Pinckney*. New York and Washington: Neale Publishing Co., 1906.

————. *Douglas; Tender and True*. St. Louis: Nixon-Jones Printing Co., 1892.

————. *In the Southland*. New York and Washington: Neale Publishing Co., 1906.

Porter, William Sidney [O. Henry]. *The Complete Works of O. Henry*. Garden City, N.Y.: Doubleday, Doran, 1928.

Portis, Charles. *True Grit*. New York: Simon & Schuster, 1968.

Powell, Philip Wayne. *The Tree of Hate: Propaganda and Prejudices Affecting United States Relations with the Hispanic World*. New York: Basic Books, 1971.

Raine, William MacLeod. *A Daughter of the Dons.* New York: Grosset & Dunlap, 1914.

Rechy, John. *The Sexual Outlaw: A Documentary.* New York: Grove Press/Dell, 1977.

Reese, John. *Blacksnake Man.* Garden City, N.Y.: Doubleday, 1976.

———. *Hangman's Springs.* Garden City, N.Y.: Doubleday, 1976.

———. *Sequoia Shootout.* Garden City, N.Y.: Doubleday, 1977.

———. *Singalee.* New York: Belmont, 1970.

———. *Sure Shot Shapiro.* Garden City, N.Y.: Doubleday, 1968.

Rhodes, Eugene Manlove. *Peñalosa,* in *Best Novels and Short Stories of Eugene Manlove Rhodes,* ed. Frank V. Dearing. Boston: Houghton Mifflin, 1949.

Rikhoff, Jean. *The Sweetwater.* New York: Dial, 1976.

Robinson, Cecil. *Mexico and the Hispanic Southwest in American Literature.* Tucson: University of Arizona Press, 1977 (originally published in 1963 under the title *With the Ears of Strangers* by University of Arizona Press).

Rogers, Rosemary. *Wicked Loving Lies.* New York: Avon, 1976.

Rubin, Theodore Isaac. "What the Movies Reveal about You, the Audience," *Glamour* 60 (October, 1968).

Rushing, Jane Gilmore. *The Raincrow.* Garden City, N.Y.: Doubleday, 1977.

Ryan, Marah Ellis. *Flute of the Gods.* New York: Stokes, 1909.

———. *Indian Love Letters.* Chicago: A. C. McClurg, 1907.

Saloutos, Theodore. *Farmer Movements in the South, 1865–1933.* Berkeley: University of California Press, 1960.

Savage, William W., Jr. *Cowboy Life: Reconstructing an American Myth.* Norman: University of Oklahoma Press, 1975.

Scarborough, Dorothy. *In the Land of Cotton.* New York: Macmillan, 1923.

———. *The Stretch-Berry Smile.* Indianapolis: Bobbs-Merrill, 1932.

Seidman, Robert J. *One Smart Indian.* New York: Putnam's, 1977.

Shelley, John, and David Shelley. *Hell-For-Leather Jones.* New York: Ace, 1968.

Sherman, Caroline B. "The Development of American Rural Fiction," *Agricultural History* 12 (January, 1938).

Shideler, James H. "The Development of the Parity Price Formula for Agriculture, 1919-1923," *Agricultural History* 27 (July, 1933).

Shireffs, Gordon D. *The Apache Hunter.* New York: Fawcett, 1976.

———. *The Marauders.* New York: Fawcett, 1977.

Shrake, Edwin. *Blessed McGill.* Garden City, N.Y.: Doubleday, 1968.

———. *Peter Arbiter.* Austin, Tex.: Encino Press, 1973.

Simon, Charlie May. *The Sharecropper.* New York: Dutton, 1937.

Slade, Jack. *Guerrilla.* New York: Belmont, 1972.

————. *The Man from Tombstone.* New York: Belmont, 1971.

Slade, Walt. *Border War.* New York: Pyramid, 1968.

Smith, C. W. *Country Music.* New York: Ballantine, 1975.

————. *Thin Men of Haddam.* New York: Grossman, 1973.

Smith, Henry Nash. *Virgin Land.* New York: Vintage, 1950.

Sonnichsen, C. L. *Billy King's Tombstone.* Tucson: University of Arizona Press, 1972 (first publication, 1943).

————. *Cowboys and Cattle Kings: Life on the Range Today.* Norman: University of Oklahoma Press, 1950.

————. *Ten Texas Feuds.* Albuquerque: University of New Mexico Press, 1957.

Steelman, Robert. *Apache Wells.* New York: Ballantine, 1974 (first printing, 1959).

Stern, Richard Martin. *Murder in the Walls.* New York: Scribner's, 1971.

————. *Power.* New York: David McKay, 1975.

Stilwell, Hart. *Border City.* New York: Doubleday, Doran, 1945.

Stuart, Colin. *Walks Far Woman.* New York: Dial, 1976.

Styron, William. *The Confessions of Nat Turner.* New York: Random House, 1966.

Swarthout, Glendon. *The Cadillac Cowboys.* New York: Random House, 1964.

————. *They Came to Cordura.* New York: Random House, 1958.

Telfair, Richard. *The Secret of Apache Canyon.* New York: Gold Medal, 1959.

Terrell, John Upton. *Apache Chronicle.* New York: World, 1972.

Tolbert, Frank X. *Bigamy Jones.* New York: Holt, 1954.

Traven, B. *The Treasure of the Sierra Madre.* New York: Knopf, 1935.

Turner, John Kenneth. *Barbarous Mexico.* Austin: University of Texas Press, 1969 (first published in 1910).

Tuska, Jon. "The American Western Cinema: 1903-Present," in *Focus on the Western,* ed. Jack Nachbar. Englewood Cliffs, N.J.: Prentice-Hall, 1974.

————. *The Filming of the West.* Garden City, N.Y.: Doubleday, 1976.

Tuttle, W. C. *Tumbling River Range.* Boston: Houghton Mifflin, 1935.

Vance, William. *Apache War Cry.* New York: Popular Library, 1955, 1960.

Venkataramani, M. S. "Norman Thomas, Arkansas Sharecroppers, and the Roosevelt Agricultural Policies, 1933-1937," *Agricultural History* 47 (September, 1960).

Villareal, José Antonio. *Pocho.* Garden City, N.Y.: Doubleday, 1970.

Vliet, R. G. *Rockspring.* New York: Viking, 1974.

Voss, George L. *The Man Who Believed in the Code of the West.* New York: St. Martin's, 1975.

Wagoner, David. *The Road to Many a Wonder.* New York: Farrar, Straus & Giroux, 1974.

Walker, Franklin. *A Literary History of Southern California*. Berkeley and Los Angeles: University of California Press, 1950.

Warren, Charles Marquis. *Only the Valiant*. New York: Macmillan, 1943.

Waters, Frank. *The Colorado*. New York: Rinehart, 1946.

————. *The Earp Brothers of Tombstone*. New York: Clarkson N. Potter, 1960.

Watson, John. *The Red Dress*. New York: Harper, 1949.

Webb, Lucas. *Eli's Road*. Garden City, N.Y.: Doubleday, 1977.

Weber, David J. *Foreigners in Their Native Land: Historical Roots of the Mexican-Americans*. Albuquerque: University of New Mexico Press, 1973.

Wellman, Paul I. *Broncho Apache*. New York: Modern Library, 1969.

West, Kingsley. *Apache Lance*. New York: Banner, 1967.

Westermeier, Clifford P. *Trailing the Cowboy*. Caldwell, Idaho: Caxton, 1955.

White, Stewart Edward. *The Killer*. Garden City, N.Y.: Doubleday, Page, 1920.

Whitman, S. E. *Captain Apache*. New York: Berkley, 1965.

Whittington, Harry. *Desert Stakeout*. New York: Fawcett, 1961.

Williams, Jeanne. *A Lady Bought with Rifles*. New York: Coward, McCann & Geoghegan, 1976.

Wilson, John W. *High John the Conqueror*. New York: Macmillan, 1934.

Wister, Owen. *Lin McLean*. New York: Harper, 1907.

————. *The Virginian*. New York: Macmillan, 1902.

Wright, Harold Bell. *The Mine with the Iron Door*. New York: D. Appleton, 1923.

Wyckoff, James. *John Slaughter's Way*. Garden City, N.Y.: Doubleday, 1963.

NEWSPAPERS AND MAGAZINES

Arizona Daily Star, July 27, 1976; February 21, May 1, 1977.

Galveston News, April 12, 13, 15, 1904; April 26, 28, 1905.

Hempstead News, April 21, 1905.

Houston Chronicle, October 3, 1964.

Houston Post, April 25, 26, 1905.

Newsweek, April 17, 1975 (review of William W. Savage, Jr., *Cowboy Life*).

Publishers Weekly, February 14, 1977 (on "comeback" of hard-cover fiction).

Time, March 20, 1959 (on "The American Morality Play"—the western).

LETTERS

Barker, S. Omar, to C.L.S., August 4, 1975 (on humorous westerns).

Gilchriese, John, to C.L.S., June 24, 1962 (on Wyatt Earp).

Wyeth, N. S., Jr., Executive Editor, Harper & Row, to C.L.S. October 8, 1968 (on sales of Larry McMurtry's *Horseman, Pass By*).

INTERVIEWS

Crook, Mrs. M. T., Hempstead, Texas, June 29, 30, 1943.
Groce, Miss Barbara, Hempstead, Texas, June 29, 30, 1943.
Scott, Mr. and Mrs. George, Houston, July 2, 1943.
Tompkins, Mrs. R. E., Hempstead, Texas, June 29, 30, 1943.

GOVERNMENT DOCUMENT

John McPherson Pinckney Memorial Addresses, Fifty-ninth Congress, First Session, House of Representatives, April 29, 1906. Washington: Government Printing Office, 1907.

Index